THE JEW OF CULTURE

VOLUME III

 SACRED ORDER / SOCIAL ORDER

KENNETH S. PIVER, GENERAL EDITOR

Publication of this volume was assisted by a generous grant from the Institute for Advanced Studies in Culture at the University of Virginia.

PHILIP RIEFF

The Jew of Culture

FREUD, MOSES, AND MODERNITY

Edited by Arnold M. Eisen and Gideon Lewis-Kraus
With an Introduction by Arnold M. Eisen

UNIVERSITY OF VIRGINIA PRESS CHARLOTTESVILLE AND LONDON

University of Virginia Press
© 2008 by Philip Rieff
Introduction © 2008 by Arnold M. Eisen

First published 2008
9 8 7 6 5 4 3 2 1

LIBRARY OF CONGRESS CATALOGING-IN-PUBLICATION DATA

Rieff, Philip, 1922–2006.
  The Jew of culture : Freud, Moses, and modernity / Philip Rieff ; edited
by Arnold M. Eisen and Gideon Lewis-Kraus ; with an introduction by
Arnold M. Eisen.
       p.   cm. — (Sacred order/social order ; v. 3)
  Includes bibliographical references and index.
  ISBN 978-0-8139-2706-0 (cloth : alk. paper)
    1. Culture. 2. Civilization, Modern. 3. Freud, Sigmund, 1856–1939—
Influence. 4. Religion and sociology. 5. Judaism and culture. I. Eisen,
Arnold M., 1951– II. Lewis-Kraus, Gideon. III. Title.
  HM621.R5339 2008
  306.6'96091821—dc22

                                                          2007045644

Contents

Editor's Acknowledgments

This volume—third in the series *Sacred Order/Social Order*—has its origins in three sets of encounters that I was privileged to have with Philip Rieff at three very different stages in my life.

The first was the seminar in sociological theory that Rieff offered, and I took part in, during the fall of 1972 at the University of Pennsylvania. It consisted entirely of careful line-by-line reading of the first several pages of Max Weber's essay "Science as a Vocation." The class began its weekly meeting promptly at 4:15, if I recall correctly, and ended when Rieff declared it over. Our professor had no patience for jargon or shows of what he called "mere erudition." Members of the class were forbidden to use words that we were not prepared to define. For some of the graduate students, new to sociology, the search to avoid jargon and supply definition at times proved difficult. I remember that the word "institution" once kept us very late into the evening. The method of proceeding line by line, word by word, reminded me of Torah study that I had been engaging in since childhood. That may well have been its source for Professor Rieff as well.

Some years later—having completed graduate work and begun teaching my own seminars at Columbia—I periodically took the train to Philadelphia for tutorials and conversation at Rieff's nineteenth-century townhouse on Delancey Street. We worked through a number of texts in the Rieffian canon together: Weber and Nietzsche, Kafka and Freud. Rieff talked about the paintings that surrounded us, the colleagues we had in common, and the two dogs yelping at our heels. He loved the dogs dearly, and frequently drew theoretical lessons from their behavior. Conversation often turned to Jews, Judaism, and Israel. We pored over passages from the Torah, debated the latest developments in the Middle East, and discussed major Jewish texts (I remember the Bible, Mishnah, and Maimonides in particular) and contemporary Jewish religious thinkers (Buber, Rosenzweig, Heschel). Rieff's wife, Alison, sometimes joined us for meals and conversation. I was (and will forever be) Rieff's student. These meetings made it clear that I had become his fellow teacher as well. He conveyed the expectations attached to that role with characteristic rigor and affection.

Rieff and I stayed in touch even after I had moved to California. He met my wife and then my children on visits back to Delancey Street, and despite poor health he made the journey to Palo Alto for my daughter's bat mitzvah. Not a few of my own seminars at Stanford prominently featured "Science as a Vocation"; those with my best students increasingly included the work of Philip Rieff as well. After my mother died I took my father—ten years older than Rieff—with me on my visits to my teacher. We took the steep staircase up to the second floor, where Rieff sat at his desk or, bedridden, met us in pajamas. It was during one of these meetings that Rieff lamented the failure of *Fellow Teachers* to reach the audience for which he had hoped, as well as the general lack of appreciation for the importance of Jewish themes in his work. I suggested there might be value in a collection of his writings built around the key conception of the Jew of culture, so central to *Fellow Teachers*. He agreed, and requested that I prepare the volume. "Arnold," he asked more than once in the months that followed, "how is the book coming along? I'd like to see it before I die." I am pleased that I can now present the volume to the new generation of readers that has been introduced to Rieff's work by the first two volumes of *Sacred Order/Social Order*. I regret only that I did not have the chance to show it to its most important reader before he died.

The book could never have been written without the encouragement and assistance of Dr. Kenneth S. Piver, general editor of the *Sacred Order/Social Order* trilogy, and one of Philip Rieff's most devoted and perceptive students. He generously shared his collection of unpublished essays with me, and consulted with me on their use in this volume. Gideon Lewis-Kraus and I are greatly in his debt. David Rieff has also offered every assistance along the way, for which we are extremely grateful. Penelope Kaiserlian and her staff at the University of Virginia Press have been a pleasure to work with from start to finish. We very much appreciate their efforts. I would like to take this opportunity to thank Professor Rieff's widow, Alison Knox Rieff, for thirty years of hospitality and wit.

Finally, I want to express thanks to my former student Gideon Lewis-Kraus, without whose learning, skills, and writer's instincts this collection would never have been completed. Gideon worked closely with me on the selection and interpretation of Rieff's writings; it is immensely satisfying to me, and would have been to Philip Rieff, that one of my best students has enabled me to know and understand one of my most influential teachers better than I ever had before.

We dedicate this book to Philip Rieff's memory, in the hope that it will help his capacious mind, heart, and soul, his insights and convictions, to remain alive in the minds, hearts, and souls of his readers. Jews of culture can aim at nothing less when it comes to fellow teachers. May Professor Rieff's memory remain a blessing for years and generations to come.

"Disraeli: The Chosen of History Uniting the Old Jerusalem and the New" was first published in *Commentary* 13 (January 1952): 22–33; it is reprinted here from *The Feeling Intellect: Selected Writings,* ed. Jonathan B. Imber (Chicago: University of Chicago Press, 1990). "On Franz Rosenzweig" was first published in the *Journal of Religion* 35 (October 1967): 262–63; it is reprinted here from *The Feeling Intellect. Freud: The Mind of the Moralist* was originally published in 1959 (New York: Viking); the preface reprinted here appeared in the second edition, published in 1961. "The Religion of the Fathers" originally appeared in and is reprinted here from *Freud: The Mind of the Moralist* (New York: Viking, 1959). "Toward a Theory of Culture" originally appeared in and is reprinted here from *The Triumph of the Therapeutic: Uses of Faith after Freud* (New York: Harper & Row, 1966). Selections are reprinted here from *Fellow Teachers*, originally published in 1972 (New York: Harper & Row). "The Impossible Culture: Wilde as a Modern Prophet" originally appeared in *Salmagundi* 58–59 (Fall 1982–Winter 1983): 406–26; it is reprinted here from *The Feeling Intellect*. "Is Not the Truth the Truth?" was written circa 1994 and is previously unpublished. All pieces are published by permission of the estate of Philip Rieff.

Introduction

ARNOLD M. EISEN

At the heart of Philip Rieff's *Fellow Teachers* (1972)—a book not only at the chronological center of Rieff's immense body of scholarship and reflection but arguably at the substantive center as well—we encounter a major concept in Rieff's theoretical lexicon, the "Jew of culture." Rieff explicitly and consistently identified with this ideal-type, named here for the first time but crucial in one form or another to everything he ever wrote. Much of *Fellow Teachers* is devoted to explaining what Jews of culture stand for and urging the reader to stand alongside them. For the rest of Rieff's long career, the "Jew of culture" would serve as foil, countertype, corrective, and adversary to the "therapeutics" who represented not only Rieff's analysands but his antagonists. The purpose of this collection of Rieff's writings, undertaken at his suggestion, is to trace the evolution of the "Jew of culture" over the course of his work. In so doing we gain particular insight into his distinctive theory of society and the self; we also come to better understand the theorist. Rieff confessed near the end of *Fellow Teachers* that he did not "pick my theories from a bag of books" (137). For this Jewish Jew of culture, the questions posed and struggled with were always more than merely academic. Rieff expected no less of his readers.

The Jews are in one sense an obvious feature of all Rieff's work—as obvious, if not as salient, as the preoccupation with culture and "anti-culture," Freud and therapy. One of Rieff's earliest published pieces (included in the present volume) analyzed Disraeli as author and statesman under the provocative title "The Chosen of History." Rieff noted on its very first page that Disraeli "played at being a Jew far more seriously than Heine played at not being a Jew. (To play at being a Jew is usually more serious.) Disraeli, who hated the universalist rationalism of his country, refused to be accepted as simply a 'man,' and yet he was certainly not simply a Jew." Rieff's prose was dense, allusive, and scrupulously careful, so comments such as this one require more than casual unpacking. The contrast with Heine is no mere witticism. Philip Rieff, like the man who dominated his scholarship and haunted his soul, was never "simply a Jew." But like Freud—and Disraeli and Marx, Durkheim and Kafka, and many other vessels for Rieff's admiration and critique—Rieff was also never "simply a 'man.'" If he were, he would not in his own eyes have counted as "serious."

That Rieff was not content to be "simply a man" is clear from the way in which the term "Jew of culture" makes its first—its decisive—appearance in *Fellow Teachers*. Rieff's analysis takes the form of overlapping and concentric circles, and he introduces the idea of the "Jew of culture" at a juncture that included Freud and his "therapeutic" successors, Marx's "On the Jewish Question," and the tormenting memory of Rieff's aunts in Dachau. It is in this layered context that Rieff writes, "A universalist culture is a contradiction in terms. We Jews of culture are obliged to resist the very idea" (110).

The resistance to universalist definitions of self or culture— definitions that would dispense with the need for particularist identities such as Jew—has of course been a major thrust of Jewish belief and practice from its very beginnings. Rieff knew the essential sources of the tradition well, and drew on them more and more (and increasingly avowedly) as the years went by. He certainly knew—and cited with approval—the biblical claims to a covenant between God and Israel that demanded exclusivity of worship and behavior no less than a universal mission to help bring justice and redemption to all the world. Rieff also identified himself with, and tried to carry forward, the rabbinic polemic against triumphalist Christian claims that the "old" covenant had been superseded by a new one open to all through faith in a savior at once human and divine. He well understood and knowingly reiterated the resistance expressed by Jewish thinkers in the modern period to the argument that modernity itself had made Jews and Judaism an anachronism—whether that argument came in the form of "reason" or "science" or "socialism" or "sociology"; whether in the name of ex-Jews such as Spinoza and Marx, self-identified Jews such as Freud and Durkheim, or non-Jews such as Hegel. For Rieff, Jews were decidedly not a fossil. Their defining commitments—carried forward by all Jews of culture, Jewish or gentile—were not at all beside the point.

To his Jewishly learned conversation partners, Philip Rieff's familiarity with the Jewish tradition was obvious. I remember long talks with him about the Bible, Mishnah, and Maimonides. His questions attested to reading that was both broad and deep, and his curiosity about the tradition was indefatigable. His early work is shot through with comments that explicitly identify with and second major claims made in those Jewish sources, but subtler references linger with resonance, as Rieff knew they would, for readers acquainted with Jewish texts. The "Religion of the Fathers" chapter of *The Mind of the Moralist* exemplifies the former, the easily apparent Jewish argumentation. It reveals a great deal about Rieff's personal and theoretical loyalties, Jewish and otherwise, at that early point in his career. But the reader who comes to the crucial theoretical chapter in *Triumph of the Therapeutic* with knowledge of Leviticus and Deuteronomy as well as of Durkheim and Weber cannot miss the fact that Rieff's canon includes the Torah as much as it does the giants of sociology. Such a reader better understands Rieff's insistence that, for example, "Durkheim's sociology was his suicide." Durkheim tried too hard to be a universalist—"simply a man." In Rieff's estimation, he had lost too much of what was theoretically precious in being a Jew.

In *Fellow Teachers* and the writings that came after it the references to Jews and Judaism, to the rabbis and even to God, are evident to all readers. Consider the following passage from *Fellow Teachers*, placed strategically in the section immediately following the introduction of the Jew of culture. Rieff is explaining why, despite his revulsion for the state of contemporary Western culture, he cannot long for a return to "some earlier credal organization," such as the Christian culture that preceded our own therapeutic order. "I am a Jew," he declares. "No Jew in his right mind can long for some variant (including the Party) of that civilization. Its one enduring quality is its transgressive energy against the Jew of culture." A Jew such as himself could not long for renewed domination by the church or wish to purchase a renewed culture of faith at the price of resurgent anti-Semitism. How could a Jew of culture—Jewish or gentile—do so either, aware of that same cost? Indeed, Rieff warns, more anti-Semitism is to be expected "as the Jews continue to resist their assigned roles and, worse gall, refuse to disappear into the universalist future 'Man.'" That is why, to Philip Rieff as a Jew of culture, "the gospels were not good news" (115).

In his later writings—the recently published *My Life among the Deathworks*, for example, or the excerpt included in this volume from his extended (and previously unpublished) meditation on Yosef Yerushalmi's book *Freud's Moses*—Rieff almost never called the type "Jew of culture" by that name. He was, however, more explicit than ever before about his own stance as committed (although unobservant) Jew—and even more unsparing than in previous works in his critique of those who oppose the commitment to what he called, echoing Durkheim, sacred order, and so to culture. Rieff repeatedly turned to Jews as the paradigmatic (but not the only) example of his "fellow teachers." For that very reason he continued to criticize, and even to single out for opprobrium, Jews who turn away from the cultural work that for centuries had been implicit in the name Jew. An elaboration of the nature of such cultural work is a central commitment of the selections included in this volume.

In a way, the reader of these late meditations has, like Rieff himself, come full circle. The later Rieff, like the author of the Disraeli piece, reserves some special scorn for Jewish self-hatred and assimilation. But his authorial voice has changed a great deal in the meantime. His theory of culture has altered somewhat as well. The now-favored term "sacred order" conveys a great deal more than it had in Durkheim's functionalism—or Rieff's. Freud, always an object of ambivalence, is now treated with untempered hostility: the enemy of culture, impresario and conductor of a war of words against the Jews. Rieff identifies far more openly and more completely with the Jew in his "Jew of culture" than ever before, writing as an insider to the Jewish community, its intellectual debates and affairs. He strongly defends the need for a Jewish "*Machtstaat*" (Israel) to safeguard the Jewish "*Kulturstaat.*" He points more insistently and directly toward the ultimate authority of God.

Let me make clear, before proceeding to introduce the eight selections included in this volume, just what I am claiming—and not claiming—about Rieff's thought. It would be wrong, I think, to call him a "modern Jewish thinker" as that term is normally employed in the fields of Jewish or religious studies. I am not trying to add Rieff's work to the corpus that includes Moses Mendelssohn and Martin Buber, Abraham Joshua Heschel and Abraham Isaac Kook. Nor would I shelve his books alongside secular Jewish thinkers (and theorists of Jewish culture) such as the Zionist Ahad Ha'am. Rieff's work, unlike theirs, is not aimed primarily at securing and interpreting the survival of Jews or Judaism; it does not draw primarily or even in large measure on Jewish history or texts; and—despite his pride at being a Jew, his oft-stated concern for the state of the Jews around the world and for "the Jewish State," and his turn in the 1980s and 1990s to an open interest in theology—he made it clear more than once in his writings (as in conversation with me) that he did not consider himself a believing Jew and had never been a practicing Jew. In this respect and others, analogies to Emmanuel Lévinas, for example, prove completely inappropriate. Rieff left us no essays on the Talmud, only a few pieces on Jewish affairs, and no sustained reflection on the relationship between his work as theorist and as Jew. Leo Strauss, perhaps a closer comparison, accomplished more on these scores than Rieff, who never devoted himself to an analysis of the Talmud as social theory, say, in the manner that Strauss meditated upon Maimonides, Spinoza, and Hermann Cohen.

I have no intention, then, of pinning labels on Rieff's thought that he himself declined to wear. The label that suits him best,

I think, is the one that he himself conceived—perhaps for that reason. He was very much a Jew of culture: the first (and perhaps iconic) example of a character type he invented and then refined. Jewish sources and commitments loomed large in his work—but never so large that they eclipsed other commitments. Jewish tropes and stances are evident throughout his writings from the earliest to the latest, but so is the persistent attempt to speak in the name of a force and truth—culture—much larger in his mind than any single faith, and arguably more enduring. This irony—characteristic of so many modern Jewish intellectuals—pervades almost all of Rieff's work. It is also notable—and likewise typical of modern Jewish intellectuals—that he sometimes criticized Christianity severely, particularly as a cause of anti-Semitism, but far more often tended to speak of and defend Christianity and Judaism as part of the same order, if not exactly of a joint "Judeo-Christian ethic."

Rieff did not want to be a "man" only. That is certain. But neither did he write only as Jew. He found his voice preeminently as Jew of culture, and seems to have decided near the outset of his career that the vocation defined by that term, even before he had begun to use it, was the work to which he had been called.

DISRAELI

The essay on Disraeli—published in *Commentary* in 1952, when Rieff must have been in the midst of his most sustained and comprehensive work on Freud and, presumably, pondering what kinds of futures were available for Jewish intellectuals—concerns itself above all with themes of identity, assimilation, and anti-Semitism that have remained central to the magazine over the past half century, as they have to much of its readership.

No subject seems of more concern to Rieff in this essay than assimilation: the Jewish drive to disappear in universal identities, whether national or truly cosmopolitan, a drive sometimes accompanied by a loathing of all things particular to Jews. Disraeli's grandmother, Rieff writes, exhibited a "nagging self-hatred." His father suffered from physical symptoms that the doctors would not diagnose as consumption. "The disease," Rieff notes wryly, "was really self-hatred." His father, said Disraeli, lacked self-esteem. Isaac d'Israeli had his children baptized, accusing Judaism (in classical anti-Semitic terms) of harboring a "lone and sullen genius" that had cut him off from "the great family of mankind." Rieff adds caustically that Isaac spent the remainder of his life "taking flight into the universal in his library." His son resolved upon a different path.

The Disraeli shown us in Rieff's heavily psychological account always bore the scars that remained from fending off schoolboy anti-Semitism, and responded to those and later wounds in part by cultivating and expressing nostalgia for the glorious Jewish past. He read up on Jewish history and even traveled to Palestine. Disraeli's novels too furthered the romance of "Old Jewry"—ironically, the location of the solicitors with whom he apprenticed—as what Rieff calls the only aristocracy superior to England's. Disraeli's fiction and public statements provide no evidence of belief in God. But his "belief in the Jew as the indestructible hero of history," Rieff writes, "led him to claim for the Jews every historical glory of Western civilization. Christianity, at its best, is a Jewish religion, and what is not best in it is not Jewish" (20).

Such claims about the "chosen people" have been and remain common among modern Jews who seek to embrace the larger cultures of the West without abandoning Jewish identity. Pride in what Jews have done in the past has often taken the place of continued obedience to the commandments. Aesthetic attachments have grown as religious loyalties have weakened.[1] Above all, the fascination with Jewish history became pronounced in Disraeli's time—witness the Anglo-Jewish Historical Exhibition mounted in 1887 at the Albert Hall. The ex-Jewish prime minister, always seen as a Jew by his gentile countrymen, was typical in this regard. Rieff's study of him follows (or, better, anticipates) one major line of investigation by historians of modern Jewry.

Most important of all, to Rieff's analysis, is the fact that Disraeli practiced the art of being an *outsider* to his country even as he scaled the heights of power. He affected the dandy, and used dandyism, Rieff believes, "to legitimate his exoticism, which was his Jewishness" (8). The two merged. His pose "gave him the perfect grip upon himself." (American Jews as recently as the 1950s reported avoiding close friendships with gentiles lest they let their guard down.)[2] Rieff is unequivocal on this point. "An outsider—an intellectual of sorts, a Jew of sorts—cannot let the insiders get too close to him." Disraeli's opportunism was of a piece with that stance. So too was his maneuvering in Parliament. "After race," Rieff writes, "all was politics." Disraeli's politics flowed from his reaction to his Jewishness. *Punch* saw in him, accurately enough therefore, "the face of old Jewry" (14).

The characters in Disraeli's novels act out these same convictions—and, one is tempted to say, tell us something about Rieff's own thinking on the matters at hand. Alroy, for example, comes to understand that his "attempt to de-Judaize himself" had been fatal to his character. He concludes that the Jews must exist alone. Sidonia's detachment, his lack of a permanent home, is what "makes him intensely interested in the problem of political and cultural stability." Disraeli, Rieff speculated, wrote as he did and what he did in part "to protect himself against the completest assimilation: the loss of his own consciousness as a Jew" (21). The same was no doubt true of Philip Rieff, who would soon urge all Jews of culture to resist assimilation to an "anti-culture" that he believed inimical to the consciousness of all that is highest.

ROSENZWEIG

The brief review that Rieff published in 1955 of Franz Rosenzweig's little book *Understanding the Sick and the Healthy*, which had just appeared in an English translation by Nahum Glatzer, is included here to demonstrate that Rieff's intellectual interests extended to Jewish religious thought. He writes knowingly that "for modern and secular taste, Rosenzweig was almost embarrassingly good"—paralyzed while still relatively young, dead at forty-three, fully at home in the Western philosophical tradition, including a dissertation book on Hegel's theory of the State. But the review tells us little about the substance of Rosenzweig's "*Büchlein*" or why Rieff himself found Rosenzweig of value. He provides us with only two clues.

"The Jew Franz Rosenzweig belongs in the company of the

sublimest characters his religion of character has produced." Rieff would soon have a lot to say about character and its relation to culture. We have already seen that he believes its developments precluded by the sort of "universalist rationalism" that *Understanding the Sick and the Healthy* also deplores. More crucial here, however, is Rieff's praise for a book that addresses human beings rather than other books. "In the contemporary hospital atmosphere of culture, theory leads nowhere except to theorizing." Rieff too would soon engage, via anti-theoretical theory, in "an attack on the academic sickliness of modern thought" (his words).

That is pretty much all we learn of Rosenzweig's little book in Rieff's pithy review. The piece stands as a sort of promissory note for the career about to be launched with *The Mind of the Moralist*. That book would begin Rieff's search for "wider inclosures" than the American academy and for a culture more normative than the one in which "all thinking people think they have to live."

FREUD

Freud: The Mind of the Moralist (1959) has proven, since it was first issued nearly half a century ago, perhaps Rieff's most enduring work; his inquiry into Freud is so rigorous, and so wide-ranging, that the book's profound promise seems inexhaustible. Rieff would continually reevaluate Freud, and his vision of Freud, as he thought about him over the years. There is no other theorist against whom his own theory of present-day culture was always measured or arrayed, no other influence who—as he wrote about Freud's attack upon religion—so called forth both his "open hostility" and his unconscious animus. *Mind of the Moralist* introduces the Rieffian notion, elaborated in *Triumph of the Therapeutic*, that Freud was far greater—more complex, more courageous, and therefore more serious—than his intellectual heirs, and, obviously, his popularizers. The "Preface to the Third Edition" (1979) praises Freud for not indulging in the "stripping away of concealments," not aiming at "lowering" to instincts in his therapy but rather at "raising" to morality, and for saying "nothing to declare a moratorium on *must*" (italics in the original).[3] Such generosity toward his master grew rarer over the course of Rieff's career. Rieff came to blame Freud more for what he had set in motion, and to hold him strictly accountable for the "one step further"— toward guilt and God—that, Rieff argued (in the new epilogue to the 1979 edition), Freud had refused to take. Our contemporary culture, to Rieff's mind a dangerous and unstable anti-culture, had followed Freud in resisting, even repressing, that step. Rieff was not inclined at the end to show mercy.

Rieff's immense respect for Freud in *The Mind of the Moralist* is attached to the set of virtues that define him as a "psychological Jew." The importance of that "mystique of membership" in Freud's own eyes is analyzed in the "Preface to the Second Edition" (1961), included in the present volume. Rieff knew well the ways in which modern Jewish intellectuals, no longer believers, manifested instead an "obedience to the authority of [their] ancestry," and in so doing found protection from what Freud called "the sickest of questions"—the meaning of life. "Freud was his own ideal Jew" (30), Rieff writes, a fantasy Moses based on a vision of the original to whose statue by Michelangelo Freud returned in a sort of pilgrimage day after day in Rome. Rieff credits Freud with a "dark vision of the embattled self . . . truer than the cheery platitudes of his revisers" and accuses the latter of "wholesale sacrifice of what is challenging and serious in Freudian insights."[4]

What had they missed? For one thing, Freud's relentless interpretation of everything the patient says, does, or dreams, including critical interpretation of the patient's own self-interpretation. Rieff introduces his chapter on Freud's "tactics of interpretation" with a brief disquisition on rabbinic interpreters of scripture. They, like other readers of other canons, practiced not only exegesis but Midrash, which reconciled scripture with their own notions, born of "different historical movement," of what the text in question had to mean. Rieff mentions the later use by philosophers of Homer and Hesiod, as well as Philo's allegorical interpretation of the Old Testament. Freud tended to the reconciliatory rather than the exegetical in his interpretation, Rieff explains, following the rabbis in his insistence that every utterance or tic carries meaning. He differed from religious interpreters, however, in the direction of his reading. "The polarity in religion between the manifest literal and the latent ethical exactly reverses the Freudian. What is hidden by the religious text is 'high' (or at least 'higher'), while what is hidden by the psychic symptom—even a normal symptom like the dream—is 'low.'"[5] Dreams are wish fulfillment, wishes are desires, and desires are not the province where ethics resides.

As Rieff rejects Freud's notion that all wishing must be for the low, so does he argue against Freud's reliance on one single "origins myth": the Oedipal murder of the father by the "primal horde" of brothers seeking to share sex with their mothers. The "primal question," Rieff suggests in correction of Freud, is not "Am I my father's son?" but "Am I my brother's keeper?"[6] But he does discern in Freud's account a "left-handed admiration for monotheism." Freud's interpretation in *Totem and Taboo* of all religion, indeed all culture, in terms of the wish of sons to slay fathers and the resultant atonement via taboos on murder and incest, awarded "Jewish monotheism the most pervasive of modern legitimations, that of psychological truth. . . . If the first father was God, then other Gods are later, and corruptions."[7]

All this *precedes* Rieff's detailed treatment (in the chapter included in this volume) of the Freudian theory of religion in general, and "Jewish monotheism" in particular; the Jews, in his reading, were much on Freud's mind throughout. It comes as no surprise by this point in Rieff's analysis that he finds the key to Freud's problematic statements on religion in his position as "psychological Jew." Freud wished—and perhaps needed—"to define 'Jew' more fundamentally, in terms of a certain kind of character rather than by adherence to a specific creed" (35). Like Freud (and much nineteenth-century liberal theology), Rieff seems to have regarded creed as less important to religion, less essential, than the emotions that give rise to the beliefs that in turn attempt to make sense of those emotions. (It is in his own voice, not Freud's, that Rieff declares earlier in the book that "religion" emerges from "religiosity"—a conviction shared not only with many scholars of religion, past and present, but with religious thinkers such as Friedrich Schleiermacher and Martin Buber. "It is proper to speak of religion only when religion has emerged from its beginnings in religiosity, undefined feelings such as awe and fear or a diffused apprehension of power."[8]) The "psychological Jew" can remain very much the Jew, therefore, despite sloughing off inherited belief in God. Belief has never been as primary as emotion in any case. The importance of this conviction for Rieff's conceptualization of the Jew of culture is apparent. There, too, character rather than creed will be decisive.

Freud, the first and greatest psychological Jew, retained "independence and cerebral rectitude," the "figure of the minority radical [who] . . . continues to understand itself on the defensive," and an "image of estrangement." Given the choice "between intellectual and physical cultivation," he will always "put the intellect first" (38). The attributes seem essential to the character type pioneered by Freud. It is also not incidental to that type that Freud treated Moses with reverence despite clear ambivalence toward his authority, while dismissing or discounting key elements of Christianity, including its founder. Freud called the martyrdom of Jesus, Rieff observes, a "repetition of the Mosaic prototype." (It echoed the original parricide and the desire of every male to repeat it.) The Son in "Freud's doctrine of the psychic trinity" was not only Father—that is, ultimate authority, incarnate God—but also Son: the rebel who defies God. Recall the climactic argument in *Totem and Taboo* in which we learn that the Eucharist is enacted faithfully not only to atone for the death of the son but to reenact it. Rieff notes the Jewish character of this Freudian move. "To conceive Christianity as a rebellion against, as well as a repetition of, Judaism, also shows psychoanalytically how Christianity itself prefigures the endemic form of resentment in our culture, anti-Semitism" (63). This sentence prefigures a theme that will become central to Rieff's own later work.

Rieff is suspicious of Freud's account of religion. He understands the appeal of the identity he calls "psychological Jew" to Jewish intellectuals (like himself) who have repudiated Orthodoxy but remain attached to their "sacred history" and want to retain the "élan" of chosenness. But he criticizes Freud for taking seriously the "inner dynamics of the old faiths" while holding that "the articles of faith matter not at all." Ironically, Rieff notes, this stance is anti-intellectual; the real believers in Freud's view are not the philosophers but the simple pious folk who need a Father in heaven to protect them from all harm. Freud's argument never confronts theology, "for which he cares nothing." It rather proceeds to attack the religion of the naïve as if religion were intrinsically naïve, all infantile wish fulfillment (40). Worse, Freud the "psychological Jew" takes the trouble, in his last work, to rob the Jews of their founder, who was to Freud "the greatest of moral geniuses, the culture savior, the 'tremendous father-imago' of the Jews"—and whom Freud exposes as really having been an Egyptian (62).

Taking away Moses is too much (or, evaluated as analysis, too little) for Rieff, since it removes the basis for his identification as a psychological Jew. He would not, however, until much later in his career, engage theology directly. It would be many years before he would begin to take seriously the truth claims of faith rather than attack the failure of "psychological man" and therapeutic culture to do so. As far as Rieff is concerned, Freud's ideas about the "religion of the fathers" discredited him. Freud has here forfeited our trust. Hence the jarring first paragraph of Rieff's chapter on the Freudian account of religion, where he declares that Freud's clinical stance was hijacked by his own unconscious hostility. On Freud's own account of such matters, we would have to say that his attitude emerged in large measure out of his relation to his own father (33). Rieff's own personal animus toward Freud's overreaction is no less apparent, of course. We will see more of it in later works.

THE THERAPEUTIC

Just as the discussion of "psychological Jew" in *The Mind of the Moralist* is crucial to the later conceptualization of the "Jew of culture," so too is the chapter called "Toward a Theory of Culture" that opens *The Triumph of the Therapeutic* (1966). Rieff's concern with religion in this next major work was more functional than theological. Faith "superintend[s] the organization of personality" (84) and—the key to that lifesaving work—provides self and society with "communal purpose." Ideally, faith performs both these tasks, "with reasons which sink so deep into the self that they become commonly and implicitly understood." Once again we find that "explicit belief and precise knowledge" are accorded less importance than the substrate of consciousness "below" and before them (81). The question that Rieff feels compelled to take up—as a sociologist "interested in assessing the quality of our corporate life"—is whether "unbelieving men can be civilized." Like Durkheim, Weber, and Freud, all of whom stand front and center in his first systematic effort to formulate a theory of culture, Rieff worries that the decline of faith may well encourage the end of culture as we know it.

For culture, in Rieff's view of it, "is another name for a design of motive directing the self outward, toward those communal purposes in which alone the self can be realized and satisfied" (83). Freud taught that the satisfaction of desire is by definition impossible. Our most basic desires are hidden from us by repression. The satisfactions we crave and pursue are poor substitutes that invariably, when slaked or blocked, give way to others. Motives not directed outward, away from the self and its desires, will therefore prove fatal to self and society alike. Rieff's theory seems to have Durkheim's account of suicide—egoistic, anomic, and altruistic—in mind as well, along with Weber's haunting depiction of Protestants (Calvinists actually) harrowed by the need to prove success in their worldly callings month after month, year after year, so as to achieve psychological certainty that God would not deprive them of success—salvation, eternal reward—in the next world. Once the care for *doing good* in God's eyes had faded, bearers of the "Protestant ethic" or the "spirit of capitalism" were left with the drive to *do well* in the world's eyes. Hence the famous "iron cage" that in Weber's sober view of things encompasses multiple realms of rationality and disenchantment—and from which Weber to the end saw no escape.

Rieff picks up the discussion of our cultural predicament where his great antecedents left off. "For the ultimate interest of sociology . . . turns on the question whether our culture can be so reconstructed that faith—some compelling symbolic of self-integrating communal purpose—need no longer superintend the organization of personality" (84). The question is more than rhetorical, but Rieff is not sanguine.

How can culture possibly do its work—that is, help organize character—without the sense of obligation that is faith? Historically, that work has been effected, the authority of culture enforced, "through the agency of congregations of the faithful." Intellectuals were enlisted to assert that authority. They have of late renounced this task in favor of analysis and criticism. Rieff believes it an elaborate act of suicide. The claim is critical to his theoretical work. Culture literally saves societies and individuals from suicide. His argument takes the form of the jeremiad, but he resists mere moralizing. He is convinced that we dare not experiment with personalities formed without the guidance and constraint of communal purpose and demands. And he is worried that, with motives and desires not only raised to consciousness but brought before the bar of analysis and criticism, culture simply cannot work as it has always done—which may mean it cannot work at all. That is the force of his quotation from the psychiatrist Harry Stack Sullivan that "if you tell people how they can sublimate, they can't sublimate" (84). If we can't ask "How are we to be saved" in the traditional way (84), we may find that we cannot be saved at all.

In Rieff's normative theory of culture, it is not the sum total of knowledge required by the members of a group in order to function inside it, nor the Geertzian webs of significance that bind them, nor the creations and performances of the arts, but the "design of motives directing the self outward." Art and music, poetry and drama, grammar and language, all serve the purpose of ordering thought and behavior in ways seen and unseen, forced and reinforced. We are shaped decisively, in our minds and far behind them, by what we may and may not do. "Every culture must establish itself as a system of moralizing demands, images that mark the trail of each man's memory; thus to distinguish right actions from wrong the inner ordinances are set, by which men are guided in their conduct so as to assure a mutual security of contact." This "higher learning," he concludes pointedly, is "not acquired at universities" (90).[9]

Thus is obedience channeled; in the manner of Durkheim, once more, Rieff argues that cultural agencies are rendered sacred not by their source in God but by "their supreme function of organizing a life worth living." This is how Rieff understands the thou-shalt-nots of culture, given in the report of what God revealed to the Israelites at Sinai. Moreover, he refers in the very same passages to a religious "demand system . . . specified by the kind of credal hedges it raised around impulses of independence or autonomy from communal purpose" (93). I suspect Rieff had in mind the fundamental rabbinic injunction voiced at the start of *Ethics of the Fathers*—right after the Law is traced back to the revelation at Sinai—to "make a hedge around the Torah." Similarly, when Rieff writes a few sentences later about "cultic therapies of commitment" that "domesticated the wildness of experience"— restraining action, curbing thought, shaping desire—he may well have had in mind the commandment handed down by God after the spies strayed in their scouting mission into the promised land, and recalled by Jews three times each day. The Israelites were to place fringes on their garments to remind them not to "stray after their eyes and heart." The fringes are to accompany and guide them during their years in the wilderness and ever after.

Christianity too tried to shape a *conscience collective* by reining in and reigning over individual desire. The "classical Christian culture of commitment" had placed restraints on the "sexual opportunism of individuals." Rieff terms this ascetic turn the "rejection of sexual individualism." That to his mind is the significance of separating pleasure from procreation. The fact that Christianity also encouraged the seeking of individual salvation did not get in the way of producing the "necessary corporate identities" (97).

Here as elsewhere in his corpus, Rieff used shorthand, dealt with ideal-types; he chose not to embark on the nuanced historical sociology required in order to distinguish Catholics from Protestants, say, or Pietists from Lutherans, in the way that Weber felt compelled to do in *The Protestant Ethic and the Spirit of Capitalism*, a work that Rieff of course knew well. Hence the use of terms such as "Christian culture" and even "Western culture." Rieff did not prove but rather suggested; he wanted to help his readers see what is—and is not—before us. He also believed the developments he discerned too recent to permit more conclusive analysis.

Rieff worried about what he saw taking shape in our culture and admitted his desire to arouse his reader's anxiety as well, lest we succumb unawares to the final deterioration of the old cultures of authority. In particular, he worried about the supplanting of a religiously sanctified order of interdiction against transgression by a remissive religion that permitted nearly all things—or by no religion at all (99). Remission is no longer a way of allowing individuals to be saved in their communities despite having done wrong. That is its classic function, often accomplished in cultures of faith through penance and atonement and properly indicated by guilt. What should never be done, having been done, can yet somehow be made right. Only thus can the order of interdiction be saved from the weight of inevitable transgression. In the emergent therapeutic culture, Rieff feared, we are all pronounced okay, and if we are not absolutely fine at the moment, therapy will help us get there. This cultural revolution, he notes, does not replace one commitment with another—the usual pattern—but is "rather a way of using all commitments, which amounts to loyalty toward none" (99).

Rieff was of course getting at a set of developments that would later receive the label "postmodernism." One can easily imagine him embracing the term "language game," for example, precisely for its reduction of all that was previously held most serious to a "level playing field." Postmodernity assumes that there are many things, an infinite number in fact, from which the self can choose, none required and none ultimately serious. Rieff had little respect for the "nominally Jewish or Christian barbarians" who embrace such a creed (unnamed as such as of his writing) and had little confidence that the social gospel, marshaled in the sixties to assist the civil rights movement, could save liberal Christianity from decline. In this he proved correct.

Triumph of the Therapeutic does not provide us with a nuanced picture of contemporary religion in America. Any attempt to do so would have to depict more than "old ideological contents . . . preserved mainly for their therapeutic potential" (104), though there is certainly a lot of that in evidence. It is also the case, as Rieff would have been the first to admit, that religion has *always* been in the salvation business. He derived his notion of the therapeutic, after all, from a religious sect that flourished two millennia ago. Weber taught that the key religious question is always what human beings need saving from and how religion proposes to save them. The crooked are made straight, the lame to walk, the blind to see; the leper is healed, the wicked repent, the lonely are succored with the balm of community.

Indeed, at key points in the chapter a skeptical voice sets the tone of Rieff's analysis. "It may be argued against this position." "Who is to say that these [Christian/religious/cultural] controls are eternal? I do not think so." Or—my favorite sentence in the chapter, the one that leads directly to *Fellow Teachers* and the personal voice that it inaugurates in the Rieffian canon: "I, too, aspire to see clearly, like a rifleman, with one eye shut; I, too, aspire to think without assent. This is the ultimate violence to which the modern intellectual is committed. Since things have become as they are, I, too, share the modern desire not to be deceived" (91). That remarkable statement is followed at once by comparison to "the culture to which I was first habituated" and by apparent regret that it "grows progressively different in its symbolic nature and in its human product," leading to "our ambivalence as professional mourners." Rieff does not expand on this statement of attachment to and distance from the Jewish culture in which he grew up. Nor does this rather weak statement of affiliation with the successor culture that Rieff shares with most of his fellow intellectuals lead to endorsement of the "systematic hunting-down of all settled convictions" (92). Quite the opposite is the case; *that* rifleman's association is one he does *not* wish to join.

Rieff seems caught, and he wants us to know it. He cannot entirely remove himself, even through criticism, from the first person plural expressed in such phrases as "We are the true revolutionaries" or "our cultural revolution" (99). The reader has a good sense, by the end of *Triumph of the Therapeutic*, of what Rieff fears and what he stands against. What he stands *for*—negation of the negation of culture, the giant "one step further" that he believes is urgently required for the survival of culture as such—awaits the formal introduction of the Jew of culture.

TEACHERS, SCHOLARS, JEWS

That introduction is made, we recall, against the background of modern claims to have surpassed all particulars of identity. "We Jews of culture are obliged to resist the very idea" (110). Rieff's argument, spelled out in passage after passage but never made linear, let alone syllogistic, is that the attempt to abandon individual identities such as "Jew" in favor of universals such as "science" or "the proletariat" or "humanity" cannot be understood outside the larger "confusion of spheres" by "modern aspirants to freedom from all authority." Therapeutics want to believe that every option is open to them, none foreclosed by any givens of who they are or should be. This bleak view of the modern situation recalls Weber's "iron cage," though its notion of our collective "disenchantment" is even more disturbing than Weber's because Rieff sees no prospect of a charismatic authority with the ability to save us all from our predicament. It is telling, I think, that Nietzsche enters Rieff's text forcefully as alternate "presiding presence." *Fellow Teachers* never achieves Nietzsche's clear and beautiful prose (indeed, Rieff prefers concealment and opacity). But the manner of presentation in other respects recalls Nietzsche rather directly: short sections rather than extended chapters, frequent reference to works of literature, wry disputatiousness and biting wit, frequent resort to hyperbole. More important, the critique of "our reeducated classes, rich consumers of everything available" brings to mind Nietzsche's warning at the conclusion of *The Birth of Tragedy* (no. 23) about our culture's homeless roving from table to table of experience. Rieff's appeal to "we teachers" directly echoes the "We Scholars" section of *Beyond Good and Evil*. Rieff too "demands of himself a judgment, a Yes or No, not about the sciences but about life and the value of life."[10] He demands it of all his fellow teachers and readers as well.

Like Jews of culture, true teachers are those who resist (119). Their profession makes them outcasts in a culture committed to overturning authority, a game that rules no position out of bounds. "True teaching can acquire its strictly limited, easily challenged authority of resistance only after it develops institutionally in teaching orders."[11] Let's unpack this sentence. Rieff cites the Jesuits as an example of the sort of teaching order that the contemporary academy lacks. He perhaps seeks to create a new teaching order of sorts by gathering together those willing to pledge allegiance to his vision of the professor's duty, unlike that of Jesuits and contemporary academy alike. That task is far from easy. The authority of the teacher is always "easily challenged" because it comes with no power of coercion attached, not even the force of logical proof. Rieff agrees with Weber that politics does not belong in the classroom. Nor can teachers, dedicated to seeking truth, obligated to criticize established verities, expert only in small areas of knowledge—and for all these reasons "strictly limited" in their authority—attach themselves to those who exercise power. "We mere teachers, Jews of culture, influential and eternally powerless, have no choice except to think defensively: how to keep ourselves from being overwhelmed" (126). The danger lies in the anti-culture evident all around them—and now especially prevalent inside the university itself.

Jews are paradigmatic of this sort of culture not only because they have always existed as a minority (Lyotard, no friend to Rieff's analysis, famously called "the jews" those who have never fit neatly into the cultures of the West)[12] but because their teachers worked normatively from inside frameworks they believed descended from their ancestors. Rieff knew and cited the first sentence of the *Ethics of the Fathers:* Moses received the Torah from Sinai and passed it to Joshua, and Joshua to the elders, etc. Even rabbis far down this chain of reception, teachers who innovated in their interpretation of law or truth, did so in the firm conviction that they were merely drawing out implications placed in their sacred texts long ago. "The great teacher is he who, because he carries in himself what is already known, can transfer it to his student; that inwardness is his absolute and irreducible authority" (128).

The preface that Rieff added to *Fellow Teachers* in 1984 cites the Talmudic passage reporting that when Rabbi Meir died, there were no more makers of parables; when Ben Azzai died, there were no more diligent students.[13] Our teachers live in us, he was fond of saying, and we live deeply, with inwardness, thanks to the norms they transmitted to us for affirmation. Rieff's practical understanding of this transmission manifested itself in the famously careful textual studies he led with his students. In my case this meant an entire semester reading just a few short pages of Weber's "Science as a Vocation." This is the way norms are passed along to the next generation: word by word, sentence by sentence.

That is not to say that cultures do not change. Rieff is clear on this point. Cultures either remain vital or they die, replaced by successors capable of doing better. He wishes good riddance more than once in *Fellow Teachers*—with a sharpness not seen in earlier work—to the Christian culture that had maligned and persecuted Jews. "Nietzsche knew that Christendom's love was a covert form of making war on culture in any form, an expression of the most terrible hatred, envy, revenge . . . Jew-hatred remains the deepest transgressive motif of Christian Love." In a quieter moment, sitting at All Souls College in Oxford, he is led to reflect on "the arbitrariness and pathos of old authority when it will not stay far enough in arrears" (138). Rieff is no caricature of a cultural conservative. His allegiance depends upon what is being preserved, for what purpose and by whom.

He certainly does not look to his fellow Jews to defy the anticultural trend. Rieff scorns those whom he calls "ex-Jews," who have abandoned exactly the virtues necessary to the tasks of the Jews of culture. "Israel cannot survive the end of faith," he declares. "The fate of our high culture is inseparable from the relation between the past of faith and the future of Israel" (118). Rieff ridicules "The New Joodeyism," reduced from thoroughgoing life commitment to an "ism" easily collapsed into general principles and combined with immersion in a life of therapy. "'Judaism' represents contemporary Jews to themselves as they are, still in their massive fugue, fleeing the interdictory genius for which the gentile world, like the Jews themselves, cannot be expected to show gratitude" (188). He taught me, a scholar of Judaism in the modern period, to see much that modern Jews have said and done as deliberate "act[s] of forgetting." (We argued good-naturedly over my use of the word Judaism in my work and self-description as a scholar. I cling to it still despite his reservations.)

Rieff did not in my estimation give enough consideration to two possible reasons (aside from therapeutic distaste for absolute noes and yesses) for the Jewish flight from "interdictory genius," though he hinted at both in the passage just quoted. There is, for one thing, anti-Semitism. Nowhere previously in Rieff's writings do we encounter such bitter hostility to this facet of Christianity and in particular to Paul. (Like many modern Jewish thinkers, Rieff identifies Jesus as a true Jew, a model Jew of culture, who came to fulfill the law not break it [129], whereas Paul loosed Jews from their bonds and assured gentiles they had no need of them.) Nowhere else in Rieff's work do we find reference to the aunts who died in Dachau rather than be sex slaves to the SS—or to their father, who survived Dachau at the price of unimaginable humiliation.

A second cause of flight from Judaism may well be reluctance—so soon after the Holocaust—to be overly distinctive from the larger society. The states and societies of the modern West frequently let Jews know—sometimes through coercive legislation, sometimes through social opprobrium—that adherence to the "ways of the land" was expected in return for the rights of emancipation. It was a price Jews were more often than not quite willing to pay, so long as it did not mean total erasure of their identity. In another of the more powerful passages in the book, Rieff joins the horrors of the Holocaust to the abandonment of the sabbath, foreshadowed and rationalized in Marx's famous distinction in "On the Jewish Question" between "the *sabbath Jew* and the *everyday Jew.*" Marx had no use for either sort of Jew, of course. The former paid homage to a God whom Marx believed part of the opiate that kept the masses from revolution, and an illusion "projected" out of human alienation to boot. The latter was a huckster, an egoist, a bourgeois. "The Revolution respects no sabbaths," Rieff writes. "How are you on the trivial old question of sabbath keeping? Is any order worthy of the name without its strict sabbaths: *No* is the first word of resistance" (130).

Most Jews of Rieff's acquaintance were without sabbaths and without regret or guilt at the loss of sabbaths; they had cast off most of their tradition's noes. As countermodel, Rieff holds up Abraham: bold enough to argue with God about the justice of wiping out Sodom and Gomorrah, but ever determined to make God's will his own. Abraham's colloquy with God also teaches the need for remissions as a safeguard for the interdicts (here Rieff explicitly passes on biblical and rabbinic lessons). Finally, Abraham provides subsequent generations with a grandfather figure who, Rieff notes, compares favorably with parents, who are always objects of ambivalence. "My parents were not nearly good enough for me," Rieff says, not entirely in jest. "I was lucky to have grandfathers." He concludes the accompanying note by saying that he cannot penetrate all the mysteries to which he refers. "I am not learned in the tradition" (141).

This statement too was not entirely ironic. Rieff was not a scholar of Judaism, nor a Jewish theologian, not even a faithful exegete. His God remains in *Fellow Teachers* what God was in *Triumph of the Therapeutic*: a functional presiding presence, originator and guarantor of sacred order, but far from a personal creator, revealer, or redeemer. A key footnote on this point in *Fellow Teachers* replaces Martin Buber's "I-Thou" of relationship and "encounter" between human beings and "the Eternal Thou" with a "we-they" that separates holy from profane (117). We might say that Rieff to this point in his career always remained on that horizontal level of covenant, perhaps because he was convinced that ascent on the vertical remains beyond human (or at least modern) capacity. For all his dissatisfaction with Weber's picture of disenchantment, he too never found his way back to the affirmation of belief.

But neither did he rest content with unbelief—or blame recourse to it, as Weber did, on the alleged requirement to sacrifice intellect in order to return to the religious fold. Rieff's complex stance is on view in a passage that alludes to the conclusion of Weber's credo essay "Science as a Vocation," where Weber quoted from Isaiah. "He calleth to me out of Seir, Watchman, what of the night? The watchman said, The morning cometh, and also the night: if ye will enquire, enquire ye: return, come." To which Weber added that "the people to whom this was said [i.e., the Jewish people] has enquired and tarried for more than two millennia, and we are shaken when we realize its fate."[14] Rieff's response is somewhat different. He is not about to distinguish himself from the Jews, even if he cannot embrace Jewish faith. "Beyond saying "'Inquire,' who dares say 'Return'? Prophetic orders and their compelling god-terms have ceased to recall us" (127).

Why was that the case? A related passage in *Fellow Teachers* suggests that the obstacle may not be modern culture—and certainly did not lie in any Jewish propensity to inquire and tarry—but was rather to be found in the nature of faith itself. "A large supply of god-terms" may be all we can attain because "our god can only reveal as he conceals himself; ask that, concealment with every revelation, and you have understood why the major questions must always continue as if unanswered" (112). The relevant source here is not Isaiah but Deuteronomy. "The hidden things belong to the Lord our God, but the revealed things are for us and our descendants forever to do all the words of this Torah" (29:28).

Deuteronomy of course offered Jews a divine revelation, mediated by Moses. This Rieff could not claim. He did the best he could without it, we might say, drawing upon reason, upon tradition, and upon the nature of culture. He was ever true to the calling and the limitations of the Jew of culture. Only in later writings would he come to speak directly of God.

Oscar Wilde

A note in *Fellow Teachers*, placed immediately before the call to sabbath keeping, alludes to an introduction Rieff had just written to an edition of Oscar Wilde's *The Soul of Man under Socialism*. A decade later he expanded the piece into "The Impossible

Culture," one of the most eloquent statements of his theory of culture. The Jews—of faith or of culture—are never mentioned in the piece, and yet they are present on almost every page. Wilde emerges in Rieff's analysis as a prophet of paganism and polytheism, an avatar of modern culture who represented everything the Jew of culture is not and so must oppose.

It had been clear from the Disraeli piece onward that English culture occupied a special status in Rieff's theory; it serves in many ways as successor to the original chosen aristocracy of culture. The Puritans had first pronounced that genealogy, and built it into the fabric of what English culture became under the impress of the King James Bible. Matthew Arnold ratified the connection with his effort to create a secularized national culture, drawn as much or more from "Hebraism" as "Hellenism." We have already observed Rieff reflecting wistfully on the link between Oxford and Jerusalem from the vantage of the towers at All Souls. And now, in Wilde, we see a great artist of English culture, one of its most brilliant products, engaged full force in an act of betrayal. Here is a man, a man of culture, who says, "I rarely think that anything is true." Far from affirming Hebraism, he is "entirely on the side of the Greeks." The idea he favors "is a pagan idea" (144). Not only is his view of culture nonnormative but he declares right and wrong antithetical to culture. No statement of the matter could be more opposed to Rieff's. It is no surprise then that Wilde serves him as such a worthy antagonist, the theorist of culture who called forth one of his own finest efforts. Rieff needed to show us, and himself presumably, that what Wilde wished for in the way of culture was nothing short of impossible.

That is because—contrary to the Torah's warning against going astray after eyes and heart—Wilde resisted the narrowing of possibility. "Sociologically, a truth is whatever militates against the human capacity to express everything. Repression is truth. God is not love, except as he is authority. When Wilde declared himself against authority, he did not know how he weakened what he was for: love. Authority will not be separate from love" (150). A more rabbinic statement could hardly be imagined. The Jewish prayer book, set in place by the rabbis, brackets the recitation of the "Hear O Israel" prayer, recital of which in their view connoted renewed acceptance of the "yoke of the kingdom of heaven," with paragraphs affirming Israel's love for God and God's love for Israel. How can one love—without distinctions? How can love exist—without claims of high and low, right and wrong?[15] What is love worth—without protection of those claims, by force if necessary, but certainly by force of argument? Pagans too were aware of this truth, Rieff argues. They could have worshiped no gods otherwise. "Wilde had a most inaccurate notion of any actually pagan idea" (151).

And if the pagan gods enforced the limitation of experience, how much more so the God of Israel! That God demonstrated supremacy by ordaining a sacred order of yes and no that is unparalleled outside monotheism. But God's god-ness was confirmed, as it were, by virtue of a so-called revelation that took the form of near-total concealment. "The guardians of any culture must constantly protect the difference between the public and private sectors. . . . Art should be expressive and repressive at the same time. This, after all, is what is meant by sublimation." Character runs deep. The self thrives on inwardness, and dissipates on surfaces (160). And here, at the very heart of who he was and where his greatness lay, Wilde betrayed the work of culture by reversing the proper spheres of public and private. "I have put my genius into my life—I have put only my talent into my work" (158). He understood, Rieff writes, "that in the established society this was an inversion of the energies appropriate to the private and public sectors." Display of the genius for intimacy still finds its welcoming public—and so trades intimacy for scandal. (Or, we might add, for mere publicity. True scandal grows ever harder to achieve.) Art captures what we want to say, and cannot. It teaches through indirection. It crosses boundaries of good and evil that in real life we dare not violate. Art thus attains heights and depths otherwise unavailable to human beings. All this so long as we know that it is not life, that we are not in this sense works of art.

Rieff argues cogently that in part "Wilde's attack on all authority [was] too easy. When authority becomes so external, then it has ceased to be authoritative" (160). Wilde questioned norms that had become open to question. The opposition was tired and easily bested in debate. Wilde knew this, though he lost his case nonetheless. He was knowledgeable enough about culture to understand as well that "whatever makes authority incarnate in our culture is no longer available to it." No creed, no symbolic, can do the job of culture half as well (161). And do the job authority must—lest we perish from sheer infinity of possibility. "Culture is a tremendous articulation of compromise between equally intolerable feelings of nothing and everything. The claim of the artist to express everything is subversive in one especially acute sense: the claim to express everything can only exacerbate feelings of being nothing" (163). That is the charge for which Rieff prosecutes Wilde, an accusation far more grave in his view than the transgression for which Wilde's "dying culture" put him in jail. The man who could have served as a consummate Jew of culture chose instead to serve the opposite god—all gods, no gods.

The story Rieff tells ends, as we would expect by now, with a confession of sorts on the part of the accused. Just as Rieff had detected Freud's (unconscious?) recognition of the truth he had for so long denied, so too now in the case of Wilde. At one level, deep within, Wilde understood his crime and his salvation. "I was buoyed up with a sense of guilt" (164). We all are, Rieff would say. He enjoyed quoting the words of the officer in Kafka's "In the Penal Colony": "Guilt is never to be doubted." Thank goodness, Rieff would add: otherwise there would be no apparent judgment in the world, and no Judge.

ONE LAST TIME, FREUD

The final selection included here is unlike all the others in many respects, most notably in the fact that it consists of passages chosen by the editors of this volume (roughly a fourth of the whole) from a manuscript Rieff wrote in the mid-1990s and never revised into final form. The prose and thinking are sometimes polished, but often not; the manuscript contains occasional notes that Rieff wrote to himself concerning points or sources that required following up or checking; at times the train of his thought moves from idea to idea in a way easily followed, but at other times his mind jumps so quickly that the reader strains to keep up. The entire manuscript takes off from, and repeatedly returns to, a study written about Freud's complex relation to Moses, to the God Moses served, and to the religious tradition of which Moses stands as founder: the historian Yosef Yerushalmi's highly acclaimed *Freud's Moses: Judaism Terminable and Interminable* (1991). Rieff greatly admired the work but had a number of reservations, and one in particular: Yerushalmi had let Freud off too easily. By this point in his life Rieff was convinced that Freud had knowingly and intentionally set out to murder Moses in his great, final work, *Moses and Monotheism*. Freud pronounced him an Egyptian, deconstructed his achievement, and reduced his God to nothing. Here, in what may have been Rieff's own final work, he mounts an attack from which nothing is held back.

The reader of *My Life among the Deathworks*, published in 2006 and written more or less at the same time as "Is Not the Truth the Truth?" will not be surprised by the tone or content of the latter work. Neither will the reader of *The Crisis of the Officer Class* (2007), the second volume in the *Sacred Order/Social Order* trilogy. In the former work, too, Jewish "lifeworks" stands in stark opposition to contemporary "deathworks." The concepts of first (pagan), second (Judeo-Christian), and third (neo-pagan; therapeutic) worlds are introduced and used to good effect. Shakespeare takes his place as a major part of Rieff's canon in both works. The sociological theorist Rieff takes what James Davison Hunter calls a decided "ontological turn."[16] (I would call it an avowed entry into theology.) The "Jew of culture" remains active. "Breuer, on the verge of the discovery that authority was a fiction of the erotic acceptance and dependence, was still so much a Jew of culture that he withdrew and opened the way for Freud's transformative understanding."[17] In *The Officer Class*—Rieff borrows the term from Kafka's *In the Penal Colony*—this cultural elite, too, plays a role directly analogous to the Jew of culture. That book, like the "Truth" essay, argues the impossibility of a culture without guilt, that is, a culture not subordinate to what Rieff now calls the "vertical in authority." In many respects, there is little that is added in the present manuscript.

And yet there is: not least the direct assault on Freud that begins on the very first page of "Truth" in the conceit that dominates the essay from start to finish. Hitler began his onslaught against the Jews in 1939. Freud finished his that same year with the publication of his book on Moses. The assault from without was paralleled by that from within. Wars of words precede and follow battles fought by bombers and artillery. Worst of all, perhaps, "the war against the Jews" is "apparently [a] permanent part" of "the foreseeable historical context in which this book will be read."

These claims are troubling, to say the least. Rieff's readers are old enough not to swear by the refrain that "sticks and stones may break my bones but words will never hurt me." And yet we are unlikely to posit the equivalence of *any* words with Hitler's actual deathwork, let alone the words of Freud. It is hard to believe that Rieff took his own words to this effect seriously, or meant for us to do so. There is a great deal in the essay that Rieff might well have revised, if given the opportunity, or eliminated. We have tried not to include any portion of the manuscript that seems entirely unthought out, preliminary, or trivial. But Rieff's thought rarely descended to the trivial. Even when patently exaggerating, he has a lot to teach. And there is more than rhetorical power, I believe, in all the selections included here. I hope and believe that Rieff would have tempered some of the claims put forth in these pages. But I hope equally, for the sake of our learning, that he would not have eliminated such passages entirely.

One argument in particular seems especially important to the conception and consideration of the Jew of culture: whether there can be such a thing as Jewishness apart from the sacred, or indeed apart from God. Rieff is convinced that there cannot be, and he faults Yerushalmi for implying the opposite through the subtitle of his book. Rieff's concern is no longer with use of the word "Judaism" but rather with the horrifying thought—conceived by Freud—that the religion it denotes might be "terminable." Consider this passage:

Yerushalmi carries his burden so gracefully that his reader would swear that the Jewish past is brought into the post-Freudian present without more than occasional noises, offstage, of the war within the Jewish camp Yerushalmi conducts. The war for the Jewish world, conducted here within the Jewish camp, is almost noiseless. Yet, hovering as the hidden reality, just off Yerushalmi's stage, is the world in all its bloody mess and gore, ourselves ever on the move in that mess. (176)

Rieff labels Yerushalmi elsewhere an "accomplice" of Freud's by virtue of that silence. He chides him for employing "Jewishness" as a "sponge word" disguising the descent to godlessness (176). He insists that any war against the Jews is a war against their "king," God. Freud had conspired to overthrow the authority of Moses, and so to challenge the primacy of God among the Jews, and Yerushalmi to Rieff's mind has let him get away with it.

There are several other high points of the study, which likewise reveal Rieff to have become well versed in Jewish concerns and conversations at the time. The essay is pervaded, as much Jewish thought was in the 1980s and early 1990s, by the Holocaust. It is also full of anxiety for Israel, and takes pains to justify the need for a "*Machtstaat*" to defend the God and faith (the "*Kulturstaat*") of Israel—this at the very same time that Rieff expresses severe unhappiness with the ultra-Orthodox Jews (*Haredim*) who hung back from commitment to the state but claimed a monopoly on legitimate Jewish worship of God. The reader is struck by Rieff's direct reference to the "Hear O Israel" prayer, which he calls, using the original Hebrew, the Shema. We are also arrested to find quotation at length from Kadya Molodovsky's bitter poem "God of Mercy" and by learned (and caring) critique of a Reform liturgy for Yom Kippur that Rieff praises for including a passage from King Lear but faults for getting Lear wrong.

Rieff, in short, is no longer defending the need for God or Jews or Jews of culture from a stance outside the Jewish tradition. He has entered the Jewish conversation enough to join in protest against God. He critiques the Reform liturgy because he has had the experience of worship inside its framework; he has even become enough of a Jew to argue—after extensive quotation from Abraham Lincoln as well as Shakespeare—that the latter "is part of a parallel canon without which my 'Jewishness' is impoverished. . . . No Jew can live in an entirely Jewish reality" (196). Rieff as always is not writing merely as a Jew. But he is more clearly than ever writing not merely as a "man."

The final passage that we have included from the manuscript explains why God must be conceived as a person, even though God's thoughts (as Isaiah insisted) can never be ours. Rieff shows God in dialogue with Abraham over how the world should be governed. "The universality of therapeutic truth opposes the particularity of sacred truth in historic Israel."

We knew this from the beginning, we might say, or rather Rieff did. It was after all the message of his essay on Disraeli, pronounced on the very first page of that piece. Look, however, at how much has changed in the meantime, much of it theorized in connection with the developing conception of the Jew of culture. The author of the Disraeli essay would not and did not speak of "sacred order," or identify so unreservedly as a Jew, or denounce Freud as an enemy of true culture, or express concern for the State of Israel, or approvingly cite a poem of protest against God. Freud was "his own ideal Jew," Rieff wrote in the 1961 preface to *The Mind of the Moralist*. He would never have said the same of himself, I believe. But he might well have agreed that not until the writing of his last works did he so fully inhabit the role of Jew of culture—because never before did he speak quite so directly, or so eloquently, about what it meant to look out at the world, and seek to change it, as a Jew.

NOTES

1. See Richard I. Cohen, *Jewish Icons: Art and Society in Modern Europe* (Berkeley and Los Angeles: University of California Press, 1998).

2. See Arnold M. Eisen, *The Chosen People in America* (Bloomington: Indiana University Press, 1995), 143-48.

3. Philip Rieff, *Freud: The Mind of the Moralist*, 3rd. ed. (Chicago: University of Chicago Press, 1979), xxiii–iv.

4. *The Mind of the Moralist*, 56.

5. Ibid., 106–9.

6. Ibid., 195.

7. Ibid., 201.

8. Ibid., 106.

9. See Philip Rieff, *The Triumph of the Therapeutic* (Chicago: University of Chicago Press, 1987), 261.

10. *Beyond Good and Evil*, part 6, section 205.

11. *Fellow Teachers*, 88.

12. See Jean-François Lyotard, *Heidegger and "the Jews,"* trans. Andreas Michel and Mark S. Roberts (Minneapolis: University of Minnesota Press, 1990).

13. Sotah 9:15.

14. Max Weber, "Science as a Vocation," in *From Max Weber: Essays in Sociology*, ed. and trans. H. H. Gerth and C. Wright Mills (New York: Oxford University Press, 1972), 156.

15. Rieff is drawing on the argument in the first half of *Civilization and Its Discontents*, where Freud argues that Christian *agape* forces us to live beyond our psychological means.

16. John Davison Hunter, introduction to Philip Rieff, *My Life among the Deathworks*, vol. 1 of *Sacred Order/Social Order* (Charlottesville: University of Virginia Press, 2006), xvii.

17. Rieff, *My Life among the Deathworks*, 130.

THE JEW OF CULTURE

Disraeli: The Chosen of History Uniting the Old Jerusalem and the New

George Saintsbury thought not only that Disraeli "founded a remarkable school of fiction" but that his politics were as romantic as his fiction. The most romantic thing in Disraeli was the motivation of both his fiction and his politics, a motivation to be found in his Jewishness—his quite particular kind of Jewishness. For it was not the Jews that claimed Disraeli—Disraeli claimed the Jews. Baptized into the Church of England in what would have been the year of his bar mitzvah, Disraeli *chose* not to forget he was a Jew. And it was not simply a reaction to the "hostile consciousness of others," as Sartre would interpret the sense of Jewishness. Rather the hostile consciousness of others was a reaction to his perverse claim to Jewishness.

The hostile consciousness of others can best be read in three unsigned articles, probably written by Goldwin Smith, the Liberal historian and polemicist, printed in consecutive numbers of the *Fortnightly Review* from April through June 1878. "The secret of Lord Beaconsfield's life," Smith wrote, "lies in his Jewish blood. . . . Lord Beaconsfield is the most remarkable illustration of his own doctrine of the ascendancy of Hebrew genius in modern Europe. . . . Certainly a century and a quarter of residence in England on the part of his ancestors and himself has left little trace on the mind and character of Lord Beaconsfield. He is in almost every essential . . . a Jew."

One of the missing essentials was that Disraeli was a member of the established church. And yet he played at being a Jew far more seriously than Heine played at not being a Jew. (To play at being a Jew is usually more serious.) Disraeli, who hated the universalist rationalism of his country, refused to be accepted as simply a "man," and yet he was certainly not simply a Jew. Sartre has developed no category for him, neither "authentic" nor "inauthentic." Disraeli neither fled from nor stayed with his Jewishness: he was pushed out too early to make either choice. But he remained a Jew in a peculiar way that deserves its own study—in his nostalgia.

The critic D. H. Harding has said that the word "nostalgia" ought not to be used "unless the quality of feeling to be described is recognizably similar to the common experience of homesickness, the feeling of distress for no localized, isolated cause, together with a feeling that one's environment is . . . vaguely wrong and unacceptable." Then the word is used quite properly to describe Disraeli. His writing is an expression of an experience recognizably similar to homesickness, and Disraeli certainly felt from the very beginning of his life to the end that his environment was vaguely wrong and unacceptable. His feeling of discomfort in his environment began at home, with his family.

Disraeli's grandfather—Benjamin D'Israeli, merchant, for whom the grandchild was named—came to England from Italy around 1748, when he was eighteen. He joined the Jewish community in London, became a member of the Sephardic synagogue of Bevis Marks, and married a Jewish girl who never pardoned him his name. Her nagging self-hatred in time drove him into retirement, but not before he had made a small fortune. Her only child, Isaac, suffered the burden of never being forgiven for being a little Jew. His existence, writes the second Benjamin in the memoir of his father, "only served to swell the aggregate of many humiliating particulars. [He] was not to be to her a source of joy, or sympathy, or solace. She foresaw for her child only a future of degradation."

Isaac D'Israeli became a "timid, susceptible" boy, in his youth and early manhood suffering from what his son later decided must be called something other than a physical illness. He put it down, in his famous memoir, as a "failing of nervous energy." Disraeli was amazed that the best medical men for a long while diagnosed his father's illness as "consumption." "The symptoms," he writes, "are physical and moral . . . lassitude and despondency." He knew the case could not have been consumption, for he had had the same symptoms in his own early manhood. The disease was really self-hatred. "One of his few infirmities," Benjamin concludes of his father, "was . . . a deficiency of self-esteem."

Disraeli remembered his grandmother, even in his later life, as "a demon," and the journeys to her home were the horrors of his boyhood. But he came to understand her very well. "My grandmother, the beautiful daughter of a family who had suffered much from persecution, had imbibed that dislike of her race which the vain are too apt to adopt when they find that they are born to public contempt. The indignant feeling that should be reserved for the persecutor, in the mortification of their disturbed sensibility, is too often visited on the victim and the cause of annoyance is recognized not in the ignorant malevolence of the powerful but in the conscientious conviction of the innocent sufferer."

His grandmother, he concluded, was "so mortified by her [Jewishness] that she lived till eighty without indulging in a tender expression." His father became an intellectual, the son of a rich Jew searching for mankind in libraries. He read Bayle and Voltaire, and especially Rousseau. When he had been a young boy he imagined his name was Emile, not Isaac. He was too mild to break with the synagogue, or to marry other than a Jewess. His wife, Maria Basevi, took over the practical affairs of the family and bore him four sons, Benjamin, Raphael, Jacob, and Naphtali, and a daughter, Sarah. Benjamin was born December 21, 1804, "or according to the Jewish reckoning the nineteenth of Tebet, 5565," as his chief biographer, W. F. Monypenny, puts it. "On the eighth day the boy was duly initiated into the covenant of Abraham, the rite of circumcision being performed by a relative of his mother's."

In 1817, when the grandfather died, Isaac agreed to have all his children baptized, and Benjamin was received into the Anglican communion at St. Andrew's Church, Holborn, July 31, 1817. Isaac had grasped at a petty reason to break with the synagogue. He gave it in an essay entitled "The Genius of Judaism": the "lone and sullen genius of rabbinical Judaism" cut him off "from the great family of mankind." Isaac D'Israeli spent the remainder of his life taking flight into the universal in his library, where he read and puttered all day and most evenings, and wrote such books as *Calamities of Authors*, which sold well to "the middling classes." But he himself did not become a Christian—that was no more "reasonable" than to remain a Jew. And the family name remained the same, D'Israeli. Indeed, D'Israeli had allowed the baptizing of his children only after considerable urging by a gentile friend, the historian Sharon Turner, who convinced him that baptism would help their careers if not their souls. Civil office and much land and business were closed to Jews, not to be opened until Benjamin Disraeli himself helped do so.

There is no evidence that the twelve-year-old boy resisted baptism. Neither is there any sign that he welcomed it. Boys do not usually have opinions on such matters. What had happened was quite simple, and sudden—and, most of all, expedient. But the young Disraeli was certainly aware of his Jewishness. Until the year he was baptized, a man came every Saturday to the Christian school he attended and gave him Jewish religious instruction. When the rest of the boys made their daily prayer, Benjamin had to go to a corner and turn his back, as was the custom developed at that time to take care of this sort of situation.

And there was always his name. Even after he had been received into the Church of England he had to fight his schoolmates to defend his name. The D'Israelis sent him to a Unitarian school, but even there he had to fight and they soon took him home. Benjamin stayed at home, alone, and read hard. The lonely boy decided he would be a famous man, and quickly. After all, Pitt had become prime minister at twenty-one, and Byron a star in Europe's culture at twenty-five. Young Benjamin made himself sick wondering what role to choose in order to be great.

Disraeli's father thought he ought to go into law; at seventeen he was articled to a firm of solicitors in Old Jewry. (A year later he dropped the apostrophe from the spelling of his name.) But he had already discovered another role, which he loved and which was to make him at least famous. He was writing a novel, *Vivian Grey*. And when it appeared it made him the literary lion of London, at twenty-one. *Vivian Grey*—and a period of deep depression—saved him from the law. Still, he could not decide what he was, or even *who* he was.

Troubled, he took his *Wanderjahre*, and returned home, irresolute. His depression drained him until he could not "write a line without effort." He wandered aimlessly about his father's house in "solitude and silence," unable to work enough to break the depression, but doing some reading and thinking. He worried about his appearance. "I grieve to say my hair grows very badly." Now his interest in dress became quite intense. He took to green velvet trousers, a canary-colored waistcoat, low shoes, silver buckles, lace at his wrists, and his hair in ringlets. He made himself into a complete dandy.

He lived "in perfect solitude for eighteen months." And he was "still suffering." It was the malaise his father had once suffered from, but Benjamin understood it better. In his letters, the word "ill" appears often in quotation marks. And his consequent reaction was quite different from his father's. What reading he did was in the history of the Jews. What thinking he did was of the Jews. Though every line was an effort, he began a second novel, to be called *Alroy*, whose hero was a Jew. But he dropped this. He could not be heroic. He began another, *The Young Duke*. The young duke is young Disraeli, and both are quite despairing, even if their despair seems unfashionably Byronic now. "The drooping pen falls from my powerless hand, and I feel—keenly, I feel myself what indeed I am—far the most prostrate of a fallen race."

Finally, the son announced to his father what had been on his mind during the despair of all his solitudes and silences: he proposed to visit Jerusalem. This would be his cure. (Disraeli sent his heroes to Jerusalem to end their malaise.) His announcement was vetoed with all the cold calm his father could muster. Almost twenty years later, in his novel *Tancred, or The New Crusade*, Disraeli imagined how his father must have reacted to his announcement. "Why should Benjamin go to Jerusalem?" the father must have insisted to himself. "Unreasonable boy!" And if he reaches there what does he think he will find? Religious truth? Political justice? Let him read of Jerusalem in travel books for restless young gentlemen. "They tell us what it is, a third-rate city in a strange wilderness." Isaac thought it was a folly, and his wife, who was a practical woman, agreed.

But Benjamin found a way to go. Some wealthy friends, the Austens, financed the trip. And he got as his traveling companion the wealthy fiancé of his sister Sarah, William Meredith. They set out for Jerusalem in June 1830. His trip was an effort to get at himself by traveling back through his past to what he considered to be his beginning. The first important stop after England was Spain, land of the Sephardim. The next, Jaffa. He passed through Ramleh, and rode into Jerusalem in February 1831.

The impact of Jerusalem upon him is recorded in his letters from that place to his sister Sarah; and, at a twenty years' remove, in *Tancred*.

Tancred, troubled young Lord Montacute, having always been fascinated by theology and troubled by the past, goes to find the mystery of that trouble in Palestine; it is his private crusade. If he is to go to the very beginning of his past, a learned Sephardi advises him, he must retrace his steps "from Calvary to Sinai." When the pilgrim comes finally "within sight of Sinai" he is "brooding in dejection, his eyes . . . suffused with tears." Tancred is in a "reverie," the style, at least, if not the condition, in which Disraeli often expressed his own Jewishness—rather, his nostalgia for it. The pilgrim Tancred stands at Sinai. "It was one of those moments of amiable weakness which make us all akin, when sublime ambition, the mystical predispositions of genius, the solemn sense of duty . . . and the dogmas of . . . [religion and] philosophy alike . . . sink into nothingness. The voice of his mother sounded in his ear, and he was haunted by his father's anxious glance. Why was he there? Why was he, the child of a northern isle, in the heart of stony Arabia, far from the scene of his birth and of his duties?"

Disraeli calls it "an awful question." But he thinks he knows the answer he ought to assign to Tancred. The answer is in one of Disraeli's favorite parliamentary devices: the rhetorical question. Was he, then, a stranger there? Uncalled, unexpected, intrusive, unwelcome? Was it a morbid curiosity, or the proverbial restlessness of a sated aristocrat, that had drawn him to these wilds?

What wilds? Had he no connection with them? Had he not from his infancy repeated in the congregation of his people the laws which, from the awful summit of these surrounding mountains, the Father of all had himself delivered for the government of mankind? And were not the wanderings of the Jews in the wilderness "the first and guiding history that had been entrusted to his young intelligence, from which it had drawn its first . . . conceptions?" Disraeli decides that Tancred is neither morbid tourist nor jaded young aristocrat. Tancred is here because he was here before he went to other lands. "Why, then, he had a right to be here! He had a connection with these regions; they had a hold upon him." He was not visiting a foreign land, like an educated and refined Hindu curious about Europe. He was visiting his own land, foreign as it was, "his fathers' land." Tancred's most passionate desire was "to penetrate the . . . elder world, and share its . . . divine prerogative. Tancred sighed."

Disraeli, who had written to John Murray that he might never return home, sighed and turned home. On their return trip, Meredith died of smallpox. Sarah never married. Instead, she became her brother's devoted sister. Her brother needed all her devotion. Having failed to find himself in journalism (at twenty-one, he had been important in pushing John Murray to publish a rival to the *Times*) or in novels, Disraeli finally decided on politics—this, while he was still in Jerusalem. He returned to England "in famous condition—better indeed than I ever was in my life and full of hope and courage."

Disraeli was twenty-eight when he returned to England. He was a famous novelist and a bad poet. Most of all, he was a young man of letters with a public, and this had given him a precarious professional income and an annoying habit of picking up large debts. But his sense of failure was still with him. A sense of failure, and something else, had driven Disraeli to Jerusalem. But Jerusalem, at this point, was a dream, and he knew he could have waking greatness only in action—on another blessed plot, that New Israel, this England.

Disraeli's position in English society in 1832, when he first stood for Parliament, was that of an intellectual, a dandy, an exotic. His novels had made him important to a society that, after all, did read novels. And his dandyism had made him even more ingratiating to a world that was, after all, a world of fashion. But the relation of the dandy to high society was that of a pacesetter of fashion who was also an outsider. The dandy might well be an aristocrat born, but if, like Disraeli, he was not one, he was never quite accepted—nor quite rejected.

"To enter high society, a man must have either blood, millions, or a genius." Disraeli thought he had at least genius. And he was in a hurry. He sought out the great with a purpose: to be great with them. They represented action and power. There was only one aristocracy above the English—the Jews', the universal, eternal aristocracy.

Disraeli used dandyism to legitimate his exoticism, which was his Jewishness. His dandyism merged with his Jewishness. This was the image the public had of him all his life, or at least until he became Lord Beaconsfield. The combination, Jew-dandy, gave him a name as a *farceur*, and he remains forever the Jew at play, overdressed and tongue in cheek, piping a cynical tune. Nothing about him was assumed to be true—except his Jewishness.

The diarist Wilfred Blunt decided Disraeli's Jewishness was the only real thing about him: "Aesthetically our good Jew was a terrible Philistine; and politically . . . a very complete *farceur*. I don't like to call him anything worse than that. . . . Only you cannot persuade me that he even for an instant took himself seriously as a British statesman, or expected any . . . to accept him so. His *Semitic* principles of course were genuine enough. For his fearlessness in avowing these I hold him in esteem—for a Jew ought to be a Jew. . . . [But] the wonder is that anyone should have been found to take him seriously . . . after such beginnings as his had been."

Disraeli's exaggerated Jewishness was a pleasure, a revenge, a resource. It was the center of his strength. Disraeli, wrote Emma Lazarus, had inherited and cultivated the pose of the Jew, "the simulated patience to submit to [humiliation, defeat, and brutality] without flinching, while straining every nerve and directing every energy to the aim of retaliation and revenge." Emma Lazarus thought Disraeli shared with Shylock, as a representative Jew of the Diaspora, "the rebellion of a proud heart embittered and perverted by brutal humiliations, and the consequent thirst for revenge, the astuteness, the sarcasm, the pathos, the egotism, and the cunning of the Hebrew usurer." As in Shylock, she found in Disraeli "the poetic, Oriental imagination dealing in tropes and symbols, the energy, or rather now the obstinacy, of will, the intellectual superiority, the peculiarly Jewish strength . . . not only to perceive and make the most of every advantage of their situation and temperament, but also, with marvelous adroitness, to transform their very disabilities into new instruments of power."

Disraeli's pose gave him his perfect grip on himself. But the price of a perfect pose is to be unknown, alone, and this was the rock-bottom price he had to pay for power. An outsider—an intellectual of sorts, a Jew of sorts—cannot let the insiders get too close to him. It would only deepen their suspicion or, at least, their confusion about him. And confusion is the same thing as suspicion in politics.

Disraeli was an opportunist. This did not strike him as being unethical, only political. He made no bones about his opportunism. After silence, it was the highest law of politics. If he was unfair to Peel in the famous debates in which he destroyed his party leader and opened the way to make over the Tories under his own leadership, he was unfair with a clear eye that this was his main, perhaps his only, chance. Politics is a game of time. And times change. Peel knew that, too. But Disraeli knew it better. When Peel attempted to change the Tory protectionist policy, Disraeli rose to defend it. It was his chance to separate the Tories from their leader, and he made the most of it. He became the leader the protectionists had to accept, finally. No one else could speak so well for them.

But this was later, after Disraeli had been elected to the House. His first stand, in 1832, failed. He was too suspect. Neither party took him seriously. Opinion had it that he was a Radical. Disraeli failed as well in his second stand, and in his third, and in his fourth. By this time he had decided to be a Tory. Failure makes conservatives out of near radicals.

The Conservative party was in a quandary when Disraeli entered it; "having rejected all respect for antiquity, it offers no redress for the present, and makes no preparation for the future." Disraeli gave English Conservatism in the nineteenth century its program and its purpose. To prepare for the future, a political movement must return to its past. So Disraeli believed all his life; he was a dynamic conservative. And the conception of a return to the past organized his own energies, if it did not supply them.

Disraeli's "active and real ambition" was to be a great man, even prime minister of Victoria's England. As his fiction was in some measure a nostalgia for his Jewishness, so his political ideology was founded on nostalgia for a past that Britain, like himself, perhaps, had never had.

Disraeli made the return to the past the guiding principle of his politics. The program of "Young England"—the label of his ideas before they acquired the later label "Imperialism"—was avowedly old: "To change back the oligarchy into a generous aristocracy round a real throne; to infuse life and vigor into the Church, as the trainer of the nation . . . to establish a commercial code [this is the age of child-labor capitalism] . . . to elevate the physical as well as the moral condition of the people, by establishing that labor required regulation [that is, protection] as much as property; and all this by the use of ancient forms and the restoration of the past rather than by political revolutions founded on abstract ideas."

This is how Disraeli viewed his political religion, from the perspective of the general preface to the 1870 edition of his novels. The return to the past—the program of Young England—was at once the expression and the distortion of his nostalgia for his lost Jewishness. Disraeli wanted to unite the aristocracy and the masses against the Whig oligarchy and the upper middle classes. He viewed the crown and the aristocracy as the protectors of the people, with the established church as the propaganda department—the praying section—of the state. In turn, legislation had to be careful not to cut the basis of power out from under the aristocracy. Disraeli well understood that property was power in his time: he became a corn protectionist to keep it so. What was needed was a hierarchy with sensibility, and with a sense of noblesse oblige; "an aristocracy that leads . . . since Aristocracy is a fact." But that Democracy—the mass age—was coming was equally a fact. Then let it be led by that older, and higher, fact—Aristocracy. In any case, this was good politics for aristocratic parties.

The industrialists and the commercial oligarchy must be rapacious in business, and so must be irresponsible in government. The Whigs cannot care for the people. Rather, they have divided England into two nations, the rich and the poor. By the coup of 1832, the Whigs had finally set up the dictatorship of the bourgeoisie. "To acquire, to accumulate, to plunder . . . to propose a Utopia to consist of *Wealth* and *Toil*, this has been the breathless business of enfranchised England for the last twelve years [since 1832] until we are startled from our voracious strife by the wail of intolerable serfage." The Whigs, according to Disraeli, had made modern history the ugly history of class struggle. But it need not be that way. A dedicated elite could change modern history. Capitalism, which is Whiggery to Disraeli, has divorced the idea of property and power from the idea of duty, and thus has divorced power from responsibility. But in the English past, responsibility was joined with power. The connecting link was a dedicated elite. Dedication is, after all, the price an elite ought to pay for its power and for its property.

Chartism was the first answer of the English masses to industrial capitalism. Among the politicians of the time, Disraeli alone was not afraid to hear it. He almost welcomed it. He thought the alliance of the true gentlemen and the good people was perhaps just around the corner. Let the sheep and the shepherds together stand off the wolves. This was Disraeli's program, and he tried to educate the Tory party to it. He was a first-rate teacher, but somehow the lessons failed to get across. His pupils were inclined to another tactic: to domesticate the wolves, who seemed to them much more manly than Disraeli. The Whigs, after all, were of the gentry. So the Tories refused to become Disraeli's gentlemen: they suspected that Disraeli did not know, really, what a gentleman was. He never belonged at Brooks's. And if he belonged at the Carlton—in fact to become enshrined there—he had to mount a great deal of pressure to get in. Even his friend Bentinck did not think he was a sportsman. Certainly, Disraeli knew little about horses.

But he knew more and cared more about politics. It was almost all of his life. Politics made his life successful, he thought. And he played politics everywhere, even where there was no politics. Disraeli was a completely political man. After race, all was politics.

As a political man with the common touch, Disraeli knew, before most of his contemporaries, the value of public opinion. He called it the "cry," and he always knew how to "play with a cry," as he put it. The novelist turned politician was an early modern master of mass manipulation and the first modern politician to assert the supremacy of his art. He used the press, then the most powerful means of mass manipulation, as no other politician before him. And he was proud of his craft. "I am a Knight of the Press," he once said, "and have no other escutcheon." This was rare in an age when politics still demanded escutcheons of a more biological, or at least economic, sort.

Disraeli discovered how to manage that new political integer, the People. One got along with the People in the same way one must get along with women—say, Queen Victoria. The trick, of course, is to flatter them; in fact, "to lay it on with a trowel." They will know it is flattery, but will love it anyway. Disraeli's best advice to politicians was always: "Talk to women. Talk to women as much as you can. This is the best school. This is the way to gain fluency, because you need not care what you say, and had better not be sensible."

If Disraeli gave Conservatism a grip on the public, he equally made Conservatism legitimate for the intellectuals, who are always anti-public. The point is clearer when American Toryism is compared with the British variety. As Crane Brinton has said, American Toryism is "dull and stuffy, singularly lacking in intellectual graces." Robert Taft is not quite bright enough to attract the bright young people, and Catholicism, in America, is still Irish. Disraeli gave English Toryism grace. He added books to good tobacco, drawings, and the University, even though he himself did not smoke and had not attended a university. Disraeli made politics respectable for young gentlemen, semi-skilled intellectuals, and old ladies who love literature. The image of the literate Conservative is Disraeli's work, after Burke.

The man who remade Conservative politics almost failed to become a politician. The cry "Shylock!" rose to meet him as he rose to speak. The public was put off by his "physiognomy," which seemed to them "strictly Jewish." If it was not "Shylock!" the alternative greeting was "Old clothes!" And some of his opponents declared to their audiences, in asides, that they could not "pronounce his name aright."

Disraeli did not complain. He could not. In any case, he had already formulated the ruling motto of his life: "Never complain, never explain." Rather, he returned insult for insult. He gained a reputation for being a very insulting young man. Later, when he was older, his reputation was as a mysterious reservoir of cynical truculence. Aristocratic ladies, in their memoirs, list as one of their constant fears that they would come under Disraeli's wrath.

After four tries, Disraeli was elected to the House of Commons from Maidstone in 1837. He stayed forty years. But the first speech of perhaps the greatest parliamentary orator of the nineteenth century ended as a humiliating farce. The hostile members met him with hoots and catcalls. It was the laughter, however, that brought him down to his seat, his speech unfinished. But his final words were a taunt he was to make good: "I sit down, but the time will come when you will hear from me."

Much of what England heard from Disraeli is outside the limits of this essay. Its task is rather to follow the voice to its origins, that is, to Disraeli as Jew.

On the surface, Disraeli seemed never to be disturbed by anything. This—and his talent for dramatic silences—was the mask that so infuriated Gladstone while it charmed England's salons. It was also the mask that gave face to the myth of the Jew Satanas, the "superlative Hebrew conjuror" who led poor old England by its nose.

"Someone wrote to me yesterday," Lord Acton said in a letter to Gladstone's daughter Mary, "that no Jew for 1800 years has played so great a part in the world. That would be no Jew since St. Paul; and it is very startling. But, putting aside literature . . . I have not yet found an answer." And further: "Let us . . . call him the greatest Jewish minister since Joseph."

Consciousness of Disraeli as a Jew appears in all English writing of the period and later. His biographers and the political writers of his day cannot shake their awareness of "that Oriental tendency in his nature." And they are made uncomfortable by his defiant outbursts of racial scorn for the "barbarians," who, of course, were the gentiles, the "flat-nosed Franks" who worship a Jew, and "who toil and study, and invent theories to account for their own incompetence." The only "barbarians" Disraeli excepted from his scorn were the ancient Greeks. Nevertheless, his advice to students of civilization is: study the Jews. In the Jews, and in the Jews alone, can the exhausted gentiles "discover new courses of emotion, new modes of expression, new trains of ideas, new principles of invention, and new bursts of fancy."

It was the impressive, death's-head face, which *Punch* saw as the sphinx or, at least, as the face of old Jewry, that exasperated Carlyle to ask how long "this Jew would be allowed to dance on the belly of [England]." Disraeli's face fascinated—and still fascinates—Englishmen. It seems to them to express the witty, ironic, dancing character of the Jew. It was not simply his dandyism. The upper classes knew and included many dandies. Rather, it was his thin face; the "lividly pale" skin; the large "black eyes"; the long nose and heavy underlip; the jet black hair, curling near the big ears; and, finally, the stoop of a thin body. It was the face and stoop of Irving's Shylock, so popular that it has been the classic portrayal of the role from that time to this.

But the disturbing question of his Jewishness can best be read in the snatches of Disraeli's memoirs and in his novels. In his novels, particularly, Disraeli lifted "the veil that hides his own personality," and opened up the "hidden motives" to deep underneath his "public pretenses," as he says of the partly autobiographical character Sidonia (who is also Lionel Rothschild) in his finest novel, *Coningsby.*

One of the more significant accounts of his secret life is in his memoir of his father, written as an introduction to a three-volume edition of Isaac D'Israeli's *Curiosities of Literature*. Most revealing is his fantasy about his name. He simply decided that his name came to be Disraeli because his ancestors "assumed the name . . . in order that their race might be forever recognized." Thus they would be forever D'Israeli—of Israel. Disraeli invented a romance by which his name became a deliberate emblem of dignity, a badge of pride, an irrevocable identity, a "we" to the world's "they." There are elements of his "ideal ambition"—of his Jewish fantasy life—in each of his novels. It is especially obtrusive in the rhapsodic *The Wondrous Tale of Alroy*. He writes in his *Diary*: "My works are the embodification of my feelings. In *Vivian Grey* I have portrayed my active and real ambition: in *Alroy* my ideal ambition . . . [it] is the secret history of my feelings." In another place, Disraeli further explains his purpose in *Alroy*: "It is meant to be the celebration of a gorgeous incident in the annals of that sacred and romantic people from whom I derive my blood and name."

Disraeli published *Alroy* soon after his return from Jerusalem. It was never one of his popular novels. The critical public judged it absurd where not unreadable. But it provoked a reaction reserved for creations less absurd than annoying. A number of parodies of Disraeli's rhapsodic attempt appeared. One opened: "O reader dear! do pray look here, and you will spy the curly hair and forehead-fair, and nose so high and gleaming eye of Benjamin Dis-ra-e-li, the wondrous boy who wrote *Alroy*, in rhyme and prose, only to show, how long ago victorious Judah's lion-banner rose." But the most furious critical baiting was done by "Thomas Ingoldsby," a famous pseudonym of the magazine world of the time. "Thomas Ingoldsby," the Reverend R. H. Barham, published a parody of *Alroy* in *Blackwood's* in 1832, calling it *The Wondrous Tale of Ikey Solomons*—Ikey Solomons was a notorious receiver of stolen goods.

Alroy is a story of the Jews of the Diaspora. David Alroy is a "Prince of the Captivity," full of Byron and brooding on the degradation of the Jews. Alroy, of the princely people, is sick—to the Byronic verge of action—of the slavery of the chosen: "God of my fathers! For indeed I dare not style thee God of their wretched sons. . . . Thy servant Israel, Lord, is born a slave so infamous, so woebegone, and so contemned, that even when our fathers hung their harps by the sad waters . . . why it was paradise compared with that we suffer."

Alroy refuses to suffer. He prefers to lead the Jews back to power, to national identity. Disraeli sets Alroy in a number of characteristically revealing conversations. One of these is with an ex-Jew who has risen to power in the gentile world. Alroy argues the problem of commitment with the ex-Jew, now high in government service.

"After all," Alroy insists, "thou art a [gentile]."

"No," the ex-Jew, called Lord Honain, answers.

"What then?"

"I have told you, a man." Honain asserts he is neither Jew nor gentile, and that most of all it is foolish to belong to a frail minority. It is better to belong to the strong majority; there is power, there is chosenness. Alroy has only one answer. Power is not the predicate of chosenness, but chosenness of power.

"We are the chosen people."

"Chosen for scoffs, and scorns, and contumelies. Commend me such a choice," Honain answers.

Alroy stubbornly commends the choice to him. Further, he insists to the ex-Jew that he cannot now understand the Jews. Honain is too well-off, too strong, and so he cannot understand why the Jews must fight for power. The fight for power is clearest to those who are powerless but superior: the Jews.

The world goes well with thee, my Lord Honain. But if, instead of bows and blessings, thou like my brethren, wert greeted only with cuff and curse; if thou didst rise each morning only to feel existence a dishonour, and to find thyself marked out among men as something foul and fatal; if it were thy lot, like theirs, at best to drag on a mean and dull career, hopeless and aimless, or with no other hope or aim but that which is degrading, and all this too with a keen sense of thy intrinsic worth, and a deep conviction of superior race; why, then perchance, [you] might discover 'twere worth a struggle to be free and honoured.

Alroy's brooding discomfort, and the guilt he feels at his inaction, are ended when he kills a Moslem who has tried to violate his sister, Miriam. He flees into the hills, to the retreat of the militant rabbi Jabaster, who is his ideologue. The rabbi instructs him in his mission: to raise the Jews first to revolt and then to independence. But first, Alroy must make a pilgrimage to Jerusalem. The fantasy at the "Tomb of the Kings" in Jerusalem is the most remarkable in the pattern of fantasies in Disraelian fiction. Solomon incarnate appears and hands down to his descendant, David Alroy, the rod of leadership. David returns to raise the revolt. With Jabaster as his chaplain, he leads the Jews to triumph. Alroy is, indeed, a Prince. But power, of course, corrupts him. He wants to be Alexander instead of David.

> The world is mine: and shall I yield the prize, the universal and heroic prize to realize the dull tradition of some dreaming priest and consecrate a legend? . . . Is the Lord of Hosts so slight a God, that we must place a barrier to His sovereignty, and fix the boundaries of Omnipotence between the Jordan and the Lebanon? . . . Universal empire must not be founded on sectarian prejudices and exclusive rights.

Seeking power for his people, Alroy has become intoxicated with it for himself. The Prince of the Captivity is corrupted by the vision of power in a gentile world. He marries a gentile, the daughter of the caliph, and makes Baghdad his capital. When it becomes apparent that he has abandoned his Jewish ambitions for other pleasures, Jabaster leads the Jews in revolt against him. This gives Alroy's wife the opportunity she has wanted to eliminate Jabaster, who is beheaded at her insistence. Finally, the Moslems defeat Alroy, and he is sentenced to death by the restored sultanate. However, he is offered his freedom if he will renounce his Jewishness. This last irony amuses him. His refusal to renounce religiously what he had already renounced politically is his near-final affirmation of Jewishness.

But his final affirmation is more positive. Failure has taught him more about his Jewishness than success. What had been fatal for him, Alroy now understands, was his attempt to de-Judaize himself. He makes what he considers to be a historical analogy: "The policy of the son of Kanesh—'twas fatal. He preferred Egypt to Judah, and he suffered." Alroy is a convinced Jew now, even more than he was when he was an ambitious Jew. His ambition is now for the Jews. In the same speech, he continues: "Sires, the Lord has blessed Judah; it is His land. He would have it filled by His peculiar people. . . . For this He has by many curious rites and customs marked us out from all other nations, so that we cannot at the same time mingle with them and yet be to Him." Alroy comes to what proves to be the final conclusion of his life: "We must exist alone." The Jews are meant to "preserve this loneliness." Loneliness is "the great and holy essence of our law."

The other side of the Jews' historic loneliness is Zionism. Alroy comes to understand this in what is perhaps one of the earliest Zionist perorations given in Western literature. He is asked what he wishes for the Jews: "You ask me what I wish? my answer is: a National existence, which we have not. You ask me what I wish? my answer is: the Land of Promise. You ask me what I wish? my answer is: Jerusalem—all we have forfeited, all we have yearned after, all for which we have fought—our beauteous country, our holy creed, our simple manners."

But Alroy is troubled by the thought, again, that the Return may be the Jews' last illusion. "Is there no hope?" he asks himself. His answer is to quote the Prophets, that religious hope exists most of all in the hopeless situation: "The bricks are fallen, but we will rebuild with marble; the sycamores are cut down, but we will replace them with cedars. . . . Yet again I will build thee, and thou shalt be built, O . . . Israel!"

Alroy is a confession. It is an assertion that the Jew is the clue to history, and its demiurge. But the most passionate statement of Disraeli's fantasy of Jewish chosenness is made by his most romantic character, the Jew Sidonia in the novel *Coningsby*. Sidonia is Disraeli's affirmation of the myth of the super-Jew, superior because a Jew. Disraeli insists: "Race is everything; there is no other truth." Sidonia is proudest that he is "pure" Sephardic—for him, the Sephardim are the purest Jews. Sidonia is Disraeli, although he is made to look like Lionel Nathan Rothschild, who was to become the first man to enter the English Parliament as a Jew; that is, without having to take his seat "on the oath as a Christian." Guedalla calls Sidonia, in a try at a joke, "Disrothschild."

As Disraeli's proudest projection, Sidonia is the most powerful, the most learned, the most shadowy man in the world. He is also the loneliest. Sidonia is an alien, detached, without intimates or a permanent home. It is his homelessness that makes him intensely interested in the problem of political and cultural stability.

Disraeli offers in Sidonia a character who has the insight of an outsider. But his insight and his power are pathetic—for they must be the insight and the power given to an outsider who can never quite use his superiority to bring him into a community. His power and insight are the masks, the weapons, of his detachment. Sidonia "was admired by women, idolized by artists, received in all circles . . . and appreciated for his intellect by the very few to whom he at all opened himself; for though affable and generous, it was impossible to penetrate him; though unreserved in his manners, his frankness was limited to the surface. He observed everything, thought ever, but avoided serious discussion. . . . He looked on life with a glance rather of curiosity than contempt. His religion walled him out. . . . He perceived himself a lone being."

This is the image Disraeli accepted for his own self: walled out, a lone being. But Sidonia chooses to remain walled out and to turn his loneliness and exclusion into a premise of insight. Disraeli turned his own loneliness into both a pride and a political tactic. Yet the lonely, proud man titillated himself with the fancy that English Jewry found a secret, private joy in him, whispering among themselves that "he is one of us." The Jewish hero, walled out from the Jews as well as from the gentiles, nevertheless is aware of his irrevocable connection with the Jews.

Disraeli, in his fantasy, saw in the Jew the demiurge, as well as the measure, of history. Sidonia expresses this: "The fact is you cannot destroy [us]. It is a . . . fact, a simple law of nature, which has baffled Egyptian and Assyrian kings, Roman emperors and Christian inquisitors. No penal laws, no physical tortures can effect that a superior race should be absorbed in an inferior, or be destroyed by it."

Sidonia insists that the Jews are not only the super-race but now and always responsible for whatever is great and good in history, despite the attempt of their inferiors to degrade and to destroy them. The Jews, according to Sidonia, are superior by more than force of intellect. The Jews are favored with genius by nature, as a divine gift. Try as the gentiles might to destroy them, the Jews are indestructible. They are the intermediaries between man and God, the divine "link" that gives to mankind its humanity, the priestly people in a world that would be best organized as a theocracy.

Disraeli avowed Sidonia's manifesto for his own in the famous twenty-fourth chapter of his political biography of his friend Lord George Bentinck, which repeats many of the same things. This chapter, quite out of place in the story of Bentinck's life, is a wholesale defense of the Jews, past, present, and future, and an unqualified assertion of their superiority over other "races." Disraeli's belief in the Jew as the indestructible hero of history led him to claim for the Jews every historical glory of Western civilization. Christianity, at its best, is a Jewish religion, and what is not best in it is not Jewish. He could not allow many pages to pass before he must repeat one of his favorite taunts: that, after all, the gentiles worship a Jew and a Jewess. This is also the taunt of his beloved heroine, the Jewess Eva in *Tancred*. The taunt was meant as a challenge delivered by Disraeli in his own name to the gentile world.

The Jew is chosen for eternity, Disraeli proclaims in the same chapter of his life of Bentinck. He does not know too much of Jewish theology or history—or of Christian theology or history, for that matter. For Disraeli, these are all lumped together as the "great Asian mystery." But knowledge, he thinks, is not so necessary to insight as faith. Neither as prime minister nor as a proto-Zionist did Disraeli allow lack of information to inhibit his certainty. He is sure that the Jews, "sustained by a sublime religion," are the chosen of the earth. Each Jew proves his chosenness. Opportunity makes him the Tory prime minister of Great Britain. Persecution makes him a revolutionary leader in Europe.

It does not matter what the world does to Jewry, Jewry always gives proof of its chosenness.

But Disraeli has still to answer a taunt returned to his own taunts: that he, D'Israeli of Israel, was a convert to Christianity. Disraeli gave a Jewish answer to an impossible question. *He* the convert? A *converted* Jew? It is the gentiles who are the converts, he answers. And that is something that in their confusion about the real nature of Christianity they quite forget. The answer is, admittedly, not equal to the question; but it has its cogency.

To Jews who thought themselves "better" converted, Disraeli showed an icy humor. He saved some of his sharpest irony for those "young ladies" who are "ashamed of their race, and not fanatically devoted to their religion, which might be true, but certainly was not fashionable." And he directed what he hoped were his most telling thrusts at the most sophisticated, and so the most vicious, type of assimilationist. This was the "animated" creature who "was always combatting prejudice" and who "felt persuaded that the Jews would not be so much disliked if they were better known." All they had to do, Disraeli minced, "was to imitate as closely as possible the habits and customs of the nation among whom they chanced to live."

Like many more modern Jewish intellectuals, Disraeli wrote partly to protect himself against the completest assimilation: the loss of his own consciousness as a Jew. Assimilated before he could choose another way, he hated assimilation. A master of practiced nonchalance all his life, he could barely tolerate the "practiced nonchalance" of the assimilationist ladies of his time. He expected a good woman to be "enthusiastic for her race" and unashamed, at least, of her religion. The first requirement for the role of heroine in his novels is that the lady be loyal to her "old faith," whatever that "old faith" be. This accounts for the affection he displays in his novels for noble old Catholic families, and for loyal young Catholic ladies.

But the Catholic heroine is simply a variation of the Jewish; of Eva, in *Tancred,* and of Miriam, the sister of Alroy. Catholicism, as a loyalty, appeals to him because it is a loyalty in the midst of disloyalties. The Jews are alone in the world as the Catholics are alone in Protestant England. Loyalty is the one characteristic a Jew cannot give up and still remain a Jew. The test of loyalty is to continue to live separately, no matter what the temptations of victory or defeat. "The Hebrews have never blended with their conquerors," says Eva to Tancred, proudly. In his novels, the heroine is the vessel of loyalty—a quality that makes his good women altogether flat, always superior and virtuous. Miriam is a better Jew than her brother, the great David Alroy; Disraeli dedicated *Alroy* to his sister, Sarah.

Finally, Disraeli made the Jew the image of what he thought to be his own politics. The Jews, he decided, "represent the Semitic principle; all that is spiritual in our nature. They are the trustees of tradition, and the conservators of the religious element. They are a living and most striking evidence of the falsity of that pernicious doctrine of modern times, the natural equality of man." The Jews are the "natural aristocrats" of man. Disraeli's entire "education" of the Tories was to recall them to the responsibility of their aristocracy, as trustees of the English political tradition. And his image of the English aristocrat was struck off from the image of the Jew. Disraeli insisted that the dynamic of English culture was its Hebraism.

> Vast as the obligations of the whole human family are to the Hebrew race, there is no portion . . . so much indebted to them as the British people. It was the sword of the Lord and of Gideon that won the boasted liberties of England; chanting the same canticles that cheered the heart of Judah and their glens, the Scotch, upon their hillsides, achieved their religious freedom. [And] who is the most popular poet in this country? Is he to be found among the Mr. Wordsworths and the Lord Byrons . . . ? No; the most popular poet in England is the sweet singer of Israel. . . . There never was a race who sang so often the odes of David as the people of Great Britain.

Disraeli's sense of the past made him a consistent advocate of aristocracy as the decisive basis of English politics, and of the Jews as the aristocracy of history. In *Tancred*, he calls the gentile world sordid, and he makes Sidonia dismiss gentile Christianity as an immature imitation of the peoples with a master past. The past and the present, as Sidonia says, "explain each other." The Christian clergy knows "nothing about these things. How can they? A few centuries back they were tattooed savages." Politics and theology, Sidonia concludes, are not yet within the mastery of Christian civilization. They require "an apprenticeship of some thousand years at least; to say nothing of clime and race."

Disraeli was often sentimental and could move himself to tears by his own words. But his sentimentalism was the hardest thing inside him. Sentimentalism, in the form of nostalgia, defines his politics and his fiction. It represents his sense of the past, and of his chosenness in it. It gives him his ideology, and has had a hand in shaping British political rhetoric, and Zionist rhetoric, since then. (Churchill's epigrammatic, nationalist sentimentalism is straight from Disraeli, not from Gibbon, as some students of Churchill's rhetoric think. Gibbon was neither a sentimentalist nor a nationalist.) Disraeli felt himself twice chosen, as a Jew and as an Englishman, a representative of the Old Jerusalem and the New, the past and the present united.

Disraeli was pleased to make his sense of chosenness the basis of his politics throughout his life. His belief in the mystery of Israel's chosenness gave him a basis for his belief in his own chosenness in English politics. It gave him the necessary aggressive mystique he needed to survive in English politics, a unique achievement for a man in his position, unrepeated in England since. Disraeli did not simply hint at the doctrine of election, he asserted it. And his prophecy to England was a romantic conservative vision, like Cromwell's, of England, that blessed plot, as a New Israel. It was Disraeli's nostalgia for his Jewishness that enabled him to present this vision in English political history.

On Franz Rosenzweig

Professor Glatzer concludes his introduction to *Understanding the Sick and the Healthy* with a perfect and necessary remark.[1] The book, he says, "is being printed and offered to the public not primarily as 'a contribution to philosophical or religious thought,' but as a part of Franz Rosenzweig's very life." Not that the philosophical or religious import of the book is in any way slight. As a thrust at the immense airiness of German idealism from Kant to Hegel—and therefore at professional theology—it is quick and brilliant. Rosenzweig was very clever; he averted getting hung out in the middle of the same vacuum as the idealists by probing idealism from within himself and for himself. This style may confuse unwary readers. A philosophical book, yet it is a personal book, even a chatty book. It has no system. But then, because German philosophical systems sealed off the life that ran inside them, Rosenzweig's jab flickers out toward all systems.

In approaching Franz Rosenzweig, Glatzer tries to resolve a destructive impasse within modern Jewish thought. On the one hand, in this volume and in an earlier one on Rosenzweig's *Life and Thought*, Glatzer has introduced the American public to a saintly man. The Jew Franz Rosenzweig belongs in the company of the sublimest characters his religion of character has produced. For modern and secular taste, Rosenzweig was almost embarrassingly good. But then he was paralyzed and died young, and this will confirm the secular prejudice that goodness is not for healthy dispositions. Dostoyevsky tried to make the character of Alyosha

1. Franz Rosenzweig, *Understanding the Sick and the Healthy: A View of the World, Man and God*, with an introduction by Nahum H. Glatzer (New York: Noonday Press, 1954).

good and his body healthy, but he succeeded at the expense of Alyosha's mind; the brother, of all the Karamazovs, was the least intellectual. Franz Rosenzweig was a saint and an intellectual too, a combination that runs against the prepossessions of the intellectuals I know.

At the same time, Glatzer has struggled to bring the reader near the intimate mind and doctrine of Franz Rosenzweig. But in the generations of its submission to German learnedness Jewry has grown intellectualized. Receptivity to the person and personal message of Rosenzweig is very low. As author of *Hegel and the State*, he would probably get longer notices in more journals than as author of *The Star of Redemption* or *Understanding the Sick and the Healthy*. *Hegel and the State* is a theoretical work and therefore a safe excitement, for theory does not demand an intimate and practical response, as dialogue does. Theory does not address another person but another book. In the contemporary hospital atmosphere of culture, theory leads nowhere except to theorizing. Indeed, we are past the creative age of theory, and for this reason Rosenzweig attacked it. But this does not mean that Rosenzweig in any way accepted the present domination of empirical attitudes as an alternative. On the contrary, empiricism has become an even thicker disguise of established and rejectable fact. For empiricism pretends merely to observe fact, as if such observation were not the grossest idolatry of fact. At least idealism pretended to go beyond fact.

Rosenzweig expected thought to lead the thinker somewhere he had never been before, to new relations as well as to altered perspectives. *Understanding the Sick and the Healthy* is therefore not an academic book. In fact, it is an attack on the academic sickliness of modern thought. It is saddening to realize that probably the present fate of this book is to be absorbed into the glutinous world of the American academy, where all thinking people think they have to live. Yet, in its very format, *Understanding the Sick and the Healthy* exhibits the original hope of the author, his editor, and their publisher that it would be read in wider inclosures. It is a beautifully produced book, with the death mask of a beautiful man on its covers to give the reader a vision of what lies within.

Preface to the Second Edition of *Freud: The Mind of the Moralist*

I have revised some passages and augmented a few others for this edition. In the main, the book stands as it first appeared in 1959. Since that time, however, another selection of Freud's letters, even more personal than those to Wilhelm Fliess, has been published.[1] Freud's intimate correspondence reveals an emotional life remarkably consonant with the intellectual life examined in the chapters that follow.

Freud wrote letters in huge quantities; only now can we see that he was supremely talented at it. On the evidence, I think, Freud is entitled to a place among the great letter writers of this century; only D. H. Lawrence and William James emerge from their personal correspondence anywhere near as man-size as Freud.

Freud's greatness of character comes through his letters swiftly, and particularly in his love letters to Martha Bernays, during the four long years between their engagement and their marriage. Great letters are written by great characters; they must be intensely personal and revealing, yet make us feel that, however familiarly we lean across the shoulder of the writer, we are in the presence of greatness. Freud's letters show that presence already there in his early twenties. Only great characters can survive this test of intimacy. Marx, for example, does not survive; his letters do not move us to respect him more as we get to know him better. How rarely do great men retain their presence when we

---

1. See *Letters of Sigmund Freud*, selected and ed. Ernst L. Freud; trans. Tania and James Stern (New York: Basic Books, 1960).

get close to them, in the one way possible across the distance of history—in their personal correspondence. Freud survives, and grows in stature.

That Freud was a great old man can be denied only by denying his achievement. Now, from his letters, we see that if he had greatness, it was in his person long before his achievement set it at large. As more of these autobiographical materials appear, Ernest Jones's biography becomes less and less adequate. In his lack of feeling for the intensity of his subject, and despite occasional efforts at depth of penetration, Jones put together a portrait that is almost Byzantine in its flatness. Given Jones's intention, to record the life of Freud, the flatness could not be avoided. It is the mind of Freud that gave his life a depth quite beyond the range Jones evidently set for himself as a biographer.

There is nothing flat about Freud's own self-portrait, as given informally in his letters. Told from the inside, Freud's life takes on depth, even heroic proportion, not because of the external pace of events, which is in fact steady, but, rather, because of the heavy burden of knowingness about life that Freud carried from the beginning, on his back, as it were. Yet he never bent over in defeat; difficult as he found the task, he forced himself to remain emotionally and morally upright to the last, "defiant" of his corrupting knowledge—although as he himself admitted, in a letter splendid with modesty, he did not know quite why he thus maintained his integrity. All he knew, at the end of his life, was that, as a moral man, he could not be otherwise.

The famous old Freud and his obscure young predecessor bear a resemblance to one another so close that, taken together, they challenge the sacred canon of development. Age did not alter Freud in any essential way; it merely gave him time to polish the intellectual instrument with which he expressed the greatness of his character. Psychoanalysis was the perfect instrument of that character. When at last he found himself, after searching around systematically in various established disciplines, Freud established a new discipline, first of all for himself. Later, as psychoanalysis became more adaptable, the hidden force of Freud's character op-

erated though the discipline, detached from his person. Psychoanalysis became a transferable art, and therefore something like a
science; others could be taught what Freud knew for himself.

The young Freud was one of those rare unlucky ones, burdened in youth with the wisdom of age. He was never really
young. When, at twenty-three, he remarks to Martha on "the
absurdity of this world," this is no passing adolescent sadness; it
carries the full poignancy of full comprehension, and only deep-
ens with time. Such strokes of wisdom often left him in one of his
"wretched moods." But his gift of understanding the world, as it
is, was, and will be, did not leave him completely exposed and vulnerable. Guarded by his self-image as a scientist, Freud's personal
wisdom hardened him just enough to permit him to remain wise
without ever falling over into the jeopardy of demanding an end
of wisdom—some synthesis of his analytic attitude that must, as
he knew, take him beyond the specific gravity of his intelligence.
The perfect nonsense of the artist, or of the religious genius,
never appealed to Freud; he chose, rather, to make imperfect
sense. One letter concludes, with final accuracy, "In short, I am
evidently an analyst."

To compel his imagination to stay put, short of synthesis, was
admittedly a severe limitation upon it. But the absurdity of this
world could not be balanced, in his opinion, by absurd ideas. To
be religious is to be sick, by definition: it is the effort to find a cure
where none can possibly exist. For Freud, religion can be only a
symptom of what it seeks to cure. Psychoanalysis does not cure; it
merely reconciles. Therefore it works best for healthy men, who
are willing to sacrifice their precious first sons of thought on the
altar of reality. For those who seek, through analysis, to avoid the
sacrifice, therapy must inevitably fail. Psychoanalysis is a therapy
for the healthy, not a solution for the sick—except so far as the
sick themselves become analysts, and find in this therapeutic their
personal solution, as Freud did. In his science, Freud overcame
the "tiredness" from which he suffered. His recurrent fatigue was,
he explained to Martha, a "kind of minor illness; neurasthenia,
it is called." Work was the one way out of this tiredness. Thus
Freud turned necessity into therapy; there was no other way out,

before death. In a sense we can now better understand, there is something to the gross charge that psychoanalysis is the perfect profession for neurotics—but only for extremely intelligent neurotics, those who can learn to inhibit successfully their religious impulse. "The moment a man questions the meaning and value of life," Freud wrote to Marie Bonaparte, "he is sick, since objectively neither has any existence." The analyst proudly needed no synthesis.

But Freud needed no synthesis because it was already there, built into his character. More easily than most, if they are truly analytical, Freud could avoid asking the essential question, for within him he had an answer that he guarded and cherished, although toward the end of his life his own ambivalence toward that answer increased so much that he could not resist both analyzing and justifying it. Finally, but with extreme reluctance, he published *Moses and Monotheism*, his own private answer. He discovered that although he was not a believing Jew, he remained a psychological one. It was, in fact, Freud's mystique of membership in the Jewish community that protected him from asking too obviously the sickest of questions. His letters are full of obedience to the authority of his ancestry. When Freud goes "every day for three lonely weeks" to contemplate the Moses of Michelangelo, in a Roman church, it is an act of piety—which must eventuate in a psychoanalytic exercise, of course.

Following in Freud's steps, not long ago, I went to that same church in Rome. But, having had the American experience of detachment from all communities, it was Michelangelo's Moses that I saw, not Freud's. Being still attached to his community, the Jew Freud could afford to be merely what he was—an analyst, and that long before psychoanalysis permitted him to cosset his sense of despair in the professionalism of his analytic attitude. At times, before his wish for genius came true, Freud experienced "something like attacks of despondency and faintheartedness." At other times, he grudgingly admits to Martha his "gray, grim despair," does nothing all day, except perhaps browse in Russian history or some other subject equally remote from his work. On one occasion, he reaches for a passage in Milton, as if it were a shield behind which he can advance again on the unconquerable enemy realities. That passage, cited by the early Freud, is appropriate in theme for Freud in his later years.

> Let us consult
> What reinforcement we may gain from hope;
> If not, what resolution from despair.

But immediately he says to Martha that he has "no use for this mood." Paradise never has been lost, and therefore cannot be regained. But what of those who are not members of Milton's mysterious community of the elect by desperate resolution? Or of Freud's even more mysterious one? Pity the poor gentile, or, if not, pity the half gentiles of American intellectual Jewry. Freud was not long on pity, and certainly had none for the gentiles. There is an early letter in which he fans his envy, suggesting to Martha that perhaps he will "try and live more like the gentiles— modestly, learning and practicing the usual things and not striving after discoveries and delving too deep." The mood did not persist. Freud was his own ideal Jew—not a half gentile of the real Jewish world but a fantasy Moses, lonely and estranged as he leads the large remainder of himself, resisting, through the "magic world of intellect and unhappiness," from one small oasis of rational insight to another, with no promises of a promised land this time around. Such a powerfully useful self-image, once deeply buried, is not easily given up.

Being, in youth and age, a lonely man, Freud sought love and loyal company with an ardor that his letters express in a permanently readable way. Martha Bernays became his first chosen person. (Later, there was Fliess.) In his love letters, the young Freud is engaged in the training of his bride-to-be. Martha did not understand him; Sigmund was determined that she should. After all, the circumstances were strained. He has proposed before he really knew her. He was twenty-three, and he had decided to marry. In the four years of their affianced courtship, he educated her to him, so that, despite the revolutions brewing in his mind, he could enjoy the safety of marriage. He "picks her to pieces," so finely that at times she must have protested; he then promises to restrain his analytic thrust. But, through all the pedagogy of his letters, he is grateful to her: the promise of her lifelong company and confidence has saved him from "the worst fate," loneliness. His gratitude permits him to unbend with her; otherwise he is never deprived of his pride in being alone.

Freud needed a standard Jewish marriage, in which the wife is queen and keeper of a standard Jewish household. From this bridgehead of tradition, Freud the theoretician invaded the whole rotten empire of the family, without running the ultimate risk of cutting himself off from the devout practice of its creed. No more compulsively moral man ever has explored the compulsiveness of morality. This prince of the modern moral quandary needed a princess remote precisely from that quandary, completely untouched by it. Not that the courtship, following the engagement and conducted through the mails, was easy. Freud was no tame Jewish doctor; he did not want his wife so tamed that she would not have an idea of what he was about. His letters to Martha function as deliberate revelations of himself, a first playing out of his tremendous intelligence upon the special case of their own relation. Freud's love letters serve a double purpose: they prepare her for marriage to him; he prepares himself for his long, tenacious contest with life, one in which he knew he could not become an old-style hero, winning through in one decisive battle with himself, but, rather, holding his own and learning how to give better than he got.

Freud was lucky the first time. Desperate loneliness can lead to errors in judgment. But when he decided to fall in love, and did so with Martha, promptly, at first sight, his gamble succeeded. His later, secondary attempts to break through his loneliness were not as fortunate. First-rate disciples can be trained, but they do not easily compose themselves into members of an intellectual family, even when that family is fathered by a Freud. That he tried, hard and genuinely, to avoid his inevitable role is evident in the patience of his relations with Jung, Rank, Ferenczi, Jones, and others. Max Eitingon actually insisted on symbolic adoption, as a son, into Freud's family. But definitive assessment of Freud's character can be attempted only as part of a history of the psychoanalytic movement. When that history is written, I suspect that Freud's personal stature will grow rather than diminish. The greatness of the man is beyond question, complementing the greatness of his mind.

The Religion of the Fathers

Why atheism nowadays? "The father" in God is thoroughly refuted; equally so "the judge," "the rewarder."

—Nietzsche

It is on the subject of religion that the judicious clinician grows vehement and disputatious. Against no other strongpoint of repressive culture are the reductive weapons of psychoanalysis deployed in such open hostility. Freud's customary detachment fails him here. Confronting religion, psychoanalysis shows itself for what it is: the last great formulation of nineteenth-century secularism, complete with substitute doctrine and cult—capacious, all-embracing, similar in range to the social calculus of the utilitarians, the universal sociolatry of Comte, the dialectical historicism of Marx, the indefinitely expandable agnosticism of Spencer. What first impresses the student of Freud's psychology of religion is its polemical edge. Here, and here alone, the grand Freudian animus, otherwise concealed behind the immediacies of case histories and the emergencies of practical therapeutics, breaks out.

I

There was no reason why Freud should have been so engaged by the problem of religion—at least no obvious, psychoanalyzable reason. He had never gone through a phase of faith; no family pieties had stifled him, so that he had to speak out. His freethinking father, emancipated from the provincial ghetto life of Galicia, raised his children in a secular atmosphere. After a childhood devoid of religious impulse and schooling, Freud was easily converted to the Darwinian gospel and a lifelong faith in science. In such a background there is nothing that promises erudition in religious questions, let alone sympathy for them; but neither is there an incentive to react strongly against the old articles or new moods of faith. Yet the animus is there.

We can gauge its extent by noting Freud's claim to encompass impartially, as a psychologist, the entire historical variety of religion. What appears in *The Future of an Illusion*, in the essay "Obsessionalism and Religious Practices," and in other writings as a generalized critique of religion is of course not impartial; nor is it evenly distributed. Aiming at religion in general, Freud's critique hits Christianity most accurately; and by Christianity he had in mind mainly the Roman Catholic Church, as he saw it in the fiercely anti-Semitic Vienna of his day.

To balance this strong animus toward Catholic Christianity, Freud's feelings about his own religious origins were tolerably hospitable. Freud viewed himself as as "little an adherent of the Jewish religion as of any other."[1] Toward a Judaism that entailed beliefs theologically distinct from Christianity, he had no attitude at all. Yet, despite his irreligion, Freud felt intensely Jewish and lived his life in largely Jewish society. His is the familiar history of the European Jewish intellectual. His friends were all Jews, his patients mostly so; his private culture—jokes and family sentiment—exemplify a Jewishness more binding than religious orthodoxy. Even some of the neurotic traits in Freud's character point to his origins in eastern European Jewry; for example, that obsessive anxiety for the health of wife and children which is a common by-product of the Jewish son's close and persistent bond with his mother. (Until a year before his marriage, at twenty-seven, Freud lived at home, and later, as husband and father, apparently transferred to his own family a good deal of his maternal anxiety.)[2] However little nostalgia he harbored for Jewish ceremonies or custom, Freud did acknowledge himself as

1. Quoted by A. A. Brill, *Freud's Contribution to Psychiatry* (New York: W. W. Norton, 1944), 195–96.

2. See Ernest Jones, *The Life and Work of Sigmund Freud*, 3 vols. (New York: Basic Books, 1953–57), 1:64, 145–46. For evidence from Freud's own dreams, see *The Interpretation of Dreams*, in *The Standard Edition of the Complete Psycho-*

a psychological Jew—and indeed he had many of the rigidities of that curious and heroic type in late European history.

It is easy to dismiss Freud's Jewishness as a residual attachment, or as a reflex against the anti-Semitism of the majority culture around him. But it deserves more serious consideration; for here concealed are a number of connections between his personal psychology and his psychology of religion. In considering himself a psychological Jew, Freud meant to define "Jew" more fundamentally, in terms of a certain kind of character rather than by adherence to a specific creed.

Freud found in the perennial Jewish character, rather than in any belief, the source of his personal integrity, his moral courage, his braininess—and, above all, his defensive attitude toward the world. As he linked the insights of his admired contemporary Josef Popper-Lynkeus into the "hollowness of the ideals of our present-day civilization" with the fact that Popper was Jewish,[3] so Freud claimed for his own moral stamina the same source. Such ethnic pride projects his desire for that unhampered critical utterance which is the religion not of the Jew integrated into his own community but of the "infidel Jew,"[4] standing on the edge of an alien culture and perpetually arrayed against it. In one respect, then, I take Freud's Jewishness as a rationale for his critical pugnacity. His minority-group loyalty reinforced his image of an embattled psychoanalytic minority.[5]

From an early age, Freud in his critical sentiments had been erecting a mystique of the Jews. Even when his admiration became fixed on a figure not actually Jewish, it served his Jewish moralism. As a boy, when he finally came to realize the consequence of

---

logical *Works of Sigmund Freud* (hereafter *SE*), ed. and trans. James Strachey (London: Hogarth Press, 1953–), 4:136 ff.

. 3. "My Contact with Josef Popper-Lynkeus" (1932), in *Collected Papers of Sigmund Freud*, 5 vols. (London: Hogarth Press, 1949–50), 5:301.

4. "A Religious Experience" (1928), *Collected Papers*, 5:244.

5. Cf. the essay "Resistances to Psychoanalysis," *Collected Papers*, 5:174: "Nor is it perhaps entirely a matter of chance that the first advocate of psychoanalysis was a Jew. To profess belief in this new theory called for a certain degree of readiness to accept a position of solitary opposition—a position with which no one is more familiar than a Jew." In his image, the minority shrinks at times to a group of one—a Moses, himself—the solitary opponent of organized error.

belonging "to an alien race," and was forced by the anti-Semitic feeling among his classmates "to take up a definite position," he invoked "the figure of the Semitic commander" Hannibal. "To my youthful mind Hannibal and Rome symbolized the conflict between the tenacity of Jewry and the organization of the Catholic church."[6] That the schoolboy Freud should have chosen Hannibal as his "favorite hero" is no more surprising than that the aged scientist should at last write of Moses. A similar feeling infuses his admiration for Oliver Cromwell, for whom he went so far as to name a son;[7] the Puritan commander, with his intellectual soldierliness and sense of certainty, appealed to the unbeliever Freud, psychologically, as a Jew. The affinity for militant puritanism, not uncommon among secular Jewish intellectuals, indicates a certain preferred character type, starched with independence and cerebral rectitude rather than with a particular belief or doctrine. The figure of the minority radical was especially compelling for Freud. During his long life he saw psychoanalysis move from its position as a minority movement, censuring what it took to be the dominant beliefs of the culture, to a point at which many of its tenets were accepted and partly incorporated into the dominant beliefs. Nevertheless, it is part of the logic of a critical theory that it can only acknowledge with reluctance its successes; so far as it is still critical, it continues to understand itself as on the defensive. It is not accidental, I think, that Freud's defiant interest in religion grew upon him late in his writing life. As he saw the critical impact of his therapeutic ideas weakened by success, he turned to the most resonant image of estrangement he could find—his Jewishness. Being a Jew helped Freud to maintain, throughout his career, his self-image as a lonely fighter.[8] Hannibal had almost brought down mighty Rome. Despite his later eminence, Freud's

6. *The Interpretation of Dreams*, 4:196.

7. Cf. ibid., *SE*, 5:447–48.

8. "To deny a people the man whom it praises as the greatest of its sons," was another stroke of genius in Freud's lifelong intellectual act of estrangement. Thus to intuit that Moses, creator of the Jews, was himself an Egyptian transformed the greatest son into the greatest stranger, a lonely fighter even against his own armies. See *Moses and Monotheism* (1939; New York: Alfred A. Knopf, 1949), 3.

object remained to bring down the mighty Romes of our ascetic civilization, now so corrupt and, even worse, ineffectual. Freud always kept his "desire to go to Rome." But he wanted to go as a Hannibal of the mind, as Lord Protector of its dark dominions.

A motif to which Freud recurs in analyzing his own dreams is ambition. Sometimes it is prosaic and career harried, as in the dream whose underlying wish, he discovered, was his desire to become a professor;[9] at other times it is a more noble ambition that he evokes, as with the recital of this memorable childhood incident:

> I may have been ten or twelve years old, when my father began to take me with him on his walks and reveal to me in his talk his views upon things in the world we live in. Thus it was, on one such occasion, that he told me a story to show me how much better things were now than they had been in his days. "When I was a young man," he said, "I went for a walk one Saturday in the streets of your birthplace; I was well dressed, and had a new fur cap on my head. A Christian came up to me and with a single blow knocked off my cap into the mud and shouted: 'Jew! get off the pavement!'" "And what did you do?" I asked. "I went into the roadway and picked up my cap," was his quiet reply. This struck me as unheroic conduct on the part of the big, strong man who was holding the little boy by the hand. I contrasted this situation with another which fitted my feelings better: the scene in which Hannibal's father, Hamilcar Barca, made his boy swear before the household altar to take vengeance on the Romans. Ever since that time Hannibal had had a place in my phantasies.[10]

Freud would have preferred a heroic father to such a prudent one; he once dreamed of him as a Garibaldi, a national emancipator.[11] To argue, as Freud was to do, that our image of God derives from the experience of the father does not preclude understanding that there are many fathers. One of his charges against Christianity

9. *The Interpretation of Dreams*, 4:136 ff., the dream of the uncle with the yellow beard. Cf. ibid., 216.

10. Ibid., 197.

11. Ibid., *SE*, 5:427–29.

is that its father-image is not sufficiently strict and demanding. Perhaps with the Roman theology in mind, Freud valued unyielding spiritual pride, such as that with which he credits the Jews. He questions the "kindness" of the Christian God, who "must lay a restraining hand upon his justice. One sinned, and then one made oblation or did penance, and then one was free to sin anew."[12] The creator of the Jews—Moses—was neither kindly nor indulgent, as Freud depicts him; soldierly and uncompromising rebels like Hannibal, Cromwell, or Garibaldi symbolized to him the moral tenacity of the Jews.[13]

Freud attributed his intellectuality, as he did his moral courage, to his Jewishness. "For various reasons the Jews have undergone a one-sided development and admire brains more than bodies." The Greek balance between intellectual and physical cultivation "is certainly preferable . . . but if I had to choose between the two I should also put the intellect first," Freud once said to Ernest Jones.[14] "For two thousand years," he declares in *Moses and Monotheism*, the Jews have exercised their "preference" for intellectual and "spiritual endeavour."[15] It is a sentiment that Jewish intellectuals who have repudiated orthodoxy but are still covertly attached to their sacred history have frequently expressed in an effort to preserve the old élan of being divinely chosen. I need not point out how self-deceptive this superiority complex, cultivated by an able and insecure European post-religious Jewish intelligentsia, has become. The setting of Jewish aspiration has shifted from the learned Germany of Freud's era to athletic and nervous

12. *The Future of an Illusion*, (London: Hogarth Press, 1928), 66.

13. Freud's feeling for the persistent character of the Jews was shared, in the Victorian and Edwardian periods, not only by marginal Jews (Disraeli's proud defensive mystique immediately comes to mind) and by Jewish self-haters like Otto Weininger, but also by friendly rationalists and liberals. Freud's remark that the Jews must have "behaved in Hellenistic times as they do today" reminds me of E. M. Forster's description, in a story with a Hellenistic setting called "Philo's Little Trip" (in *Pharos and Pharillon*), of "six Hebrew gentlemen of position and intelligence, such as may be seen in these days filling a first-class carriage in the . . . express on their way up to interview the government." Freud's partisanship is of course Hebrew, while Forster sides with the Greeks. Both take for granted a persistent Jewish character.

14. Ernest Jones, *Life and Work*, 1:31.

15. *Moses and Monotheism*, 181.

America. In the American environment, Jewry has altered its inherited preference for intellect. Several generations and suburbs away from the dismantling of orthodoxy, many Jews have become too comfortably aware of their purely psychological—or, for that matter, sociological—Jewishness to remain Jews or become intellectuals. According to the Freudian assumption, to become self-conscious about a prototype helps dissolve it. Among educated Jews in Europe and now in America, from whom it has chiefly drawn its partisans, Freudianism may be seen as breaking the last painful strands of religious identification. Under psychoanalytic tutelage, the felt ambiguity of being a Jew without religion can be understood as part of a neurotic submission to an exhausted authority, and dispelled. Freud himself retained more loyalty to his Jewishness than his doctrine permits.

II

That doctrine has proved the least answerable of recent adversaries to both Judaism and Christianity, just because it takes so seriously the inner dynamics of the old faiths. The articles of faith matter not at all. Freud's own Jewish attitudes illuminate, better than any atheist posture, the entirely anti-intellectual approach of the psychologist to religion. In *The Future of an Illusion*, Freud's major essay on religion, where he appears in such a sharp polemical mood, his greatest contempt is reserved for the philosophers of religion—those who try to make religion intellectually, as well as emotionally, attractive. In view of the strategy of peeling off manifest contents that is generally characteristic of his therapeutic method, it is not surprising that Freud decried the subtleties of the philosophers of religion. He accuses them of stretching "the meaning of words until they retain scarcely anything of their original sense." Philosophers of religion may call "some vague abstraction which they have created for themselves" God, and "pose as deists, as believers." But the "higher and purer idea of God" which they "pride themselves on having attained . . . is nothing but an insubstantial shadow and no longer the mighty personality of religious doctrine."[16]

16. *The Future of an Illusion*, 57.

Freud has little to say of religious inquiry. His argument never confronts theology, for which he cares nothing, but is based strictly on a view of religion as a certain emotional set. The rational theology of Saint Thomas, Calvin's cutting logic, the entire inquisitive and speculative bent of Western religion, remain unacknowledged. This intellectual superstructure Freud saw as merely a disguise or rationalization for the deeper emotions, which were as much political or moral as religious. Like Schopenhauer and Nietzsche before him, and like D. H. Lawrence and others after, Freud interprets the cognitive pith of religion as a displacement of the emotion toward authority.

Rejecting the religion of the intellectuals, Freud went about his main business, the attack on the religion of the naïve. Yet his rejection of the intellectual content of religion, his charge that religious intellectuals were trying to fill the expanding silence of God with their own voices, accords with the main defense of religion in the last century as well as with the main attack. For a growing number of the thoughtful, from Pascal to Harnack, no bridge seemed long enough to reach from the God of Aristotle and Saint Thomas to the God of Abraham, Isaac, and Jacob. Freud found the crossing easy—and irrelevant. The conceptual God was simply a pale abstraction of the living God. The bridge led nowhere; it was only the cleverest way of leaving the scene of the old God's death. Yet all this cleverness had little to do with religion. White peacock and bull father, totems marched out before tribal brothers, sovereign kings of families covenanted together, communion rites and fertility images—these are religion. Not even the God of Abraham and Isaac would do as the authentic deity. The God of Freud's polemic is still less cognizable. Behind the One God of Judaism, as he explained in *Moses and Monotheism*, stands the remote figure of a bloody mountain deity; and behind that deity looms the awesome figure of the primal father, the missing link between anarchy and culture.[17] Freud conceived of no God not originally mortal, none that did not incarnate the

17. Freud based his view upon the origins fiction proposed by Darwin and Atkinson.

human craving for authority—just as in the social sphere he could conceive of no political unity based on anything other than erotic attachment to a personal leader.

What Freud contributed to the discussion of religion was not a critique of orthodoxy. To disparage theology as merely intellectual sums up the genius of that liberal and sentimental piety—the evasive religion of the heart—which, in the nineteenth century, had succeeded large segments of Protestant orthodoxy. When in midcentury, after many premature announcements, the old fatherly God did really die, he was replaced by a model man, compounded of the highest moral sentiments and sweet reason. In order to avoid the finality of death, the mighty anthropomorphic personality was dismissed respectfully as a poetic but not exclusively valid representation of God—for the many. Thus Matthew Arnold, one of the most thoughtful representatives of liberal religion, wrote:

> It is undeniable that the old anthropomorphic and miraculous religion . . . no longer reaches and rules as it once did. . . . [But] it is not to be imputed merely to the inadequacy of the old materializing religion, and to be remedied by giving to this religion a form still materializing, but more acceptable. It is to be imputed, in at least an equal degree, to the grossness of perception and materializing habits of the popular mind, which unfit it for any religion not lending itself, like the old popular religion, to those habits; while yet, from other causes, that old religion cannot maintain its sway. And it is to be remedied by a gradual transformation of the popular mind, by slowly curing it of its grossness of perception and of its materializing habits, not by keeping religion materialistic that it may correspond to them.[18]

Arnold's polite faith, which he hoped could somehow be spread from the cultured few to the uncultured many, is precisely the solution to the religious problem with which Freud began. Assuming that such a dematerialized God cannot, as Arnold hoped, attract the naïve and uneducated, Freud taunts us with the old personal

18. Matthew Arnold, *Last Essays on Church and Religion* (London, 1877), vii–viii.

God, the true God of the naïve. For the Freudian psychologist, with his unquestioned assumption that individuals are motivated only through an appeal to the emotions, God can hardly be a first principle or an abstract composite of moral enthusiasms. In Freud's view, religion excluded any cognitive function; it was as purely associated with feeling as science was with reason. By this application of his psychology, Freud accepted a major trend of nineteenth-century belief and interpretation of belief, rejecting the theology of the mind for the religion of the heart—in order to move on from this to the rejection of religion altogether.

Such a tactic characterizes all modern attempts at a psychology of religion, even that made in a work as complex and persuasive as William James's *The Varieties of Religious Experience* (1903). James was aware of the reductive import of the psychological approach to religion; by distinguishing *varieties* of religious experience he tried to mitigate this reductionism, as Freud did not. But James, too, for all his analytical delicacy, was still a psychologist, with a psychologist's one-eyed interest in religion. Like Freud, later, he found the emotions of the naïvely religious more interesting, more fundamental, than the intellectualized responses of those who have experienced faith more subtly, though no less power-fully.[19] Freud was, however, more polemical than James, and he was less impressed by the therapeutic value and moral authority of religious belief.

Further, Freud's analytic apparatus is less complex than is James's; it consists largely of connecting religion with the emotional need for authority. His geneticism lies behind this connection. Through religion, the needs of the past revive. Adults feel their helplessness in the world at large, as if still children. In "the child's defensive reaction to his helplessness" Freud found what he thought a perfectly adequate model for the adult religious experience of "unknown and mighty powers."[20] Religion is linked

19. Studying the phenomenon of conversion, for example, James passed over evidence of the conversion experiences of intellectuals, or conversions based on doctrinal grounds, in favor of the experiences of untutored and disturbed minds swayed by revivalist fervor.

20. *The Future of an Illusion*, 42. One may compare Freud's idea of religion as deriving from the timid propitiation of the "all-powerful Father" with Spen-

with the weakness of childhood and contrasted with the heroism of true maturity. "There is no question that religion derives from the need for help and the anxiety of the child and mankind in its early infancy." Freud's point is that adults are only a little less helpless today, but that at least they need not convert helplessness into a fantasy of some beneficent relation to power. To the rejoinder that man *is* weak, Freud would reply that religion does not overstate the weakness of the human condition but expresses too much pride in it. Religion corresponds to the childhood of the human mind and is suitable to ages of intellectual weakness; the evolutionist moral of Freud's description is that we must grow up, develop beyond religion.

The rhetoric of Freud's analysis depends almost entirely upon evocations of "childishness." By religion he appears to have in mind the famous feeling of dependence, with God conceived as the sovereign father of the extensive human family. Even less generalized religious feelings, those not attached to apprehension of a personal deity (the image of the father enlarged), are reduced to childishness. Take, for instance, the well-known passage in *Civilization and Its Discontents* where Freud summarizes a correspondence with the novelist Romain Rolland.[21] Rolland had inquired whether Freud would admit the sense of an all-embracing, indefinite consciousness, an "oceanic feeling," as a genuine variety of mystic experience. Freud answered no; and, as we would expect from his unfailing recourse to origins as a therapeutic (and at the same time scientific) mode of explanation, he played on the positivist affront of childishness. He called Rolland's religious feeling primitive; this sense "of belonging inseparably to the external world as a whole" is nothing but a survival of the primitive

---

cer's theory that all forms of religious worship are derived from the propitiation of deceased ancestors, and that our idea of the deity derives from our fear of ghosts (*Principles of Sociology*, 1897). Both Freud's father-theory and Spencer's ghost-theory are ways of discounting religion as a form of "projection"—a type of analysis which received its classic statement in the writings of Ludwig Feuerbach, especially *The Essence of Christianity* (1841) and *The Essence of Religion* (1854).

21. *Civilization and Its Discontents* (London: Hogarth Press, 1930), 7–9. Rolland is not mentioned by name in the text.

ego-feeling which is normal to infancy. Here, as elsewhere, Freud shows how far he is from sharing that sentiment for childhood which unites Christian orthodoxy with modern Romanticism, old faith with new sensibility. Christian and Romantic alike refuse to regard a childlike simplicity of vision simply as a mode of immaturity, holding that children may know something—of morals, of beauty—which adults with their complex and limited experience have forgotten.

What Freud disparages as infantile feeling could plausibly be treated as a saving inclination of the self to assay some simple reconciliation with the world. Surely reconciliation is a universal motive. Freud had self-consciously echoed[22] the mythological notion asserted by Plato that even the orgiastic impulse was an attempt to overcome the duality of the sexes and restore their original unity. But he treats the interior movement toward reunion as regressive. The mystic's cherished break through the sense of individuality is treated by Freud as a regression, a flagging of the ego in its irresolvable struggle with the alien world. Every such reconciliation merely evades the permanent conflict between self and not-self. The permanence of conflict is Freud's leading theme, and part of his hostility to religion stems from an awareness that religion somewhere assumes a fixed point—in Christianity, the figure of Christ—at which conflict is resolved. In contrast, Freud maintains an intractable dualism; self and world remain antagonists, and every form of reconciliation must fail.[23] Indeed, nothing so well represents Freud's own irreligion as his feeling for the irreconcilable. It also explains how he could make an exception, in his antireligious critique, for the Jews, whom he so admired for their tough, uncompromising monotheism and their "usual stiff-necked obduracy"[24] in the face of persecution and reproach.

To his disparaging view of religion as derived from the dependent sentiments of childhood, Freud subjoined another charge,

---

22. *Beyond the Pleasure Principle, SE* 18:57–58.

23. See the concluding passage of *Civilization and Its Discontents,* 144, on the two "immortal adversaries," Eros and Thanatos; and *Collected Papers,* 5:346.

24. *Moses and Monotheism,* 142.

that religion is basically a "feminine" preoccupation. He was not referring by this last to any institutional fact, such as the female monopoly on lay devoutness which is an important feature of the history of Christianity, at least of Catholic Christianity, in the West. He intended, rather, a psychological judgment beyond all the facts of religious history—a further caricature of religion as being beneath the masculine dignity of reason. Freud is concerned to show the pathos of the religious *man* who is, like a woman, "forced to obey unconditionally."[25] To be religious, as Freud sees it, is to be passive, compliant, dependent—essentially feminine traits. This is the main point he saw illustrated by the paranoiac seizure of an eminent Dresden jurist, Dr. Paul Schreber, on whose memoirs Freud commented in a lengthy essay (1915). One feature of the intricate messianic delusion to which Schreber fell prey, while confined in a mental hospital, was the belief that he had changed his sex, Schreber's desire to be a woman submitting to the masculine God Freud took as an exemplary case of the submissiveness that defined the religious attitude. Again, in his own case, the "Wolf Man," Freud explained his patient's childhood streak of piety as a projection of the boy's feminine attitude toward his own father. Not only is a spontaneous religiosity inconceivable to Freud, he even gave religion a sexual character in order to convey the power of religious thralldom.

These genetic disparagements of the religious spirit are, I should say, the least viable part of Freud's psychology of religion. Resembling all too closely the "nothing but" argument by which animus is sanctified as science, Freud's reasoning is actually tautological: he will admit as religious only feelings of submission and dependence; others are dismissed as intellectual dilutions or displacements of the primary infantile sentiment. (A like objection applies to the analogy he drew between religious acts and the obsessional ceremonies of neurotics.)[26] What is chiefly interesting in Freud's critique is not its blunter tactic of scientistic name-

25. "The Economic Problem in Masochism," *Collected Papers*, 2:258.
26. "Obsessive Acts and Religious Practices," *Collected Papers*, 2:25.

calling—religion as childish, feminine, obsessional—but the general implications of a *psychology* of religion, as a cultural symptom as well as a mode of diagnosis. I have noted earlier that Freud largely rejected as irrelevant the philosophic and historical study of religion that flourished among the postorthodox minds of the nineteenth century. But notice the source, and the power, of that rejection. In the Freudian rhetoric of faith as childishness, and of religion as a political device representing the oppressive claim of the community over the individual, we may detect a revival of the great tradition of Enlightenment criticism. It is this animus of the Enlightenment that has gained, under the aegis of Freud's intellectual authority, a new precedence among the educated but religiously illiterate of our time. The basis of Freud's critique of religion is now old enough to have been forgotten; through his writings the superseded standards of the Enlightenment take on a new freshness.

The fact that Freud was confronting not religious orthodoxy but a defense of Christianity (and today in America, of Judaism) that had already receded and merged with a vague defense of religious feeling as such gives his critique an aptness and novelty that a close look at its actual texture does not sustain. This apologetics—the repudiation of dogma for experience, of creed for feeling—seems virtually to invite a final, psychological reduction. Further, it seems likely that the rapidly accumulating data of anthropology lent new sense to the Enlightenment quest for an original, or "natural," form of religion, behind all variety and complication. Freud's lack of respect for the historicity of religions is comprehensible only if we see behind it his acceptance without question of the value of this quest.

This reduction of the liturgy and doctrines of historical religion to representations of universal "natural" (i.e., psychological) motives was first proposed in the eighteenth century by deists and rationalists. In the nineteenth century, when comparative religion emerged as a mature discipline, it was carried on chiefly by missionaries and other church-affiliated researchers. One of the earliest was the German pastor-scholar Friedrich Wilhelm Ghillany, who in 1842 published a book in which he derived the Passover from a rite of human sacrifice, and portrayed the Christian Eucharist as a modified Jewish sacrament of god eating (theophagy).[27] The post-religious implications of such study became evident only slowly, so that these church-affiliated scholars could study religion comparatively and yet insist that creed and faith remain untouched.[28] When the study of comparative religion was taken over by secular scholars and absorbed into the rising and more inclusive discipline of anthropology, conclusions overtly hostile to religion were drawn. Belief in a variously represented God was succeeded by an interest in various beliefs about God. It was at this point that Freud put forth his own contribution. Accepting the reduction broached in the Enlightenment and documented by the sciences of comparative religion and anthropology, he added to it the category of projection. Both the doctrinal essence and the ritual manifestation of religion were interpreted by Freud as projecting the revolt against, and subsequent acceptance of, the father. To the "identity," established by the anthropologists, "of the totem feast, the animal sacrifice, the theanthropic human sacrifice and the Christian Eucharist," he adds a unifying motive: that each rite is "at bottom" nothing but "a new setting aside of the father, a repetition of the crime that must be expiated."[29]

27. In *Die Menschenopfer der alter Hebraer.* See also the work of Ghillany's friend Daumler.

28. Their disclaimers were, however, not always convincing. Robertson Smith was tried by the elders of the Scottish Church for advancing a thesis much like Ghillany's.

29. *Totem and Taboo, SE,* 13:154–55. The original commemorative rite of parricide, "the ancient totem meal," is "revived again" in the Christian communion, a new totem feast "in which the company of brothers consumed the flesh and blood of the son—no longer the father—obtained sanctity thereby and identified themselves with them" (ibid., 154). "The memory of the first great act of sacrifice thus proved indestructible, in spite of every effort to forget it." The prototype of rebellion persists deeply in the memory of its defeat, when "at the very point at which men sought to be at the farthest distance from the [parricidal] motives that led to it, its undistorted reproduction emerged in the form of the sacrifice of the god" (ibid., 151–52). In this way, Freud sought to encompass what his predecessors, such as Robertson Smith, had already established sociologically as the priority of "cultus" to "doctrine"—a psychological version of the religious ritual as (in all its variations) expressive of the original alienation from authority. Ritual commemorated the original crystallization of

The challenge of Freud's critique, by which the differences of history are bleached into a sameness of motive, is more thoroughgoing than that posed previously by generations of erudites in search of the common faith underlying the complex historical varieties of religion. By tracing parallel occurrences of the myth of the dying Savior, outside Christianity, in Greek mystery cults and Mithraism; by exposing the patchwork of biblical texts; by showing how liturgy was shaped by ecclesiastical politics—in these ways the historical method shook Christianity. But outside the enclaves of biblical literalism, the shocks could be absorbed. Liberal Christianity could let go of the historical Christ and keep only the personal Jesus. Indeed, liberal Christianity absorbed the historical method into its own canon of argument, taking its stand on a universal and inherently spiritual "need," of which dogma was one plausible if limited historical expression. Not just the intellectual justification for tolerance in a variety of liberal denominations but also the great nineteenth-century, largely middle-class Protestant religion of culture developed out of Enlightened, comparisoned, and scienced Christianity. Indeed, that Christ should have emerged as "Christ, Scientist," as in one remarkable upgrading of his professional title, marks the bathetic climax of Enlightenment therapeutics in America.

The style of attack that reached its climax in Freud was more damaging than historicism, more damaging than Christianity as mind cure. A psychology of religion cannot be fended off in quite the same way, by partial incorporation. Embracing the findings of the comparative—that is, historical—study of religion and adapting as well the liberal refutation, psychology can reject the universality of the "religious need" in human nature by dissolving that specific need into emotions characteristic of more than religion. There is no distinctively religious need—only psychological need. The psychologist still has the option, however, of being friendly or hostile. If friendly, he will argue that religion is

---

the dual impulses of human nature into the character of culture as such. "We can recognize in all these solemn occasions the effect of the crime by which men were so deeply weighed down but of which they must none the less feel so proud" (ibid., 154–55).

"psychologically" valuable; this is the position of Jung. If hostile, he will counter that the need can be satisfied by something better, more mature, than religion; this is Freud's view. That "something better" is rational science, in the service of a less wasteful development of human satisfaction.

III

Freud is a popularizer of the religious problem, speaking in the authoritative voice of science, to an audience on the whole post-religious[30] and unfamiliar with the lines of self-criticism laid down by the theologians themselves. Upon many brought up within a weak or defensive religious environment, his arguments for atheism have had a great emancipating impact, giving them reasons for a break already in process.

On religious minds, however, he has a different effect—one of those reversals to which the psychoanalytic method is liable. Given the intellectual poverty and lame spirit of organized religion today, it is ironic but not surprising that Freud should be understood by a number of influential clerical spokesmen as contributing new authority to their side of the old argument between the rationale of faith and faith in reason. One of the more curious turns in the history of Freud's reception is that by which his atheist psychology, despite the indignation with which it was first greeted by professional guardians of morality, has been taken up by a number of eminent religious minds as if it were a prop and not an assault. Whatever is serious in the current revival of religion is evocatively, if not substantively, Augustinian in temper; it proclaims the wretchedness of the human condition and rather muffles the voice of God. For this sort of religiosity Freud performs a delicate service. His atheism being dismissed as a personal aberration, Freud's psychology has been pressed into service, mainly as independent testimony to the religious "depth" for those no longer persuaded of its existence by theological rhetorics. Again, Freudianism may buoy up those who recoil from the

30. By "post-religious," I mean an attitude so far removed from ultimate concern that neither piety nor atheism can appeal to it. "Religion" is accepted, like any other service, as another good to be consumed by those who have a taste for it.

optimism of liberal religion. Chastened by decades of failure to convince themselves that every day in every way they are getting better—under Christ and/or the prophets—liberal Christians and reformed Jews now flock to a moral psychology that, in Freud's own ironic words, confirms "the habitual pronouncement of the pious: we are all miserable sinners."[31] It is stressed that Freud did acknowledge a native moral evil (in the instincts). He did assume a universal sense of guilt. His view of nature was pessimistic. These things are taken as evidence of the affinities between the religious and psychological view.[32]

Freud merits respectful treatment by the theologians; they can use him more than they can any other thinker who has ever been fundamentally hostile or indifferent to them. Today a Christian anthropology that does not incorporate large quantities of Freudianism cannot serve Christianity. Nevertheless, the theologian who subjoins psychoanalytic to theological conceptions is foolhardy. The irrationalities to which Freud drew our attention are to be mastered through rational self-control; he does not enjoin faith. He detected neither accident nor mystery in the world. Even its "depths" conform perfectly to the laws of nature, those laws which it is the business of science to extend. To be sure, Freud was not sanguine about the average man's powers of reason. But he never wavered in his attachment to the public fellowship of science and its powers of explanation. In contrast to Jung's, nothing in Freud's theory supports the claim of any intuitive system of explanation or response.

It is just those Freudian terms with a religious resonance—

31. *Totem and Taboo*, SE, 13: 72.

32. I speak here only of the theoretic appeal of psychology for religion, and vice versa. There is also a less obtrusive trend of rapprochement going on—and, to my mind, a more dangerous one, since it stakes its claim below the level of theological argument and psychological theory. I refer to the affinities that have been discovered between the pastoral techniques of religion and the therapeutic techniques of psychiatry. Here, both sides have contributed to the new amity: ministers and theologians attempting to repair the encroachments that psychiatrists have made on their professional preserve as the authority who is consulted when people are in emotional and moral straits; psychiatrists anxious to repudiate the unavoidable doctrinal implications of their clinical practice by a new generosity toward the successes of the religious "cure of souls."

such words as "guilt," "anxiety," "conscience"—that reproach the corresponding religious notions. Take, as a case, Freud's treatment of conscience. While not denying the natural development of a moral sense, he offers little support to the religious conception of it. In Freud's usage conscience is an instrument of parental dominance, the accretion of ordinances by which, as the sociologists say, a child is "socialized" and its resentments "internalized." It is precisely the religious view of conscience as intelligent and reflective as well as passionate that here comes under attack, for Freud argues that conscience is furnished by social authority and remains, unreflectively, at authority's disposal. This refusal to acknowledge that conscience may be at odds with its social sources surely simplifies the moral process. Because he views society reductively, as the family-in-large, Freud overestimates the degree of consistency in the ethical injunctions to which people are exposed. (This error mars his therapeutic writings, as well as his general consideration of the superego.) He assumes that parents, as well as "teachers, authorities, [or] self-chosen models and heroes venerated by society,"[33] all preach the same line; he underestimates the cynicism and cleverness of the young and exaggerates their naïve impressionability. For Freud, however, freedom of conscience is a contradiction in terms; there are only alternative submissions.

In place of such freedom there is the empirical capacity for aggression—a capacity without which Freud cannot explain the moral order and the individual's need for religion. For him the instinct of aggression plays the same role, formally, that Christian psychology assigns to free will. Thus aggression is the psychological potency that enables man to rebel against authority, in the person of the primal father (as, in the religious account, free will allows us to rebel against God), and at the same time it supplies the means by which men can end their rebellion. Freud's idea of the "introjection" of aggression formally resembles the religious idea of the free act of faith; it reconciles the subject to authority. He did not hold the comforting view that aggression is

33. "The Economic Problem in Masochism," 265.

a secondary emotion, a consequence of the frustration of love. On the contrary, as he saw it, aggression is as original as sin. Again, this metainstinctual strain in Freudianism, these dark expectancies concerning the permanence of aggression, have appealed to those for whom psychology is religion touched with science. But Freud's view does not invite this response, for what the religious think of as moral evil—these aggressive feelings and the reaction to them—he discusses as entirely natural. His remedy, too, is far from a religiously acceptable one. To reduce human aggressiveness he recommends that we reduce our overextended moral aspirations, since aggression is, in part at least, a reaction against too fervent a desire for personal virtue.

The gulf between psychoanalytic and Christian psychologies appears even more sharply in the related idea of guilt. Though Freud saw guilt as in some degree inevitable and objective—as the religious do—any further likeness to the religious prepossession is deceptive. Guilt may be innate, original, natural, a feeling prior to action. But this Freudian conception of guilt is cast strictly within the critical language of pathology. First of all, in Freud's account, repression forces a backward flow of the destructive instincts upon the self. And apart from the externally imposed restraints exercised by civilization (the repressions), everyone inherently suffers from a residue of the "death instinct," so that hostilities which are not directed outward upon others turn back upon the self in the form of "an intensified masochism" and feelings of guilt.[34] Its origins having been explained thus naturalistically, the sense of guilt can hardly be considered a reliable index of real felony and warrantable remorse. Since no distinction is drawn in the Freudian scheme between natural and moral evil, no room is left for guilt as distinct from ignorance. The overscrupulous and conscience-ridden person is in the grip of certain prepossessions of which he is unaware; and the presumption is that his guilt will dissolve in the rational self-consciousness fostered

---

34. Ibid., 267. When the positive redirection of the death instinct outward takes place, Freud wrote, "it is then called the instinct of destruction, of mastery, the will to power" (*Collected Papers*, 2:260).

by therapy. Guilt indicates lack of self-understanding, a failure of tolerance toward himself on the part of the natural man.

However, as Karen Horney has pointed out, even after analysis (after the patient "knows"), patients may still have feelings of guilt. She is mistaken, though, when she accuses Freud of seeing guilt as merely private and missing the all-pervasive weight of ideology. That this is not his view Freud makes clear in *Totem and Taboo* and thereafter. He supposed guilt the normal attitude of an individual toward authority, social as well as individual. One of his favorite theses is that human beings have an ineradicable social heritage of guilt. The great religions are attempts to solve the problem of guilt; they are all "reactions to the same great event," the murder of the primal father, "with which civilization began and which, since it occurred, has not allowed mankind a moment's rest."[35] Religion attempts to appease the sense of guilt; at the same time, only by perpetuating it (by such commemorative repetitions of the parricidal act as the Christian communion) does the authority of faith continue. Morality too stands under the sign of guilt. The best behavior of which we are capable is "at bottom" an attempt "to conciliate the injured father through subsequent obedience." The social and religious meaning of guilt is summed up by Freud in the following formula: society was "based on complicity in the common crime; religion was based on the sense of guilt and remorse attached to it; while morality was based partly on the exigencies of this society and partly on the penance demanded by the sense of guilt."[36] The sense of guilt is thus the pivot for Freud's conception of morality and religion. Religion, he says elsewhere, proceeds by "fomenting an ever-increasing sense of guilt."[37]

The Christian theologians—especially liberal Protestants—who have expressed a certain fondness for Freud's affirmation of the saving sense of guilt are mistaken to see any support in this for their own position. Freud held that religious sentiment is a phase resulting from certain historical processes of repression

35. *Totem and Taboo*, 145.
36. Ibid., 144–46.
37. *Civilization and Its Discontents*, 121.

(and subject to historical fluctuations); for him the sense of guilt is a flexible instrument, and "it is possible that cultural developments lie before us, in which yet other wish-gratifications, which are today entirely permissible, will appear just as disagreeable as those of cannibalism do now."[38] Aldous Huxley makes Freud's point effectively when he shows the horror with which the inhabitants of *Brave New World* regard us, their ancestors, for our obscene practice of bearing children alive, like mammals, instead of in a civilized fashion, out of test tubes. The strength of Christian culture has depended on the use it has made of the funded potential of human guilt feelings, and Freud argues that, whatever its value in the past, the "creative sense of guilt"[39] has now increased beyond all use. Religion itself has become the sort of collective neurosis by which we can no longer save ourselves from a personal one.

Man is a remorseful killer, and religion is the history of his guilt. But why "guilt" at all? The animals feel none. Guilt is incurred by the infraction of a law or principle. And how powerful must that *Schuldgefühl* have been, if the whole complicated, infinitely anguished story of religion grew out of that feeling. But Freud refused to go the one step further, to admit the universal objectivity of guilt. So, too, Otto Rank held that without the repression of the incest urge, civilization was unthinkable. But it did not occur to him to ask why man should have repressed the incest urge. Whatever so evidently tore man out of the context of nature was itself repressed.

"When an instinctual trend undergoes repression," reads one formula in *Civilization and Its Discontents*, "its libidinal elements are transformed into symptoms and its aggressive components into a sense of guilt."[40] That guilt about which Freud writes is above all the *sense* of guilt, a psychological not a moral fact. In the Freudian rhetoric repression has a very special meaning, both individual and social; indeed, it is the conception at which psy-

38. *The Future of an Illusion*, 18.
39. *Totem and Taboo*, 159.
40. *Civilization and Its Discontents*, 132.

choanalysis meets Christianity back-to-back, so to speak. In the Christian psychology what is supposed to have been repressed, causing bad conscience, is one's higher nature—the moral sense. In the Freudian psychology what was repressed, causing a sense of guilt, is one's lower nature—the instinctual desires. Thus, in Christianity the sense of guilt is characteristically a sign of augmented moral delicacy; in Freudian psychology the sense of guilt is a source of private illness. In a culture undergoing the final reversals in religious meaning and value, the psychoanalytic inversion of Christianity's saving sense of guilt has had a curious appeal. Freud's meaning and that of Christianity are indeed close but completely at odds.

Having so redefined guilt as the repression of one's lower nature, Freud could demonstrate how treacherous was the floor under conventional piety. The sense of guilt as defined by Christian culture seemed to Freud a sandy foundation for morality. Indeed, he noted, it was possible precisely out of a "conscience phobia" to commit the most horrible crimes. Freud was aware of the morality, so highly praised in modern fiction, of the holy sinner. As a reader of Dostoyevsky, he noticed "in so many Russian character types" a special odor of sanctity around sin. "Russian mysticism has come to the sublime conclusion that sin is indispensable for the full enjoyment of the blessings of divine grace, and therefore, fundamentally, it is pleasing to God."[41] Of course, even though he mildly caricatured this theological fancy, Freud respected the necessity in a repressive culture of incorporating sin into the larger doctrine of grace. Moral dualism could be a conscious expedient of cultural coercion. "The priests could only keep the masses submissive to religion by making these great concessions to human instincts."[42]

Holy sinning, Freud recognized, is not simply a religiously permitted outlet for natural impulses, sponsored chiefly by certain historical forms of Christian (Catholic and gnostic) belief. The phenomenon of holy sinning might occur in any individual

41. *The Future of an Illusion*, 66. See also "The Economic Problems in Masochism," 266.
42. *The Future of an Illusion*, 66–67.

whose masochism, the cumulative backwash of the death instinct, "creates a temptation to 'sinful acts' which must then be expiated by the reproaches of the sadistic conscience or by the chastisement from the great parental authority of Fate." Since guilt is really pathological, a guilty conscience may not necessarily imply a turn to the good. Certain unmotivated crimes may be explained as a kind of suicide of conscience.

> An individual may, it is true, preserve the whole or a certain amount of his morality alongside his masochism, but, on the other hand, a good part of his conscience may become swallowed up by his masochism.[43]

The "pale criminal"[44] whom Freud had in mind commits his crimes in order "to provoke punishment" from authority. His acts are attempts to justify a preexisting sense of guilt. Convinced that he has committed some crime (the nature of which is left uncertain), he feels he "must do something inexpedient, act against his own interest, ruin the prospects which the real world offers him, and possibly destroy his own existence in the world of reality."[45]

Such an interlocking of weakness, rebellion, and obedience has been examined with extraordinary intensity in the modern novel. Raskolnikov (*Crime and Punishment*) and Stavrogin (*The Possessed*) are both ethical criminals, holy sinners. The type has not only fascinated the great Russian novelists and introspective Roman Catholics such as Bernanos, Mauriac, and Graham Greene but has also summoned Existentialist ideologues to a strenuous defense of writers with personal histories of criminal offense. The Existentialist characterization of writer-criminals—de Sade, Rimbaud, Jean Genet—as inverted men of faith draws upon the idea that crime can be an ethical act, more admirable than merely conforming to the proprieties. I doubt if Freud would have agreed

43. "The Economic Problem in Masochism," 266.

44. Nietzsche "on the Pale Criminal" is mentioned in *Collected Papers*, 4:342–44.

45. "The Economic Problem in Masochism," 266–67. For another discussion of crime from a sense of guilt, see *The Ego and the Id* (London: Hogarth Press, 1923), 76. Concept of guilt is prior to the concept of crime, *Totem and Taboo*, 13:159.

with the Existentialists that such crimes may be freely and coolly chosen, without compulsive residue—as an *acte gratuite*.[46] But a similar admiration for the antinomian character—the figure of the instinctual hero who is guilty of "presumptuousness and rebelliousness against a great authority"[47]—is a basic theme of Freud's work.

To resist the demands of conscience may be an act of maturity, since conscience may be a source of crime as well as of piety. The aim of Freudian psychiatry is, however, not the triumph of instinct over moral feelings but the reconciliation of instinct and intelligence. The intellect is set to helping the instincts develop, tolerantly, like a prudent teacher.[48] Conscience, however, directs us to repress the instincts. The conscience-stricken thus do not appear by Freudian standards to be very intelligent. By viewing conscience as in opposition to intelligence, Freud exhibits a prejudice against virtue fairly common among secular intellectuals— the idea that the merely good person is not likely to be either very clever or very strong.[49] "Morality," the sadism of the superego, appears as a stupid alternative to "the will to power," the sadism of the ego.[50] (Recall that Dostoyevsky, really a very secular intellectual, did not make the saintly Alyosha the cleverest of the brothers Karamazov.) Subscribing to the weakling theory of conscience so

46. See Sartre, *Saint Genet* (1952), and the studies of Simone de Beauvoir and Maurice Blanchot on de Sade. I should argue that the capacity for gratuitous crime does not necessarily testify to inner liberty. One might find, for instance, in the very surrealistic repetitiveness of the atrocities (and the interminable speeches justifying them) in de Sade's novels an index of the irrational and compulsive. The ethical criminals of de Sade and the Existentialists seem no less compulsively motivated than the wretched Stavrogin.

47. *Totem and Taboo*, 156.

48. The metaphor of psychoanalysis as pedagogy is one of the most significant Freud uses. See, e.g., *The Future of an Illusion*, 14.

49. The snobbishness in Freud's attitude toward the conscience-stricken is also suggested in his little essay "A Religious Experience" (1928). Freud had received an evangelistic letter from a young American medical student who reported how his realization that God must exist came to him one day while watching a "sweet-faced dear old lady" being wheeled into the cadaver room. Freud replied tartly that if he wanted to be a first-rate doctor he ought to get rid of his mother image (*Collected Papers*, 5:243–46).

50. "The Economic Problem of Masochism," 267.

popular in nineteenth-century literature, Freud shows once again in his conception of the guilt feelings how entirely opposed to Christian religious psychology is his psychology of religion.

IV

There is one curious exception to the general negative in Freud's psychology of religion; it is to be found in his underrated study *Moses and Monotheism*. Despite his prevailing idea of religious experience as the training ground of suppliant personalities, in this profound little book on the origins of monotheism Freud allowed for revolution from above as well as for instinctual resurgence from below.

He fixed on the Cromwellian aspects of the eleven-year reign of the young Egyptian pharaoh Amenhotep IV (1375 B.C.). The pharaoh's conversion to the monotheistic cult of Aton (in whose honor he changed his name to Ikhnaton) set off an unsuccessful attempt by a high-minded minority at a drastic imposition of new ideals upon both people and priesthood. Ikhnaton's lieutenant Moses—for so Freud identifies him—continued the revolutionary effort. Freud conjectures that, in despair after Ikhnaton's death, the Egyptian Moses turned to an alien Semitic community that had immigrated to Egypt several generations before. He left Egypt with them, accompanied by his immediate followers, hallowed them by the Egyptian custom of circumcision, gave them laws, and introduced them to the Aton religion—in an even more exacting version than that taught by his master Ikhnaton, for Moses relinquished the connection of Aton with the sun god of On. As Freud reconstructs the story, Moses was repudiated by his adopted people, the Jews. Yet precisely on the ostensible failure of the moral hero depends the success of his doctrine. On this point Freud's entire reconstruction of Hebraic monotheism, and (in less detail) the origins of Christianity, turns: a deposition of the moral hero and the subsequent remorse. For at one time, Freud boldly conjectures, the Jews must have killed Moses,[51] throwing off the

---

51. In the Old Testament narrative, of course, Moses dies a natural death, but in several noncanonical accounts, among them that of Origen, he is murdered. Freud says he found this suggestion, that Moses was actually murdered, in the writings of the great biblicist Ernst Sellin.

puritan faith as the Egyptians had done before them. If monotheism may be seen as a repressive revolution conducted by Moses from above, the murder of Moses represents a counterrevolution, a popular reassertion of the instincts in old cultic forms. After the death of Moses—Freud continues his conjecture—the Jews relaxed into the religious habits of their neighbors, taking up the debased worship practiced by the Midianites. But still an obscure memory of the Mosaic religion lingered. Remorse for the killing of Moses continued to work underground, until in time the Midianite tribal deity, Jahve, was divested of his original warlike attributes, becoming more like the old pacific God of Moses, Aton.[52] Thus the suppressed puritanism eventually reasserted itself. At least, in *Moses and Monotheism*, Freud acknowledged that civilization can be moved by spiritual as well as instinctual discontents.

Freud's conception of the relation between Moses and the mob assigns to discontent a different value from the one we get in *Civilization and Its Discontents*, a book that deals with consciousness in its painful transition from the religious to the scientific stage. In the prophet, the seer, the moral genius, discontent can still be spiritual, at odds with the libidinal discontents of the mob. By the time the psychologist appears, discontent must be libidinal, at odds with the overextensions of civilization. The discontent of Moses and the prophets was of another time. To Freud the issue is different now and discontent has another object—the spirit, not the flesh. Freud's praise of spiritual discontent as once being

52. Although *Moses and Monotheism* has been much derided by professional historians, some of Freud's purely imaginative reconstructions have received independent support from recent biblical scholarship, particularly the Swedish. The way in which Freud's reconstruction justifies the disagreeable paradoxes of the Old Testament idea of divinity seems, if a bit overformal, quite convincing. There were, originally, two different Gods: one the God of the Egyptian Moses, "as all-loving as he was all-powerful, who, averse to all ceremonial and magic, set humanity as its highest aim a life of truth and justice," the other a "rude, narrow-minded . . . violent and blood-thirsty" invention of the Midian priest whom the Bible also calls Moses (74–75, 78). All the canonic writings of Jewish religious history can be reinterpreted, in the Freudian view, according to the manner in which they go about concealing the gap between the Mosaic law giving and later Jewish religion, the gap that was filled by the worship of Jahve—the manner in which they not only conceal but also carefully cover over the duality.

a critical force can hardly flatter religions strong chiefly in their prophetic and critical resources and not in their priestly overlay. The sentiments of bitter and personal opposition to the world, which give an innominate tension even to orthodox religious expression, pass unnoticed by Freud. It is a major omission. Freud took the traditional religious posture of obedience to the divine at face value, at the same time failing to grasp the emancipated potential in that posture. No more rugged individualist has ever existed in Western culture than the religious virtuoso. Had Freud applied his presuppositions consistently to religion, he would have noticed the other side of religious experience, the achievement of unyielding individualism in opposition to current social sanctions. Prophetic denunciation of society counts for something in the Western tradition—for as much, in fact, as the persistent civic submissions that Freud prefers to consider.

Mythologizing on the origins of monotheism, Freud does admit the possibility of a rebellion against moral conformity on behalf of an even more stringent ideal. On the whole, however, he assumed religion to be conformist; the idea of it as subversive of the established tyrannies of compromise is one that Freud never entertained except in *Moses and Monotheism*. Even there, he was giving vent to the aristocratic bias that supplied what little was sympathetic in his attitude toward religion. The only defense he could entertain for religion was that, in virtue of its social function, religion is a force for order. And religious leaders like Moses are for Freud sympathetic figures so far as they elevate the moral standards of the rabble. Far from admiring instinctual revolt, Freud's own identification is with the benevolent culture despots of the prescientific ages who raised the level of popular aspiration and occasionally succeeded in transforming their own superegos into law.[53] When a culture ceases to venerate its great men, Freud

53. The drama of the teaching struggle, death, and posthumous triumph of Moses had a special significance in Freud's inner life. The teacher is, for Freud, the universal martyr image—characterized by his charisma and wisdom, suffering the resentment of his students and public, who are his children. There is no doubt that Freud, as a great teacher, identified himself with Moses. He writes that Michelangelo's "Moses," in the Church of San Pietro in Vincoli in Rome, attracts him irresistibly. "No piece of statuary has ever made a stronger impres-

feared the onset of that *misère psychologique* which conservative critics of the nineteenth century found to be endangering our civilization.[54] But Freud's faith in the moral genius as the founder of the culture went further than most. As he sought the Moses at the heart of all going systems and creeds, he hypostatized the founder of founders—the primal father—and assumed a natural moral system based on the story of this figure's death-sacrifice to the resurgent masses.

The life of the race is, I should say, much slower and more secular than Freud imagined. Each case of progressive despotism can be matched by scores in which the benevolence of despots rots culture and misdirects progress. Refinement is rarely a matter of sudden personal impulsions or emancipations by clever dedicated chiefs. Among high cultures, the Greek was conspicuously lacking in moral geniuses. The Olympian gods were all too human, and even the euhemeristic myths supporting them were discredited by the Periclean age. Only in that meanest of all Greek nations, Sparta, did a Moses figure arise: Lycurgus, the lawgiver. Freud's own Moses is altogether too statuesque. Little that is recognizably Old Testament in feeling gets into *Moses and Monotheism*. It is a study of the moral hero putting a higher civilization over on the rabble with the burning-bush trick and the tactic of the mountain retreat. Moses is the only rugged individualist Freud ever described, stronger and more successful than Nietzsche's Zarathustra, who also came down from a mountain retreat to elevate the popular Vedic polytheism into a high-minded ethical dualism. While Nietzsche's great man fails, Freud's great man even in his death succeeds: though the Jews rebel against the tenacity

---

sion on me than this. How often have I mounted the steep steps of the unlovely Corso Cavour to the lonely place where the deserted church stands, and have essayed to support the angry scorn of the hero's glance! Sometimes I have crept cautiously out of the half-gloom of the interior as though I myself belonged to the mob upon whom his eye is turned—the mob which can hold fast no conviction, which has neither faith nor patience and which rejoices when it has regained its illusory idols" (*Collected Papers*, 4:259–60). Perhaps this is the most intimate self-image the new Moses ever committed to paper, addressing it to the unconvinced, impatient, illusion-ridden, idolatrous mob that is the public.

54. *Civilization and Its Discontents*, 93.

and intellectual fierceness of Moses's character, and abandon the religion he has taught them, after his death they are bound to it all the more. Compared with the realism, in Nietzsche's book, of Zarathustra's ultimate philosophic failure, Freud's *Moses and Monotheism* is a triumph of psychological romance.

Freud insists that it was the Egyptian Moses who chose the Jews, not the Jews who chose Moses. Moses stamped the Jewish people with its special character. He is to Freud the greatest of moral geniuses, the culture savior, the "tremendous father-imago" of the Jews. The Jewish masses, who are "his dear children," live under his authority, if they live as Jews.[55] Before Moses they were like all others—that is, not Jews. Freud strangely ignores Father Abraham and his Covenant: "It was one man, the man Moses, who created the Jews." What the Jews came to understand as their chosenness by God reflected the fact that Moses had stooped to the Jews; they were his "chosen people."[56] To Moses, finally, the Jews owe their character—their tenacity, their moralism. Moses first and thereafter definitely fixed the Jewish type.[57]

Compare Freud's reverential treatment of Moses with his remarks on Christianity in *The Future of an Illusion*. While the Jews remained in his imagination what Moses had made of them, he never allowed to Christianity the revolutionary emblem of the character of Jesus. Christianity meant always the Church,[58] a repressive social institution engaged in a highly ambivalent ritual preservation of an imago that the participants have never really trusted. He discounts the martyrdom of Jesus by calling it a "repetition of the Mosaic prototype." Jesus is "the resurrected Moses"

55. *Moses and Monotheism*, 173.

56. Ibid., 166, 168.

57. See esp. the subsection on "The Great Man," ibid., 168–75.

58. Freud always saw religion in an authoritative (i.e., political) mode, and the Roman Church, with its highly bureaucratized militancy, was the nearest fit to his theory. When he turned to an analysis of political institutions, he considered that we might "with advantage take the Catholic Church as a type." In the Roman Church, as in an army, what is important is that "the same illusion holds good of there being a head—in the Catholic Church Christ, in an army its Commander-in-Chief." Though churches and armies may differ "in other respects," they share the same psychology of militancy and unity around the person of a leader (*Group Psychology, SE*, 18:93–94).

and of course "the returned primal father."[59] Because the killing of Christ postdates, and (psychologically) reproduces, the killing of Moses, Freud concludes that Christianity operates less imperatively than Judaism—a form of genetic discounting in reverse. Surely Christ was no mere epigonal repetition of the Mosaic prototype. Nothing of the singular and exemplary power of Christ attaches to the image of Moses. Yet Christianity, for Freud, is a "Son religion," Judaism is a "Father religion." In its inner meaning Christianity is the institutionally organized remembrance and recapitulation of the deposing of the father by the son. Freud sides with the father. In his view, Judaism stands for the true father, against the spurious assumption by the Christians of the son. The Christian tradition, however, does something more than again projecting the filial revolt. Freud's doctrine of the psychic trinity—Father, Son, and People—has Christ as an ambivalent figure in the mythos of history. In one sense, Christ is the incarnate God, himself father of the rebellious sons (the mob—who must kill him), thus recapitulating the primal crime. In another sense, equally true, Christ is the Son of Man, defying the Father God. Here the father of the people becomes as well the son, dying by the wish of the father. This is the double role of all tragic heroes, Oedipus and Hamlet as well as Moses and Christ: to die the representative deaths of both son and father.

To conceive of Christianity as a rebellion against, as well as a repetition of, Judaism, also shows psychoanalytically how Christianity itself prefigures that endemic form of resentment in our culture, anti-Semitism. The Jews, Freud observed, refuse to acknowledge their relation to a newer authority. "The poor Jewish people, who with their usual stiff-necked obduracy continued to deny the murder of their 'father,' has dearly expiated this in the course of centuries." Envy of such freedom from guilt becomes a reproach against it. "Over and over again" the Jews "heard the reproach: 'You killed our God.'" Freud concludes: "And this re-

59. Ibid., 142. Like Christianity, the founding of Mohammedanism is also "an abbreviated repetition of the Jewish one" (146). Both successor religions, according to Freud, lack the heroic suffering and achievement, the "lofty heights of spirituality to which the Jewish religion had soared" (139).

proach is true, if rightly interpreted. It says, in reference to the history of religion: 'You won't admit that you murdered God,'"[60] as if any person can be free of parricidal guilt in the civil wars of the mind.

V

Although he never considered the truth of either Jewish or Christian faith to be viable—except as the truth of any psychological record—Freud did not underestimate the social function of religion. Against this social function, indeed, he posed his final devastating critique.

The Enlightenment critique, to which Freud owes much, ascribes a natural origin to religion.[61] From this basic idea Enlightenment polemicists drew the most varied conclusions. Voltaire, for instance, dismissed all historical religions as superstitious and mistaken, corrupt and dangerous; against them he set the "religion of reason," unconnected with any supernatural hopes or appeals. Others, like Leibniz in his *Theodicy*, Locke in the *Deus*, Lessing in the *Education of the Human Race*, took a more accommodating position—regarding Christianity as but one historic stage in the approach to a purified or absolute religion, still to be revealed. Freud combines these two strains, the hard and the soft Enlightenment attack. In the bitterness of his invective against the worn religious patina of authority, in his insensitivity to differences among historical religions, and specifically in his underestimation of the originality of Jesus as a religious leader,[62] Freud is quite Voltairean. On the other hand, in his respect for the civilizing achievements of religion we catch sight of a progressive Feuerbachian Freud, one for whom even Christianity might

60. Ibid., 142.

61. See, for instance, Hume's *Natural History of Religion*, which Freud quotes in *Totem and Taboo*, 77.

62. Psychologically, the redeemer is always the same figure, the tragic hero, "the chief rebel and leader" against the primal father. "If there was no such leader, then Christ was the heir of an unfulfilled wish-phantasy." If, on the other hand, there was such a historic event as the overthrow of the father by the son, then Christ was one of a number to take the role, the "successor" to it, the "reincarnation" of it (*Moses and Monotheism*, 137).

appear a step forward in the education of the human race. Of course, in both interpretations Christianity loses its uniqueness. As Leibniz asserts in the introduction to the *Theodicy*, Jesus had only finished what Moses started. Christianity expressed a natural feeling, one of several ways, the deist Locke declares, "of atoning the merciful Father." Deistical criticism was polite to Christianity, granting it a high place in the ascending line of progress. But the evolutionary principle could not accept Christianity as its final incarnation, and by Freud's time the Enlightenment temper was shorter and the treatment of religion less polite. In the course of development, Christianity had overstayed its time. For this reason Freud, in *The Future of an Illusion*, "singled out one such phase of development, which more or less corresponds to the final form of our contemporary Christian culture in the west."[63]

Freud refers not to Christianity but to "Christian culture"; the difference, a most important one, is his view of Christianity as the chief instrument of coercion in the larger system of coercions defined as culture. To his readings in anthropology Freud probably owed his understanding of religion as an externalization of moral authority, thus transforming it into social control.[64] Earlier it had been decided by Kant that the "numinal" sphere is unapproachable rationally; only the moral sphere, the relevance of religion to society, is comprehensible. This notion was taken up and driven to one logical conclusion by the new science of anthropology: beginning with Feuerbach and including Durkheim and his epigones, it was accepted as axiomatic that the numinal serves significantly as an instrument of social control. This was not a conspiracy of priests but a universally self-imposed limitation on the freedom of man. Religion became, therefore, the representative constraint with which humanity had hobbled itself. Thus the anthropologist

63. *The Future of an Illusion*, 34. Cf. *Moses and Monotheism*, 67.

64. To externalize moral authority meant to weaken it, Freud thought. For the churches had to make "great concessions" to human instinct. Here Freud is attending only to the Catholic idea of the Church, and not, for example to the modern Protestant. (See *The Future of an Illusion*, 66–69.) Given his sense of the parallels between structures of religion and power, Protestantism as such scarcely enters Freud's horizon. Because he saw religion always in a political way, the Roman Church adequately filled his need for example.

Salomon Reinach, at one time widely read, defined religion as "a body [*ensemble*] of scruples which puts obstacles to the free exercise of our faculties." With this notably one-sided view Freud, on the whole, agreed. The cultural value of religion, he insisted, has been purchased at too high a cost.

It was a distinction made by the anthropologists that gave Freud his most delicate instrument for assessing the exact cost of religion. Frazer, his chief mentor in anthropology, had advanced the following account of the difference between "magic" and "religion." In the earliest stage, argued Frazer, only magic existed. More exactly, magic and religion were identical; the functions of sorcerer and priest were combined or, at least, not yet differentiated from each other. But eventually, as society developed and religion with it, magic and religion became distinct—indeed antagonistic—as religion attempted to monopolize magic and render it routine. (The Eucharist would be an example of this.) Frazer's argument thus implicitly distinguishes the professional magician who is also a priest (Moses as he appears in the Bible before the Exodus might serve as an example) from the freelancing magician who later sets himself up in competition with the organized cult. Avoiding the Voltairean error of reducing religion to magic, Frazer emphasized the difference between public magic, which may be a part of but not identical with religion, and private magic, which operates in competition with priesthoods.[65]

65. Frazer's argument is tortuous, and I have simplified it. The preface and pp. 65–70 of vol. 1 of *The Golden Bough* sum it up best.

Nevertheless, if the association is not made pejorative then a great deal can be said for the erasing of Frazer's distinction between magic and religion. No one has been able to find the culture in which magic in fact preceded religion. It was in order to guard the notion of religion from the pejorative rationalist association with primitive culture that Frazer insisted on an original distinction. Thus his anthropology saved "religion" for beliefs in personal divine beings, or charismatic moral teachers. But religious experience plainly attached to all sorts of impersonal forces and to intuitions of sacred orders beyond the social and natural. Thus, in Freud's sense, the breaking of a taboo established mythically is at once magical and religious. Here Freud does well not to follow Frazer. Nevertheless the ethical religions of the West to which Freud attends are not simply tangles of myth and magic. They are founded religions, with charismatic moral virtuosi of high rational capacity as their founders. This makes a great

Set in its proper context, the distinction between magic and religion, Freud's blending of neurosis and religion appears very Frazerian. Neurosis was to Freud an equivalent to the private magic of the sorcerer, a kind of irrationality that can compete or blend with the brands of magic incorporated into public practice. As Frazer thought that "in the evolution of thought, magic, as representing a lower intellectual stratum, has probably everywhere preceded religion,"[66] so Freud puts neurosis, logically and emotionally, prior to religion. Religion offers one solution to neurosis. It may incorporate, stabilize, and resolve a neurosis, as it did for a patient of Freud's known as the "Wolf Man." In this case the child's homosexual regard for his father was appeased and alleviated by the sudden onset of religious piety in his eighth year. The fact that his birthday was on Christmas Day made it easy for him to identify God with his father. In this way he could love his father by loving God "with a fervour which had sought in vain to discharge itself so long as his father had been a mortal." He could bear witness to his extravagant love for his father in ways "laid down by religion," and these expressions "were not haunted by that sense of guilt from which his individual feelings of love could not set themselves free."[67] Thus religion, rather than fomenting guilt, may drain it off—in this case by transposing the child's sexual anxiety into higher, public terms.

Once understood as shared magic,[68] religion, in Freud's view, is shared neurosis. Yet for Freud religion is not simply reducible to neurosis. When large numbers of people share it, a delusion takes on a different meaning. As great a difference obtains between neurosis and religion as between the neurotic who indulges

---

deal of difference in the psychology of religion, and partly justifies Frazer's distinction of religion, although not in terms of successive spooks.

66. Frazer, *The Golden Bough*, 2nd ed., 1:xx. See also 70.

67. "Case of the 'Wolf Man,'" *SE*, 17:115.

68. Freud accepted the view that magic is prior to religion. See *Totem and Taboo*, 91–92: "Whereas magic still reserves omnipotence solely for thoughts, animism hands some of it over to spirits and so prepares the way for the construction of a religion." In the Freudian interpretation, religion, since it is shared, includes ceding part of one's personal power—includes, that is, an element of renunciation absent in magic.

in wasteful, private reverie and the poet who manages to sell his daydreams on the market of culture. Of course Freud could not entirely resist the temptation to reduce religion to neurosis, as he tended so to reduce art. The individualism of his psychology led him to grant a very limited bill of health to any shared illusion. He inclined to treat a public emotion like religion or a socially approved activity like art simply as a multiple of private emotions— ignoring the fact that a belief or act is not simply enlarged but fundamentally altered by being shared. Yet Freud nowhere makes the identification of religion and neurosis facilely, as has been often charged against him. His understanding is to this extent historical: the neurotic contents which in former times flourished under religious auspices (see his analysis of a seventeenth-century neurosis of demoniacal possession) are today more commonly elaborated in isolation. While today "neuroses appear in a hypochondriacal guise, masked as organic diseases . . . the neurosis of olden times masquerad[ed] in demonological shape."[69]

Freud's interest in the transition in Western culture from publicly shareable fantasies—e.g., religion—to private hypochondrias is thus not so remote from his interest in so-called primitive religion. In both the anthropological and the Freudian view, when religious belief declines, the old magical (or neurotic) energies hitherto stabilized will be dissolved and freed for anarchic reenactment independent of public sanction. Frazer's theory was that religion is historically later and ethically "higher" than magic, and most of his contemporaries, though their interest in primitive belief was characteristically accompanied by personal atheism or agnosticism, conceded, as he did, that religion was an advance on magic. In a guarded sense, Freud shared this view of religion as higher than (in his terms) neurosis, for he judged neurosis negatively, as the crumbling of religious commitments. Like other nineteenth-century critics of culture, he approved the familiar correlation between "the extraordinary increase in neuroses" and

69. "A Neurosis of Demoniacal Possession in the Seventeenth Century" (1923), *Collected Papers*, 4:436.
70. "The Future of Psycho-Analytic Therapy," *SE*, 9:146.

the waning of religious faith.[70] Religion is a way to keep from falling into a personal neurosis or may be a way beyond neurosis; or, as in the case of the "Wolf Man," where the child's sudden access of religious piety, however neurotic its roots,

> put a restraint on his sexual impulses by affording them a sublimation and a safe mooring; it lowered the importance of his family relationships, and thus protected him from the threat of isolation by giving him access to the great community of mankind. The untamed and fear-ridden child became social, well-behaved, and amenable to education.[71]

That religion may still give men confidence, comfort, and a sense of security may seem justification enough for it; it is not enough for Freud. In his view, religion bestows the very fears and anxieties that it then appeases. Religion may have been the original cure; Freud reminds us that it was also the original disease. And the cure is doubtful. Appeasement feeds what needs to be fought. Were it not for religious encouragements of anxiety, the individual would feel less anxious; the effect of this palliative is to remind the patient that he is ill. "It seems very unlikely," writes Radcliffe-Brown, "that an Andaman Islander would think that it is dangerous to eat dugong or pork or turtle meat if it were not for the existence of a specific body of ritual the ostensible purpose of which is to protect him from those dangers."[72] Freud thought only reason could resolve this pull between social functions and disfunctions. The lingering effects of early human weakness, to which religion was a response, can, he maintained, be rationally understood and attended, and the ancient response thus rendered unnecessary.

In an earlier stage of human development religion gave what Freud called its "value." But Freud took it as demonstrated that the main religion of the West was no longer authoritative; it had nothing more of worth to give this culture. Christianity was now

71. "Case of the 'Wolf Man,'" 114–15.
72. A. R. Radcliffe-Brown, *Structure and Function in Primitive Society* (Glencoe, Ill.: Free Press, 1952), 149.

nothing more than a painful "historical residue" of those valuable "repression-like processes which took place in antiquity."[73] In its own creative time, Christianity had deflected the brutality and aggressiveness of late pagan culture; it had turned the energies of Western man inward and refined in a new way his pugnacious energies. Christianity did heal over, if only like a cicatrice, the open life-and-death struggles of antiquity. But, Freud believed, the scar only hides the wound in our nature. The elevating of moral aspiration had lasted too long; the wound had begun to fester. Christianity, the remedy, had become religion, the symptom—a set of "neurotic survivals."

It was Freud's belief that now, after two thousand years of Christian culture, we are entering a new, scientific, phase of development in which the instinctual renunciation he considered indispensable for man's communal existence has a chance of being maintained by rational means. As the chief instrument of culture, religion was an irrational means. Thus, as the logical outcome of inevitable development struggling against unconditional demands, Freud saw Christianity under the sign of its exhaustion. There is no more ambitious theme in the entire Freudian text; it announces that Christian culture is played out. This particular incarnation of the prototypal relation to authority has lost its energy. Failing as a system of repressions, Christian culture continues to exist only as a problem. Freud viewed himself as treating specific cases of the mental suffering produced during the interregnum between the failure of one system of authority and the establishment of another. It is to a new system of moral authority that Freud looked forward and into which he foresaw that psychoanalysis would be integrated.

Freud had a shrewd feeling, never quite articulated, for the incompatibility of the modern sense of self with our historic religious legacy. Individuals could no longer, "by accepting the universal neurosis" of humanity, be "spared the task of forming a personal neurosis."[74] In a civilization dominated by religious

73. *The Future of an Illusion*, 76–77.
74. Ibid., 77.

authority, we all suffered from the same neurosis and thus were saved from the alienation of private sickness. But as religion declined, Freud noted, neuroses increased, until modern morality—having lost the coercive backing of religion—became itself the problem of neurosis. I must emphasize that Freud condemned the religious repressions for instrumental reasons—not so much in themselves but because they were failing. Because religion could no longer compel character but only distract it, Freud dared suggest, in the name of science, a new ethical straightforwardness. Neuroses bespeak the specifically post-religious condition of men, produced by the abdication of religiously grounded moral authority. Faith has become a form of anxiety. Despite his occasional protests about its neutrality and limited purposes, Freud hoped his own science would contribute in a major way to the working out of an alternative to the historical systems of anxiety. Hence his prediction that the therapeutic effectiveness of psychoanalysis would increase as the "authority" of science increased, and would include finally heavy doses of suggestion for those who could not be treated analytically.[75]

VI

The psychological foundation of religion at which Freud aimed his attack appears at first too familiar to bear reviewing. In brief, he refurbished the old fallacy that the genotype of belief repeats the phenotype of dependence, and the more general fallacy that the origin of a thing determines its end. But Freud's scorn of our repetitions seems strangely contradictory, for at the same time that he saw religious belief as the inevitable result of childhood dependence and fear of parental authority, he also thought that we could outgrow our origins. The part of Freud's analysis that seems to be worth repeating is its evolutionist conclusion that by the inexorable and natural law of development we are losing our historical religion as a child normally loses his childishness. While regressions have to be reckoned with, Freud held, they do not affect the normality of development but rather make clear

75. "Lines of Advance in Psycho-Analytic Therapy," *SE*, 17:168.

the necessity of the individual's keeping pace to avoid falling ill. "Is it not the destiny of childishness to be overcome?" he asks, his voice carrying all the coldness of the early positivist evangel. "Man cannot remain a child forever."[76]

This preferring of movement to fixation evokes a familiar response, one Freud has helped to apply in new ways. The nineteenth-century faith in progress, discredited in its straightforward historical version, prospers none the less in the form of the prevailing psychology of development. In this form Freud put forth his analysis of religion; it is, like other parts of his analysis, a critique of arrestments in development. I say Freudian analysis is at the same time a critique, not only to indicate how far from late positivist notions of value freedom Freud considered his science, but also to show again how every point in his analysis is premonitory of all; one can always get from description to judgment in a single short step. Indeed, because in his case histories Freud never *reported* the facts but *interpreted* them, what passes for description in the Freudian method is already judgment.

Because faith claims exemption from the law of development, Freud judged that it is inappropriate to the present and has become by virtue of its self-exemption the most grandiose case of neurosis. However, Freud admits that he is, perhaps without warrant, "optimistic enough to assume that mankind will overcome this neurotic phase."[77] Of course religion has served culture well, shepherding mankind through its infancy. But as the mind matures, it appeared to Freud, every religion must die of disenchantment. Freud shared the Comtist hope that theologies would die a natural death from old age and exhaustion. He knew that science cannot kill them; they must wither from within. Death does not come all at once but slowly, and in parts. The signs of life in contemporary theology are, in the scientific view, those parts of the religious organism not yet aware that death is the general condition within which it lives. It is the function of Freud's psychology of religion to emphasize the general dying within which each specific revival must run its short course.

76. *The Future of an Illusion*, 86.
77. Ibid., 92.

After the euthanasia of religion,[78] only those unconsoling scientific myths Freud mentions near the end of *Group Psychology* will remain—deliberate intellectual constructions and conjectures. But how far down through the class levels of culture can scientific disenchantment safely be allowed to penetrate? Freud did not share unambiguously the confidence of progressive rationalists, from the French Encyclopedists to Marx, that the ethical advances of the old faiths could be preserved in a scientific era. His particular doubt arises from his own adherence to a notion insisted on by modern critics, from Matthew Arnold to Ortega y Gasset, that parallel and superior to the struggle between *economic* classes there is a struggle between *culture* classes. In the case of the cultured, Freud argues, religious motives for decent behavior may safely be replaced with secular ones. But the masses, inherently hostile to culture and held in check only by the authoritarian mysteries of traditional beliefs, may accept the liberating conclusions of scientific enlightenment "without having effected in themselves the process of change which scientific thought induces in men." What authority will hold them in check? "Is there not a danger," Freud asks, expressing the standard alarm, that "if they are taught there is no Almighty and alljust God," the masses "will feel exempt from all obligation to follow the rules of culture?" Then "everybody will follow his asocial, egoistic instinct" and "will certainly kill without hesitation."[79]

How to save the achievements of culture from falling along with their nonrational sanctions? Involved in our spreading concern to preserve good conduct without mythic rationalization, Freud indicated a certain sympathy for the defense of religion as a necessary illusion. In *The Future of an Illusion*, he conducted a dialogue on the subject. Notice that for Freud no conversation with a true believer is possible. The only defense of religion he could take at all seriously is what we may call the sociological one;[80]

78. Schopenhauer's phrase.

79. *The Future of an Illusion*, 60–69.

80. For the most part the English anthropological critics of religion (Frazer, et al.) remained untempted by any explicit faith, or by the sociological defense of faith. A notable exception was Ernest Crawley, author of *The Mystic Rose* (1902), a study of primitive marriage to which Freud had recourse in *Totem*

he could have understood de Maistre but not Pascal. In the dialogue he has his interlocutor readily admit that religion has only a "practical" value—namely, that without the illusion of a divine order the social order would disintegrate into barbarism. "One should conceal the fact" that faith is a necessary hoax—"in the interests of the preservation of everybody" and "for the protection of culture."[81] Freud's imaginary interlocutor is a tertiary of the Grand Inquisitor's Order. He does not argue very well against Freud, for he is plainly a secular intellectual, making a defense not of this or that creed or church but of religion in general.

A great modern example of such a conversation is Schopenhauer's *Religion: A Dialogue.* I should guess that Freud had read it, so closely does his own dialogue in *The Future of an Illusion* follow it. The friendly disputants created by Schopenhauer raise exactly the problem Freud raised. Both take for granted the absurdity of religious belief for rational men. The issue is only whether belief is necessary to control the unenlightened many (this is the position of "Demopheles") or whether the value of religion, now declining anyway, has not been overestimated and is not actually a force obstructing the Enlightenment goals: reason, progress, the true betterment of mankind (the position of "Philalethes"). Schopenhauer has Demopheles argue in much the same terms as Freud's interlocutor in *The Future of an Illusion:*

> *Demopheles:* ". . . The first thing to do is to control the raw and evil dispositions of the masses, so as to keep them from . . . committing cruel, violent, and disgraceful acts. If you were to wait until they had recognized and grasped the truth, you

---

and Taboo. Crawley conceded that nothing in Christianity is historically new or dogmatically true—that it is in fact a patchwork of paganisms. Still, he argued in another work, *The Tree of Life* (1905), religion is all more or less productive of "vitality," and therefore precious, so that no critical analysis finally matters, except to a few scholars who are willing to bear the burden of disillusion. That the critical analysis of religious ideology nevertheless included an appreciation of its social functions and value is a paradox reached by a line of French positivists from Comte to Durkheim. In a tumid form, the interest of modern sociology (cf. Karl Mannheim at the end of his life) in creating a "faith" appropriate to our time continues this earlier positivist ambivalence toward religion.

81. *The Future of an Illusion,* 61, 91.

would undoubtedly come too late; and truth, supposing that it had been found, would surpass their powers of comprehension. In any case an allegorical investiture of it, a parable or myth, is all that would be of any service to them. As Kant said, there must be a public standard of Right and Virtue; it must always flutter high overhead. It is a matter of indifference what heraldic figures are inscribed on it, so long as they signify what is meant."[82]

Later in the dialogue, the position held by Freud is thus defended by Schopenhauer's Philalethes:

> Philalethes: ". . . We won't give up the hope that mankind will eventually reach a point of maturity and education at which it can on the one side produce, and on the other receive, the true philosophy."
> Demopheles: "You've no notion how stupid most people are."
> Philalethes: "I am only expressing a hope which I can't give up. If it were fulfilled . . . the time would have come when religion would have carried out her object and completed her course; the race she had brought to years of discretion she could dismiss, and herself depart in peace: that would be the *euthanasia* of religion."[83]

The issue debated by Schopenhauer is reopened by Freud in terms that remained unchanged between 1851, the year of Schopenhauer's dialogue, and 1928, when *The Future of an Illusion* was published. There is an important difference, however. In Schopenhauer's dialogue, Demopheles, who claims that religious illusions must be maintained for the sake of culture, has much the better of the argument. Freud, on the other hand, awards to the position weakly advanced by Philalethes, that religion can and must be overcome, the victory in the debate. The defense of religion as a priestly lie, which Freud puts in the mouth of his imaginary opponent, is acknowledged as compelling. Yet Freud

82. Arthur Schopenhauer, *Essays*, trans. T. Bailey Saunders (New York: A. L. Burt Co., n.d.), 213.
83. Ibid., 220, Schopenhauer's italics.

is prevented from assenting to it—he says—by his conviction that, however gravely the loss of religious belief threatens culture, there is no halting an "inevitable transition," not by all the half measures and insincerities philosophers can devise. According to Freud, "we are just now in the middle" of this "abandoning of religion [which] must take place with the fateful inexorability of a process of growth." If finally Christianity can be defended only as a necessary illusion, then the religious intellectual must "despair of everything, of culture, and of the future of mankind," for he will then be defending a "lost cause." Those anxious over the fate of culture need neither despair nor "oppose the new development." More sensibly, they should seek "to further it and to temper the force of its onset." With God the father killed for the last time by the development of his youngest son, Science, Freud suggests to the cultured classes that the only way they can save themselves is by a "fundamental revision of the relation between culture and religion," in which the Christian coercions would be replaced by the rational obligations of science. The only alternative to such a revolutionary pedagogic program would be "the most rigorous suppression of these dangerous masses and the most careful exclusion of all opportunities for mental awakening."[84]

The portrait of our culture that Freud sketches, showing the awkward distance between an educated class of atheists and a mass of faithful, is, surely, oversimple. Today both classes and masses are emancipated from official rhetorics of submission to the divine. Freud's prophecies are inadequate to the lessons of modern history. Matters have turned out more horribly: the classes have shown a capacity for fresh barbarisms, and the masses have proved no less docile in their unbelief than they ever were in their belief.

84. *The Future of an Illusion*, 68–69, 76, 93, 95. Much of the secondary literature of the psychoanalytic movement ranges itself around this conflict between the declining authority of religion and the rising antiauthority of science. For an influential compromise, see Erich Fromm's *Psychoanalysis and Religion* (1950). Freud's harsh rationalist exhortation that science replace religion is translated by Fromm into the ideal of a "humanistic religion" without authority.

More important, however, is Freud's misunderstanding of religion itself as social. All sociology, and now psychology as well, has been repeating Kant's mistake in regarding religion as the apprehension of our moral duties as divine commands. Religion provides that "solemn air of sanctity" which has been the established way of pledging allegiance to the laws of culture.[85] It is on this original identity of religion and authority that Freud's rejection of religion is based.

But such a sweeping identification of religion with its social function ignores one of the strongest and most valuable of Christian distinctions—between faith and the institutions and attitudes by which it is transmitted at any given time. Just as the early Christians were boorishly suspicious of the material plenitude and alien aesthetic and philosophic culture of their own time, there have been Christians fully as suspicious of Christendom. Kierkegaard diagnosed the malaise of the nineteenth century as such a confusion between religion and culture; and he warned that Christianity cannot survive unless detached from the abuses and distortions of a social order living under the faded title of Christendom.[86] By taking the identity of the churches with Christianity at face value, Freud did something he would never have countenanced in the analytic situation, where he was always alert to the differences between manifest and latent contents.

Had Freud not entirely subordinated religion to culture, he would have avoided the related error that religion is always consolatory, the chief mode of escape from the hardness of reality. His somewhat opaque distinction in *The Future of an Illusion* between religion and what is taken to be the scientific ethic—"resignation"—springs from this error. There is no necessary polarity between consolation and resignation; certainly neither term takes into account the calculated defiance that religious temperaments have displayed in the face of powerful antagonists. Freud's favorite example of tenacity and moral courage, the Jews,

85. Ibid., 77–78.
86. Kierkegaard's knife-edge distinction between Christianity and Christendom lives on in Paul Tillich's division between the "Protestant principle" and Protestant middle-class churches.

ought to have suggested to him the limits of his own analysis. The prophets' announcement of doom for Israel could have been consolatory only in a very severe sense—even for the remnant. From any social point of view the prophetic denunciations were truly subversive. That these mavericks renewed the basis of community does not mean they assumed authoritarian functions in any sensible usage; the prophet, even as he renews the repressions, destroys conformism. Nor does the religious feeling of dependence on providence support Freud's easy genetic reduction of it to an original social deference. As among the Anabaptist and Puritan rebels, one dependency may be used to contradict the other. Consolation, if such it be, of the religious sort is frequently charged with the most critical social and ethical potentialities.

If to equate religion with "consolation" is an error, it is equally misleading to equate science with "resignation." Science is inseparable from the rationalist aims of Western culture, which are as utopian as any vision of heaven.[87] Freud's conclusion that religion is a narcotic, and that they who learn the lesson of science will be "brought up soberly" does not stand much examination. Science has its own mysteries and enthusiasms; attached by an umbilical cord to technology, science can only drift with the drifts of power in society. At least the clerics have a tradition of hostility to the state behind them; the scientists have only just begun to learn that they must fight, and they are embarrassed by their own bursts of ethical enthusiasm. Sobriety—moderation in all things, including worship—used to be the appeal of respectable religion against the sectarian waste of emotion. Today it is the appeal of a conformist technology against the painfully held standards of

87. Thus the widespread idea that we are inexorably moving forward to a time, perhaps a thousand years hence, when people will become truly rational and all social problems will be solved by scientific engineering.

Though he rejected the religion of the highbrow, Freud felt no compulsion to reject the science of the highbrow. Religion is always an illusion, science never (*The Future of an Illusion*, 98). But might one not argue that science is—no less than religion—in the class sense, a matter of feeling? The popular science of the day by which the utopian hope for a robot man is marched round the totem test tube is as naïve as, and surely more reprehensible than, the yielding to God's will.

critical enthusiasm in both religion and science. From its transcendental consolations (e.g., the idea that gospel is superior to law), religious sentiment had at least the possibility of criticizing the social order, while scientific energies, by the facile transformation of the objectivity necessary to science into "value neutrality" or "value freedom," are easily enlisted to the aims of society, whatever these may be.

The success of Freud's own doctrine is probably as good a refutation as any of his sharp separation between "religion" and "science." Psychological doctrine, filtered down into textbooks, daily newspaper columns, salesmanship manuals, and the mental-hygiene movement, overtly antireligious and carrying all the pomposity of an immature science in its train, actually now teaches mostly the character virtues of resignation and adjustment. With their powers of "positive thinking," their ethics of "living on a twenty-four-hour basis," the psychological cults in which America currently abounds do not even aspire to the halfhearted criticism still occasionally to be found in the churches. The popular drift of psychological science aims at freeing the individual most of all from the burden of opposition. On the other hand, religion, with its symbols of remembrance, may be that very submission to the past that will preserve in us some capacity for a radical criticism of the present.

Toward a Theory of Culture

Things fall apart; the centre cannot hold;
Mere anarchy is loosed upon the world,
The blood-dimmed tide is loosed, and everywhere
The ceremony of innocence is drowned;
The best lack all conviction, while the worst
Are full of passionate intensity.

Surely some revelation is at hand;
Surely the Second Coming is at hand.
The Second Coming! Hardly are those words out
When a vast image out of Spiritus Mundi
Troubles my sight: somewhere in sands of the desert
A shape with lion body and the head of a man,
A gaze blank and pitiless as the sun,
Is moving its slow thighs, while all about it
Reel shadows of the indignant desert birds.
The darkness drops again; but now I know
That twenty centuries of stony sleep
Were vexed to nightmare by a rocking cradle,
And what rough beast, its hour come round at last,
Slouches towards Bethlehem to be born?

—Yeats, "The Second Coming"

Literature and sociology have long supplied eloquent and knowing professional mourners at the wake for Christian culture. After
Matthew Arnold, much of modern poetry constitutes an elegiac
farewell (mixed with powerful feelings of good riddance) to the
religious culture of the West. After Auguste Comte, much of
modern sociology has struggled for diagnostic ideas refined and
yet wide enough to encompass the spectacle of a death so great
in magnitude and subtlety. Now the dissolution of a unitary system of common belief, accompanied, as it must be, by a certain

disorganization of personality, may have run its course. The long period of deconversion, which first broke the surface of political history at the time of the French Revolution, appears all but ended. The central symbolism of personal and corporate experience seems to me well on its way to being differently organized, with several systems of belief competing for primacy in the task of organizing personality in the West. Beyond its concern with the dynamics by which Christian culture has been displaced, the present volume [*The Triumph of the Therapeutic*] will concentrate upon a struggle within the camp of one among these displacing systems of belief; I intend drawing certain implications for the reorganization of Western culture and personality from the divergence between Freud and those of his most powerful successor-critics studied in this book—C. G. Jung, Wilhelm Reich, and D. H. Lawrence. In Freud's analytic attitude and in the efforts exerted by his successor-critics to go beyond it, to post-communal faiths, there are concentrated some aspects of a theoretical problem that interests me greatly, well beyond the limits of this book: the problem of explaining cultural change. These preliminary studies in the psychohistorical process are not aimed primarily at fellow theorists interested in the problem, but at those troubled readers in whose minds and hearts one culture is dying while no other gains enough power to be born.

As cultures change, so do the modal types of personality that are their bearers. The kind of man I see emerging, as our culture fades into the next, resembles the kind once called "spiritual"— because such a man desires to preserve the inherited morality freed from its hard external crust of institutional discipline. Yet a culture survives principally, I think, by the power of its institutions to bind and loose men in the conduct of their affairs with reasons which sink so deep into the self that they become commonly and implicitly understood—with that understanding of which explicit belief and precise knowledge of externals would show outwardly like the tip of an iceberg. Spiritualizers of religion (and precisians of science) failed to take into account the degree of intimacy with which this comprehensive interior understanding was cognate with historic institutions, binding even the ignorants of a culture to a great chain of meaning. These institutions are responsible for conveying the social conditions of their acceptance by men thus saved from destructive illusions of uniqueness and separateness. Having broken the outward forms, so as to liberate, allegedly, the inner meaning of the good, the beautiful, and the true, the spiritualizers, who set the pace of Western cultural life from just before the beginning to a short time after the end of the nineteenth century, have given way now to their logical and historical successors, the psychologizers, inheritors of that dualist tradition which pits human nature against social order.[1]

Undeceived, as they think, about the sources of all morally binding address, the psychologizers, now fully established as the pacesetters of cultural change, propose to help men avoid doing further damage to themselves by preventing live deceptions from succeeding the dead ones. But, in order to save themselves from falling apart with their culture, men must engender another, different and yet powerful enough in its reorganization of experience to make themselves capable again of controlling the infinite variety of panic and emptiness to which they are disposed. It is to control their dis-ease as individuals that men have always acted culturally, in good faith. Books and parading, prayers and the sciences, music and piety toward parents: these are a few of the many instruments by which a culture may produce the saving larger self, for the control of panic and the filling up of emptiness. Superior to and encompassing the different modes in which it appears, a culture must communicate ideals, setting as internalities those distinctions between right actions and wrong that unite men and permit them the fundamental pleasure of agreement. Culture is another name for a design of motives directing the self outward,

1. From its beginnings, sociological theory has argued against dualist oppositions of human nature and social order, and against individualist conceptions of the self. For a discussion of these arguments, see my two studies on the thought of Charles Horton Cooley, published as introductions to reprints of his major works, *Social Organization* (New York, 1962), v–xx, and *Human Nature and the Social Order* (New York, 1964), ix–xx. Both essays are thematically related to the present volume.

toward those communal purposes in which alone the self can be realized and satisfied.

A reorganization of those dialectical expressions of *Yes* and *No* the interplay of which constitutes culture, transforming motive into conduct, is occurring throughout the West, particularly in the United States and in England. It is to be expected that some instruments appropriate to our inherited organization of permissions and restraints upon action will not survive the tension of fundamental reorganization. But, suppose the tension is driven deeper—so deep that all communications of ideals come under permanent and easy suspicion? The question is no longer as Dostoyevsky put it: "Can civilized men believe?" Rather: Can unbelieving men be civilized?

To raise again the question of nihilism, as sociologists since Auguste Comte have done, demonstrates a major change in tone: the note of apprehension has gone out of the asking. We believe that we know something our predecessors did not: that we can live freely at last, enjoying all our senses—except the sense of the past—as unremembering, honest, and friendly barbarians all, in a technological Eden. Comte would have substituted a religion of humanity for its enfeebled predecessor; Max Weber proposed no substitute religion. Matthew Arnold could still listen for distant echoes of the sea of faith; Yeats knew there was a desert where once that sea might have been. To raise up faith from its stony sleep encourages the possibility of living through again the nightmare history of the last half century. Yeats did not hope for either restoration or parody of the established faiths. Rather, he prayed for a very modern sort of Second Coming, in which men would recover their innocence, chiefly by accepting the fact that it is self-delighting, self-appeasing, self-affrighting—"and that its own sweet will is Heaven's will." In our recovered innocence, to be entertained would become the highest good and boredom the most common evil.

The best spirits of the twentieth century have thus expressed their conviction that the original innocence, which to earlier periods was a sinful conceit, the new center, which can be held even as communities disintegrate, is the self. By this conviction a new and dynamic acceptance of disorder, in love with life and destructive of it, has been loosed upon the world. Here literature and sociology converge; for the ultimate interest of sociology, like that of psychiatry when it is not lost in a particular patient, turns on the question whether our culture can be so reconstructed that faith—some compelling symbolic of self-integrating communal purpose—need no longer superintend the organization of personality.

So long as a culture maintains its vitality, whatever must be renounced disappears and is given back bettered; Freud called this process sublimation. But, as that sage among psychiatrists Harry Stack Sullivan once said, "if you tell people how they can sublimate, they can't sublimate." The dynamics of culture are in "the unwitting part of it."[2] Now our renunciations have failed us; less and less is given back bettered. For this reason, chiefly, I think, this culture, which once imagined itself inside a church, feels trapped in something like a zoo of separate cages. Modern men are like Rilke's panther, forever looking out from one cage into another. Because the modern sense of identity seems outraged by imprisonment in either old church or new cage, it is the obligation of sociologists, so far as they remain interested in assessing the quality of our corporate life, to analyze doctrinal as well as organizational profiles of the rage to be free of the inherited morality, the better to see how these differ from what is being raged against. I shall attend to a few of the exemplarily enraged, and to the sense in which it may be said that they express general sentiments.

If the question "How are we to be saved?" cannot be asked in traditional ways, or need not be asked at all, then it is still the professional obligation of sociologists, who are specially interested in the behavior of collectivities, to investigate the ensuing honest silence in which the communal gods have imitated the most cultivated men. And, indeed, this is the sort of investigation that so-

2. Harry Stack Sullivan, "The Illusion of Personal Individuality," *Psychiatry* 13, no. 1 (1950): 323.

ciologists have pursued ardently, from the time of Comte through that of Weber to my contemporaries.[3] Perhaps no other problem than that of the changing moral configuration of modern culture has so engaged the interest of sociological theorists.

3. Alfred Weber's contributions to *Kultursoziologie* merit more attention than they have received. It was Alfred Weber's judgment (a judgment shared by his older brother, Max) that the "inherent forms" of our culture "seem to be dissolving . . . into something new: utter decline or the emergence of another historical organism."

It is helpful to have Robert K. Merton restate the established position beyond which sociology has not yet advanced: that the "key concept" in sociological theory, "bridging the gap between statics and dynamics," is "that of strain, tension, contradiction or discrepancy between the component elements of social and cultural structure." (Robert K. Merton, *Social Theory and Social Structure*, New York, 1962, p. 122.) Perhaps, in order to understand how tensions *between* social and cultural structures exert "pressures for change" (ibid.), it may be necessary to develop a theory of tensions *within* a culture. Suppose it is from the superior level of the cultural system that organizing (and disorganizing) higher principles thrust into the social structure. That thrust of higher (cultural) principles into the myriad particular activities of men, enacted by cultural elites even in the most highly differentiated social structure, would then establish the modalities of societal integration and disintegration. Moreover, the study of smaller units of the social self would also take its direction from these modalities. But, further discussion would carry me too far from the immediate subject of the present volume, and too near the twin subjects of another book: on sociological theory as ineluctably normative and on the "structure" of culture. These twin subjects are merely adumbrated here.

See A. L. Kroeber and C. Kluckhohn, *Culture, A Critical Review of Concepts and Definitions* (New York, 1963), for a compendium of culture theories that repeats the deficiencies of approaches from the social sciences, while too easily dismissing important contributions from the humanities.

Freud's position on the importance of a theory of culture is well summed up in the following passages. First on the normative aspects of Freudian theory, the famous passage on the therapeutic "intention" of psychoanalysis, "to strengthen the ego, to make it more independent of the super-ego, to widen its field of perception and enlarge its organization, so that it can appropriate fresh portions of the id. Where id was, there ego shall be. It is a work of culture." Then, second, on the explanatory potential of a theory of culture—and on its scientific base—"we must not forget that the mass of human beings who are subjected to economic necessities also undergo the process of cultural development—of civilization, as other people may say—which, though no doubt influenced by all the other factors, is certainly independent of them in its origin, being comparable to an organic process and very well able on its part to exercise an influence on the other factors. It displaces instinctual aims and brings it about that people become antagonistic to what they had previously tolerated. Moreover,

During the nineteenth century, when sociology helped in a major way to construct the central experience of deconversion toward an anticredal analytic attitude, that discipline suffered from a vast overconfidence both about its own advance and about the progress of the culture, which it understood as undergoing varieties of such deconversions. "Progress," wrote Spencer, "is not an accident, but a necessity. Surely must evil and immorality disappear; surely must men become perfect."[4] A basic transformation of culture appeared both inevitable and desirable.

Running parallel with and in the opposite direction from the process of deconversion was that process of conversion to a superior system of symbols—Science—which would supply the next predicate for the cultural organization of personality. Comte, for example, understood his own time as one of transition between two cultures. It was more generally proposed by students of our collective condition not merely that the old religious culture was dying but that the new scientific one had quite enough power already to be born.[5] Thus Comte concluded that only because of the "coexistence" of these two cultures did the "grand crisis now

the progressive strengthening of the scientific spirit seems to form an essential part of it. If anyone were in a position to show in detail the way in which these different factors—the general inherited human disposition, its racial variations and its cultural transformations—inhibit and promote one another under the conditions of social rank, profession, and earning capacity—if anyone were able to do this, he would have supplemented Marxism so that it was made into a genuine social science. For sociology too, dealing as it does with the behaviour of people in society, cannot be anything but applied psychology. Strictly speaking, there are only two sciences: psychology, pure and applied, and natural science." Sigmund Freud, "New Introductory Lectures," *SE*, 22:80 and 179. Note Freud's vacillation between a reductionist (to the psychological level) theory of culture and one in which culture is a phenomenon *sui generis*. This vacillation he never resolved. But there is everything still to be gained, I think, from using Freudian models in further developing a theory of culture.

4. Herbert Spencer, *Social Statics* (London, 1892), 32. Some doubts occurred to Spencer about the pace of progress toward a culture freed from faith, but not about its inevitability or eventual terminus. (See the note he added to the passage quoted.)

5. The birth pangs might be those caused by a proletariat emerging out of the womb of history, as Marx thought. But this proletariat would dominate a culture even more scientific in its substantial nature and social organization than that envisaged by Comte.

experienced by the most civilized nations" persist.[6] Freud was less sanguine. He believed that the crisis of coexistence was probably a permanent mode of the relation between personality and culture.

I question whether the "grand crisis," our deeper trouble, can be attributed to "coexistence," as major figures among the nineteenth-century intellectuals, culminating in Freud, insisted. It is less the lingering of the old culture than the emergence of the new that needs diagnosis. In fact, evil and immorality are disappearing, as Spencer assumed they would, mainly because our culture is changing its definition of human perfection. No longer the Saint, but the instinctual Everyman, twisting his neck uncomfortably inside the starched collar of culture, is the communal ideal, to whom men offer tacit prayers for deliverance from their inherited renunciations. Freud sought only to soften the collar; others, using bits and pieces of his genius, would like to take it off. There have been forerunners of this movement—Rousseau, Boehme, Hamann, or Blake. But never before has there been such a general shifting of sides as now among intellectuals in the United States and England. Many have gone over to the enemy without realizing that they, self-considered the cultural elite, have actually become spokesmen for what Freud called the instinctual "mass." Much of modern literature constitutes a symbolic act of going over to the side of the latest, and most original, individualists.[7] This represents the complete democratization of our culture.

6. Auguste Comte, "Plan of the Scientific Operations Necessary for Reorganizing Society," in *Early Essays of Comte*, ed. Frederick Harrison (London, n.d.), 88.

7. But not all modern literature, of course. There remains a strong mood of dejection at the passing of the old culture, that mood memorably expressed by Rose Macaulay, in her novel *Potterism* (London, 1920). "It was a curious age, so near and yet so far, when the ordered frame of things was still unbroken, and violence a child's dream, and poetry and art were taken with immense seriousness. Those of us who can remember it should do so, for it will not return. It has given place to the age of melodrama, when nothing is too strange to happen, and no one is ever surprised. That, too, may pass, but probably not, for it is primeval. The other was artificial, a mere product of civilisation, and could not last." But Rose Macaulay was mistaken. Her nostalgia was itself a Potterism, a snobbish and mean dislike of the fact that poetry and art were to

It was in order to combat just such talented hostility to culture that Freud emphasized coercion and the renunciation of instinct as indispensable elements in all culture. Freud was neither an eroticist nor a democrat. His theory of culture depended upon a crossing between his idea of moral authority and an elitist inclination. "It is just as impossible," he writes, "to do without control of the mass by a minority as it is to dispense with coercion in the work of civilization." By "mass" Freud means not merely the "lazy and unintelligent" but, more importantly, those who "have no love for instinctual renunciation" and who cannot be "convinced by argument of its inevitability." That such large numbers of the cultivated and intelligent have identified themselves deliberately with those who are supposed to have no *love* for instinctual renunciation suggests to me the most elaborate act of suicide that Western intellectuals have ever staged—those intellectuals, whether of the left or right, whose historic function it has been to assert the authority of a culture organized in terms of communal purpose, through the agency of congregations of the faithful.

Of course, this suicide is intended only as an exciting pose. Renunciations of instinct, as Freud wrote, "necessarily must remain." For these renunciations, the individual must be compensated by pleasures at once higher and more realizable than the pleasure of instinctual gratification. In compensation, and in place of where faith once was, men are offered Art and/or Science. It is true that new religions are constantly being born. But modern culture is unique in having given birth to such elaborately argued antireligions, all aiming to confirm us in our devastating illusions of individuality and freedom. I suspect the children of Israel did not spend much time elaborating a doctrine of the golden calf; they naïvely danced around it, until Moses, their first intellectual, put a stop to the plain fun and insisted on civilizing them, by submerging their individualities within a communal purpose. Now,

---

be taken, as they are now, with immense seriousness—piously—by the many as well as the few. It is the truly catholic character of the modern religion of art that annoys old catholics, such as Miss Macaulay and Bernard Berenson, not the religion itself.

although there is some dancing again, the intellectuals mainly sit around and think in awe about the power and perversity of their instincts, disguising their rancorous worship of self in the religion of art. Confronted thus with a picture gallery as the new center of self-worship, civilized men must become again anti-art, in the hope of shifting attention toward modalities of worship wholly other than that of self.

In my chapters on Reich and Lawrence, I shall represent some ways in which art and science have come to serve the contemporary aversion to culture. This aversion has grown less naïve, more doctrinal, and therefore more dangerous. For these are doctrines of psychological man—the latest, and perhaps the supreme, individualist—opposed in depth to earlier modes of self-salvation: through identification with communal purpose. Jung is the most interesting case. As a cultural conservative, his psychology is para-religious, striving as it does to reestablish various corporate identities and communal purposes as purely therapeutic devices. In contrast to the conservative Jung, Reich and Lawrence are moral revolutionaries in a more straightforward way: neither proposes to defend common purposes which once persisted through the individualization of those energies called "conscience," generated for the saving of selves precisely by means of a communal purpose.

The debts incurred by conscience through warped and atrophied communal purposes are now being paid off at a usurious rate of interest. The lingering death of authoritarian love has left behind hatred and violence, twin widows of dead love, free to stimulate in the culturally impoverished or disenchanted energies emancipated from conviction. It is not class or race war that we have to fear so much as deadly violence between the culture classes. But the upper culture classes have already lost this most fundamental of all class struggles by their admiration for the "vitality" of the lower, that vitality being a mirror image of their own earlier dynamism. A social structure shakes with violence and shivers with fears of violence not merely when that structure is callously unjust, but also when its members must stimulate themselves to feverish activity in order to demonstrate how alive they are. That there are colonies of the violent among us, devoid of any stable sense of communal purpose, best describes, I think, our present temporarily schizoid existence in two cultures—vacillating between dead purposes and deadly devices to escape boredom.

A full transition to a postcommunal culture may never be achieved. It is a persuasive argument, still, that maintains there are safeguards, built into both human nature and culture, limiting the freedom of men to atomize themselves. Perhaps human nature will revolt, producing yet another version of second nature with which to fend off and curb the vitality of the present assault upon the moralizing functions of our past. Every culture must establish itself as a system of moralizing demands, images that mark the trail of each man's memory; thus to distinguish right actions from wrong the inner ordinances are set, by which men are guided in their conduct so as to assure a mutual security of contact. Culture is, indeed, the higher learning. But, this higher learning is not acquired at universities; rather, it is assimilated continuously from earliest infancy when human beings first begin to trust in those familiar responses others make to their overtures. In every culture there stands a censor, governing the opportunity of recognizing and responding to novel stimuli. That governor, inclined always to be censorious about novelty, we may call "faith." Faith is the compulsive dynamic of culture, channeling obedience to, trust in, and dependence upon authority. With more or less considered passion, men submit to the moral demand system—and, moreover, to its personifications, from which they cannot detach themselves except at the terrible cost of guilt that such figures of authority exact from those not yet so indifferent that they have ceased troubling to deny them.

Now, contradicting all faiths, a culture of the indifferent is being attempted, lately using a rhetoric of "commitment" with which to enlarge the scope of its dynamism. Such a credo of change amounts to a new faith—more precisely, to a counterfaith. This counterfaith intimates the next culture; for faith, or its negative, is always and everywhere the generating and corrupting agent of culture. This is not to say that contemporary culture is corrupt; what appears to some as corruption indicates the generation of yet another culture, for none is immortal. While disassociating itself from the high costs of old doctrinal serious- ness and lonely lives, the emergent culture nevertheless produces books and music, art and science, an endless ambiance of fun and boredom—everything in fact, including moral passion and com- munal purpose, as varieties of an antitypal therapy of self. To call corrupt a culture purchased at lower cost to our nerves, and at larger magnitudes of self-fulfillment, would show a lamentable lack of imagination. The look of the future need not be blank and pitiless. Intelligence may work more efficiently, after all, than compassionate solidarity. Countertransference may succeed where less calculated loves have failed. If the religious imagina- tion is purblind, and its obstinate visionaries take risks resulting in such personifications of the Parousia as Yeats saw slouching toward Bethlehem, then we will have to make our way to a more pleasant city, using our secular vision of comforts that render all salvations obsolete.

I, too, aspire to see clearly, like a rifleman, with one eye shut; I, too, aspire to think without assent. This is the ultimate violence to which the modern intellectual is committed. Since things have become as they are, I, too, share the modern desire not to be de- ceived. The culture to which I was first habituated grows progres- sively different in its symbolic nature and in its human product; that double difference, and how ordained, augments our ambiva- lence as professional mourners. There seems little likelihood of a great rebirth of the old corporate ideals. The "proletariat" was the most recent notable corporate identity, the latest failed god. By this time men may have gone too far, beyond the old deception of good and evil, to specialize at last, wittingly, in techniques that are to be called, in the present volume, "therapeutic," with nothing at stake beyond a manipulatable sense of well-being.[8] This is the

8. Yeats's "A Prayer for My Daughter" makes an immediate pendant to "The Second Coming":

I have walked and prayed for this young child. . . .
Considering that, all hatred driven hence,

unreligion of the age, and its master science. What the ignorant have always felt, the knowing now know, after millennial distractions by stratagems that did not heighten the more immediate pleasures. The systematic hunting down of all settled convictions represents the anticultural predicate upon which modern personality is being reorganized, now not in the West only but, more slowly, in the non-West. The Orient and Africa are thus being acculturated in a dynamism that has already grown substantial enough to torment its progenitors with nightmares of revenge for having so unsettled the world. It is a terrible error to see the West as conservative and the East as revolutionary. We are the true revolutionaries. The East is swiftly learning to act as we do, which is anticonservative in a way non-Western peoples have only recently begun fully to realize for themselves.

In the regular acting out of mandatory therapies of commitment[9] built into the charter of his society, man, as a creation of affection-

---

The soul recovers radical innocence
And learns at last that it is self-delighting,
Self-appeasing, self-affrighting,
And that its own sweet will is Heaven's will. . . .

9. Nietzsche, the greatest of the nineteenth-century moral revolutionaries, generally opposed all mandatory systems of commitment. Yet even he cannot but proclaim, at times, the cultural necessity of such systems:

In contrast to *laisser-aller*, every system of morals is a sort of tyranny against "nature" and also against "reason"; that is, however, no objection, unless one should again decree, by some system of morals, that all kinds of tyranny and unreasonableness are unlawful. What is essential and invaluable in every system of morals, is that it is a long constraint. In order to understand Stoicism, or Port-Royal, or Puritanism, one should remember the constraint under which every language has attained to strength and freedom. . . . How much trouble have the poets and orators of every nation given themselves . . . [to be free] "from submission to arbitrary laws," as the anarchists say, and thereby fancy themselves "free," even free-spirited. The singular fact remains, however, that everything of the nature of freedom, elegance, boldness, dance, and masterly certainty, which exists or has existed, whether it be in thought itself or in administration, or in speaking and persuading, in art just as in conduct, has only developed by means of the tyranny of such arbitrary law; and in all seriousness, it is not at all improbable that precisely this is "nature" and "natural" and not *laisser-aller!* . . . The essential thing "in

ate and censorious authority, once organized for himself modes of willing obedience, or faith, in which he found his sense of well-being and, also, his freedom from that singular criterion. Culture without cultus appears, in almost all historical cases, a contradiction in terms. Within the mechanisms of cult, culture was organized, consisting mainly of ritual efforts to elicit and produce stable responses of assurance to more or less fixed wants—fleshly and spiritual, as it used to be said. There was, then, a standard range of expectations from which reassurance was elicited, even though the responses of the eliciting agencies, rendered "sacred" by their supreme function of organizing a life worth living, might at any moment offer admonitions rather than consolations to the seeker. Thus the sacred socializing agencies composed a moral order.

One main clue to the understanding of social organization is to be found in its symbolic of communal purpose; this, in turn, operates through a social system enacting that symbolic in a way at once admonitory and consoling. Each culture is its own order of therapy—a system of moralizing demands, including remissions that ease the pressures of communal purposes. Therapeutic elites before our own were predominately supportive rather than critical of culture as a moral demand system. Admonitions were the expectable predicates of consolations; that is what is meant, nowadays, by "guilt" culture. Whenever therapeutic elites grow predominately critical then a cultural revolution may be said to be in progress. Ours is such a time. The Occident has long been such a place.

Until the present culture rose to threaten its predecessor, our demand system could be specified by the kind of credal hedges it raised around impulses of independence or autonomy from communal purpose. In the culture preceding our own, the order

---

heaven and earth" is apparently (to repeat it once more) that there should be long obedience in the same direction; there thereby results, and has always resulted in the long run, something which has made life worth living.

In *Beyond Good and Evil*, trans. Helen Zimmern (London, 1907), sec. 188, p. 106–9.

of therapy was embedded in a consensus of "shalt nots." The best never lacked binding convictions, for they were the most bound, mainly by what they should not do—or even think, or dream. "Thou shalt" precipitated a sequence of operative "shalt nots." Cultic therapies of commitment never mounted a search for some new opening into experience; on the contrary, new experience was not wanted. Cultic therapy domesticated the wildness of experience. By treating some novel stimulus or ambiguity of experience in this manner, the apparently new was integrated into a restrictive and collective identity. Cultic therapies consisted, therefore, chiefly in participation mystiques severely limiting deviant initiatives. Individuals were trained, through ritual action, to express fixed wants, although they could not count thereby upon commensurate gratifications. The limitation of possibilities was the very design of salvation.

To the ironic question "And, being saved, how are we to behave?" Western culture long returned a painfully simple answer: "Behave like your Savior." Christian culture, like other organizations of moral demand, operated, however imperfectly, through the internalization of a soteriological character ideal carrying tremendous potentials for fresh intakes of communal energy; the highest level of controls and remissions (which together organized systems of moral demands) experienced a historical and individualized incarnation. Such euhemerist processes may have been indispensable to the vitality of the old culture. To adjust the expression of impulses to the controlling paragon, or character ideal, defines the primary process in the shaping of our inherited culture; the arts and sciences define the secondary process, in which exemplary modes of action are extended further, into a central moralizing experience, thus transforming individual into institutional action.

In the classical Christian culture of commitment, one renunciatory mode of control referred to the sexual opportunism of individuals. Contemporary churchmen may twist and turn it while they try to make themselves heard in a culture that renders preaching superfluous: the fact remains that renunciatory controls of sexual opportunity were placed in the Christian culture very near the center of the symbolic that has not held. Current apologetic efforts by religious professionals, in pretending that renunciation as the general mode of control was never dominant in the system, reflect the strange mixture of cowardice and courage with which they are participating in the dissolution of their cultural functions. Older Christian scholarship has known better than new Christian apologetics.[10]

> At bottom, only a single point was dealt with, abstinence from sexual relationships; everything else was secondary: for he who had renounced these found nothing hard. Renunciation of the servile yoke of sin (*servile peccati iugum discutere*) was the watchword of Christians, and an extraordinary unanimity prevailed as to the meaning of this watchword, whether we turn to the Coptic porter, or the learned Greek teacher, to the Bishop of Hippo, or Jerome the Roman presbyter, or the biographer of Saint Martin. Virginity was the specifically Christian virtue, and the essence of all virtues; in this conviction the meaning of the evangelical law was summed up.[11]

Historically, the rejection of sexual individualism (which divorces pleasure and procreation) was the consensual matrix of Christian culture. It was never the last line drawn. On the contrary, beyond that first restriction there were drawn others, establishing the Christian corporate identity within which the individual was to organize the range of his experience.[12] Individuality was hedged round by the discipline of sexuality, challenging those rapidly fluctuating imperatives established in Rome's remissive culture, from which a new order of deprivations was intended to release the faithful Christian believer. Every controlling sym-

---

10. J. A. T. Robinson, *Honest to God* (London, 1963) is an excellent example of that mixture of cowardice and courage in contemporary Christian apologetics.

11. Adolf von Harnack, *History of Dogma* (London, 1894–99), 3:128.

12. Genius strives to dramatize and clarify the symbolic which is its predicate. Augustine tried to formulate the Christian symbolic in a motif of polarized images that occurs over and over again in Christian tradition. "Two loves have built two cities: the love of self carried unto the contempt of God has built the city of this earth; the love of God carried unto the contempt of self has built the heavenly city." *The City of God*, 14:28.

bolic contains such remissive functions. What is revolutionary in modern culture refers to releases from inherited doctrines of therapeutic deprivation; from a predicate of renunciatory control, enjoining releases from impulse need, our culture has shifted toward a predicate of impulse release, projecting controls unsteadily based upon an infinite variety of wants raised to the status of needs. Difficult as the modern cultural condition may be, I doubt that Western men can be persuaded again to the Greek opinion that the secret of happiness is to have as few needs as possible. The philosophers of therapeutic deprivation are disposed to eat well when they are not preaching. It is hard to take Schopenhauer at his ascetic word when we know what splendid dinners he had put on, day after day, at the Hotel Schwan in Frankfort.

The central Christian symbolic was not ascetic in a crude renunciatory mode which would destroy any culture. Max Scheler described that culture accurately, I think, when he concluded that "Christian asceticism—at least so far as it was not influenced by decadent Hellenistic philosophy—had as its purpose not the suppression or even extirpation of natural drives, but rather their *control* and complete *spiritualization*. It is positive, not negative, asceticism—aimed fundamentally at a liberation of the highest powers of personality from blockage by the automatism of the lower drives."[13] That renunciatory mode, in which the highest powers of personality are precisely those which subserve rather than subvert culture, appears no longer systematically efficient. The spiritualizers have had their day; nowadays, the best among them appear engaged in a desperate strategy of acceptance, in the hope that by embracing doctrinal expressions of therapeutic aims they will be embraced by the therapeutics; a false hope—the therapeutics need no doctrines, only opportunities. But the spiritualizers persist in trying to maintain cultural contact with constituencies already deconverted in all but name. Even the Roman Catholic clergy must now confront their own constituencies, as their Protestant and Jewish colleagues have had to do long before. Nevertheless, the religious professionals have reason to

13. Max Scheler, *Vom Umsturz der Werte* (Bern, 1955), 114 (my trans.).

hope for survival, precisely because they have come to be aware of their situation and are seeking ways to alter it, in the direction of a fresh access of communal purpose, centered in the Negro protest movement, or in some other movement of protest against the effects of that very dead culture which they think, by protesting so belatedly, to survive.

The death of a culture begins when its normative institutions fail to communicate ideals in ways that remain inwardly compelling, first of all to the cultural elites themselves. Many spokesmen for our established normative institutions are aware of their failure and yet remain powerless to generate in themselves the necessary unwitting part of their culture that merits the name of faith. "Is not the very fact that so wretchedly little binding address is heard in the church," asked Karl Barth, rhetorically, in 1939, "accountable for a goodly share of her misery—is it not perhaps *the* misery?"[14] The misery of this culture is acutely stated by the special misery of its normative institutions. Our more general misery is that, having broken with those institutionalized credibilities from which its moral energy derived, new credibilities are not yet operationally effective and, perhaps, cannot become so in a culture constantly probing its own unwitting part.

It may be argued against this position that Western culture was never deeply believing—at least not in the Christian manner which, in a number of its most persuasive varieties, encouraged the seeking after individual salvations at the expense of a collective one. Even so, Christian culture survived because it superintended the organization of Western personality in ways that produced the necessary corporate identities, serving a larger communal purpose institutionalized in the churches themselves. Ernst Troeltsch was correct in his institutional title for the moral demand system preceding the one now emerging out of its complete ruin: a "church civilization," an "authoritarian and coercive culture." What binding address now describes our successor culture? In what does the self now try to find salvation, if not in the

14. Karl Barth, *The Church and the Political Problem of Our Day* (New York, 1939), 82–83.

breaking of corporate identities and in an acute suspicion of all normative institutions?

Western culture has had a literary canon, through which its character ideals were conveyed. What canons will replace the scriptural? None, I suppose. We are probably witnessing the end of a cultural history dominated by book religious and word makers. The elites of the emergent culture—if they do not destroy themselves and all culture with a dynamism they appear unable to control—are being trained in terminologies that have only the most tenuous relation to any historic culture or its incorporative self-interpretations.

It needs to be noted that in particular on the geographic margins of our moral demand system, and in the Orient, the rejection of religious culture, even in principle, is far from complete. By contrast, the communist movement may be viewed as culturally conservative,[15] belonging to the classical tradition of moral demand systems. The revolution in the West is profoundly cultural, whereas that in the East, withal its defensive doctrine of the cultural as a mere superstructure of the techno-political class system, has been less certainly so. Of the two, our revolution is, I think,

---

15. Communism, both doctrinally and institutionally, is here taken in its Leninist form, in which the Party takes up functions once performed by the teaching church, as the dominant *cultural* as well as *political* institution in Russian society. It is impossible to conceive of a vital Christian culture without a teaching church. As the inheritor of the churches' ambition, the Communist Party has sought to function as a normative institution, unlike Western political parties.

In documenting his assertion that Lenin's elder brother, Alexander (Sasha), was a Marxist, Louis Fischer has unwittingly helped demonstrate the validity of analyzing communist movements as primarily cultural—however strenuously and systematically Marxist theory itself contradicts the proposition, and persists in turning the truth upside down. Fischer quotes from Sasha's trial, when the elder brother proclaimed that "every change in the social system is a result of a change in the consciousness of society." The original Marxist Ulyanov thus expressed the true revolutionary doctrine, from which Marxists, entrapped in a moral indifferentism derived from the rejection by Karl Marx of the "utopianism" and moralism of Moses Hess and other early communist theorists, have long drawn their implicit knowledge, of what revolutions really are. See Louis Fischer, *The Life of Lenin* (New York, 1964), 15.

the more profound one. Communist culture, no less than the Christian, is in trouble; it cannot stave off a revolution coming out of the West, in part as a repercussion, in that it renounces the renunciatory mode of communism. The Russian cultural revolution is already being signaled by the liberation, however grudgingly, of the intellectuals from credal constraints.

The new religiosity is remissive. It represents no mere literary challenge, as in the time of the Enlightenment. The would-be instinctual Everyman and his girlfriend are the enlightened ones now; a Freud would be quite superfluous, especially in view of the fact that he sought to find ways other than neurotic of supporting renunciations.

Indeed, Freud has already receded into history. His problems are not ours. The psychoanalytic movement, no less than its rationalist predecessors, has been ruined by the popular (and commercial) pressure upon it to help produce a symbolic for the reorganization of personality after the central experience of deconversion, of which Freud was the last great theorist, had been completed. Fixed as they are at the historical stage of deconversion, responsible psychotherapists continue to struggle confusedly to discover their own proper attitude toward renunciatory moral demand systems even as the normative character of their abandonment has altered both the theoretical and working conditions of clinical practice. So confused, psychiatrists and clinical psychologists, in their hospitals and consulting rooms, stand almost as helpless as their functional predecessors and sometime cultural opponents, the clergy. But other therapeutic elites are not in a better condition, as I have tried to bring out more elaborately in the final chapter.

Our cultural revolution does not aim, like its predecessor, at victory for some rival commitment, but rather at a way of using all commitments, which amounts to loyalty toward none. By psychologizing about themselves interminably, Western men are learning to use their internality against the primacy of any particular organization of personality. If this restructuring of the

Western imagination succeeds in establishing itself, complete with institutional regimens, then human autonomy from the compulsions of culture may follow the freedoms already won from the compulsions of nature. With such a victory, culture, as previously understood, need suffer no further defeats. It is conceivable that millennial distinctions between inner and outer experience, private and public life, will become trivial. The individual heart need have no reasons of its own that the corporate head cannot understand and exploit for some augmentation of the individual's sense of well-bing. Thinking need not produce nausea or despair as its final answer to the assessment of communal purpose because men will have ceased to seek any salvation other than amplitude in living itself. Faith can then grow respectable again, as one entertainable and passing personal experience among others, to enhance the interest of living freed from communal purpose. The significance Marx attached to the division of labor for the organization of society may have bearing in our emergent culture on the variety of entertainments. To paraphrase Marx and Engels, all morality, be it ascetic or hedonistic, loses its force with a therapeutic outlook.

Like its predecessors, the emergent culture must formulate its own controls, no less than the preceding one defined its own remissions; it is in the process of doing so already. We are, I fear, getting to know one another. Reticence, secrecy, concealment of self, have been transformed into social problems; once they were aspects of civility, when the great Western formulary summed up in the credal phrase "Know thyself" encouraged obedience to communal purposes rather than suspicion of them. Self-knowledge again made social is the principle of control upon which the emergent culture may yet be able to make itself stable. Indeed, with the arts of psychiatric management enhanced and perfected, men will come to know one another in ways that could facilitate total socialization without a symbolic of communal purpose. Then the brief historic fling of the individual, celebrating himself as a being in himself, divine and therefore essentially unknowable, would be truly ended—ending no less certainly than the preceding personifications of various renunciatory disciplines. Men already feel freer to live their lives with a minimum of pretense to anything more grand than sweetening the time. Perhaps it is better so; in cultures past, men sacrificed themselves to heroic and cruel deceptions, and suffered for glories that once mirrored their miseries. Not until psychological men overcome lives of squalor can they truly test their assumption that the inherited ideals of glory are no longer required. Affluence achieved, the creation of a knowing rather than a believing person, able to enjoy life without erecting high symbolic hedges around it, distinguishes the emergent culture from its predecessor. The new anti-culture aims merely at an eternal interim ethic of release from the inherited controls.

Who is to say that these controls are eternal? I do not think so; even Christian theologians no longer say so with any confidence—and some are saying, rather, that new releases are holier than old controls. Yet even among churchmen there are those who understand anew that their religion is nothing if not the organization of communal purpose and the conservation of inherited culture; they therefore place desperate hope in the movement of which Dr. Martin Luther King is chief spokesman. Increasing numbers of churchmen have allied themselves with the Negro religious leader in what they have reluctantly understood must be a common struggle, for the rebirth of their moral demand system, against vastly superior numbers of nominally Christian (or Jewish) barbarians. This slowly reforming Christian cultural elite, apparent fellow travelers of the movement of Negro non-violent protest but in reality its critical aggregate, may yet save the United States from a barbarism long evident in the conduct of their own churches' members, in ordinary American commercial activity, and in the extraordinary incivilities of the American social manner. Yet there may be little power of Christian renewal in the movement of Negro protest. For the American Negro has been a focus for *releasing* images in the dominant white culture. Affluent white society, as it grows more affluent, may draw nearer their *idea* of the Negro as a model enjoyer of the relaxed life, but that idea is profoundly prejudicial to the renewal sought by the religious leadership, black and white.[16]

The present releases, in growing more dominant, must achieve institutional affirmations of the prevalent feeling. Critically to elaborate such affirmations has been the historic function of Western intellectuals. But, not yet able to produce imagery that would mark a trail for many memories, contemporary writers and artists, all those intellectuals slightly ahead of their time, mainly produce moods of solicitude about themselves, as if they could not bear the weight of the freedom from their inherited role upon which they themselves insist. This temper against moralizing has its justifications. The Germans recently manipulated all corporate identities and communal purposes with a thoroughness against which the analytic attitude may be our surest protection.

Under such protection, it may not be possible to organize our culture again as an unwitting dynamic of moral demands claiming the prerogatives of truth, exercised through credally authoritative institutions. Where family and nation once stood, or Church and Party, there will be hospital and theater too,[17] the norma-

16. Compare the white idea of the Negro with their idea of the Jews, who, throughout Western cultural history, have been feared and hated as personifications of *controlling* motifs. In the light of their personifications in terms of releasing motifs, American Negroes are stuck with a double-edged motto: "Freedom Now" aptly expresses the nervousness and furtive envy of white American ideas about Negro behavior.

17. In a passage of his *Italienische Reise* (Stuttgart, 1862) dated May 27, 1787, Goethe remarks: "Speaking for myself, I too believe that humanity will win in the long run; I am only afraid that at the same time the world will have turned into one huge hospital where everyone is everybody else's humane nurse." See the translation by W. H. Auden and E. Mayer (New York, 1962) p. 312. This is the earliest prophecy of the emergent culture of which I am aware. But Goethe was not the last member of a cultural elite to dread or wish for such an institutional development. Coleridge once suggested, in a letter, the founding of a

new charitable institution . . . for lunacy and idiocy of the *will*, in which, with the full consent of, or at the direct insistence of the patient himself, and with the concurrence of his friends, such a person under the certificate of a physician might be placed under medical and moral coercion. I am convinced that London would furnish a hundred volunteers in as many days from the gin-shops, who would swallow their glass of poison in order to get courage to present themselves to the hospital in question. And a similar institution

tive institutions of the next culture. Trained to be incapable of sustaining sectarian satisfactions, psychological man cannot be susceptible to sectarian control. Religious man was born to be saved; psychological man is born to be pleased. The difference was established long ago, when "I believe," the cry of the ascetic, lost precedence[18] to "one feels," the caveat of the therapeutic. And if the therapeutic is to win out, then surely the psychotherapist will be his secular spiritual guide.

However one may judge the validity of the multiple truths at which science and history arrive, my interest is in their social viability. The next culture may be viable without being valid; on the other hand, the old faiths could be judged valid even by those who consider them now no longer viable. In order to attend fairly to the competing beliefs and unbeliefs, one must struggle to use neutral terms. A sociological vocabulary keeps a certain distance from both new permissions and old inhibitions. This distance is the only possible justification for such jargon as I have used in the present volume; except as a device for gaining perspective, sociological jargon is a curse, first of all upon the intellectual lives of sociologists. Sociological writing itself is ineluctably part of the psychohistorical process, engaged as it is in persuasive redefinitions of action that alter the action.

Can the present releases become the predicates of new controls? Viewed traditionally, the continuing shift from a controlling to a releasing symbolic may appear as the dissolution of culture. Viewed sociologically, the dominance of releasing motifs, in which the releasers themselves evolve as new modes of control,

---

might exist for a higher class of will-maniacs or impotents. Had such a house of health been in existence, I know who would have entered himself as a patient some five and twenty years ago.

Quoted in Kathleen Coburn, ed., *Inquiring Spirit: Coleridge from His Published and Unpublished Prose Writings* (New York, 1951), 36–37.

18. For example, it is evident in the apologetics preached by Friedrich Schleiermacher to the cultured despisers of religion at the end of the eighteenth century; Schleiermacher's *Reden* (1799) were a brilliant effort to turn the deconversion experience of the highly cultured against itself.

with patterns of consumption as our popular discipline, implies a movement of Western culture away from its former configuration, toward one in which old ideological contents are preserved mainly for their therapeutic potential, as interesting deposits of past motifs of moralizing. No imperative can then develop a monopoly on sentiment, because none will be backed by a deeply ingrained system of inner ordinances.

I do not refer to a "sensualist" culture but to one that prepares for adaptability in matters of the "spirit." There is no special affection reserved in this volume for the superiority usually claimed for "spiritual" over "sensual" concerns. In the emergent culture, a wider range of people will have "spiritual" concerns and engage in "spiritual" pursuits. There will be more singing and more listening. People will continue to genuflect and read the Bible, which has long achieved the status of great literature; but no prophet will denounce the rich attire or stop the dancing. There will be more theater, not less, and no Puritan will denounce the stage and draw its curtains. On the contrary, I expect that modern society will mount psychodramas far more frequently than its ancestors mounted miracle plays, with patient-analysts acting out their inner lives, after which they could extemporize the final act as interpretation. We shall even institutionalize in the hospital-theater the *Verfremdungseffekt*, with the therapeutic triumphantly enacting his own discovered will.

The wisdom of the next social order, as I imagine it, would not reside in right doctrine, administered by the right men, who must be found, but rather in doctrines amounting to permission for each man to live an experimental life. Thus, once again, culture will give back what it has taken away. All governments will be just, so long as they secure that consoling plenitude of option in which modern satisfaction really consists. In this way the emergent culture could drive the value problem clean out of the social system and, limiting it to a form of philosophical entertainment in lieu of edifying preachment, could successfully conclude the exercise for which politics is the name. Problems of democracy need no longer prove so difficult as they have been. Psychological man is likely to be indifferent to the ancient question of legitimate authority, of sharing in government, so long as the powers that be preserve social order and manage an economy of abundance. The danger of politics lies more in the ancient straining to create those symbols or support those institutions that narrow the range of virtues or too narrowly define the sense of well-being; for the latter seems to be the real beatitude toward which men have always strained. Psychological man, in his independence from all gods, can feel free to use all god-terms; I imagine he will be a hedger against his own bets, a user of any faith that lends itself to therapeutic use.

Culture as therapy becomes realizable in part because of the increasing automaticity of the productive system. But without the discipline of work, a vast reritualization of social life will probably occur, to contain aggression in a steady state and maintain necessary levels of attention to activity. The rules of health indicate activity; psychological man can exploit older cultural precepts, ritual struggle no less than play therapy, in order to maintain the dynamism of his culture. Of course, the newest Adam cannot be expected to limit himself to the use of old constraints. If "immoral" materials, rejected under earlier cultural criteria, are therapeutically effective, enhancing somebody's sense of well-being, then they are useful. The "end" or "goal" is to keep going. Americans, as F. Scott Fitzgerald concluded, believe in the green light.

I am aware that these speculations may be thought to contain some parodies of an apocalypse. But what apocalypse has ever been so kindly? What culture has ever attempted to see to it that no ego is hurt? Perhaps the elimination of the tragic sense—which is tantamount to the elimination of irreconcilable moral principles—is no tragedy. Civilization could be, for the first time in history, the expression of human contents rather than the consolatory control of discontents. Then and only then would the religious question receive a markedly different answer from those dominant until recently in our cultural history.

Selections from *Fellow Teachers*

We teachers now easily accept, so long as our jobs and affluence are not threatened, that same cultureless society into which
our students have been born. Affluence is becoming only for
restrained people. We Americans have never learned to reject
enough new things; absence of restraint is the key to our affluence and to our populist inclinations. Very American, we teachers
have no cause for complaint about our students. We are up on
the latest and have become ex-somethings—ex-Marxists, ex-Jews,
ex-bourgeois, ex-straights, ex-kin. How can we complain that the

On March 26, 1971, Philip Rieff came to Skidmore College to submit to an extensive public interview conducted by Robert Boyers, the editor of *Salmagundi*
magazine, and Robert Orrill, at the time a member of the magazine's editorial
board. Although it was agreed that an edited transcript of the three-hour-long
interview would later be published in a special issue of *Salmagundi* devoted to
the subject of "psychological man" and built largely, though not exclusively,
around Rieff's work, Rieff was unhappy with the transcript submitted to him.
He indicated that, no matter how it was edited, it would not represent "for all
time" what he intended to convey. He decided to write in place of the interview
document "Fellow Teachers," at once an essay, a polemic, and a letter, invoking
the public interview but going on to address a wide range of matters beyond
what his two interlocutors had asked him to discuss at Skidmore. That lengthy
paper—eighty pages in the Summer–Fall 1972 issue of *Salmagundi* entitled
"Psychological Man: Approaches to an Emergent Social Type"—was soon expanded to a book-length volume entitled *Fellow Teachers*, likewise addressed to
his two Skidmore interlocutors and drawing upon the same occasion. For the
interview, Boyers and Orrill had "assigned" to Rieff several texts, which would
be referred to in the course of the interview. These included Kafka's "In The
Penal Colony" and John Barth's "End of the Road," both of which figure in
Fellow Teachers. Our selections here are fragmentary in nature and may seem to
lack much in the way of a linear structure, but the original text was composed
in a similarly elliptical mode, and we believe these stitched-together fragments
well reflect the tone and style of argumentation of Rieff's complete text.—*Eds.*

chain of interpretation has been broken? All new links must appear as forgeries if only the self is authentic. Our acceptances of experience are thought to be most satisfying when they are without precedent. We have no stable old ruling ideas and, therefore, can have no stable old presiding class.

We cannot simply dismiss the argument that the struggle for power, revealed for all to see, makes our kind of work at best irrelevant. It has been argued that our transferable interpretations are now so contradictory that they can never again prepare for soul-making and ethics, but only generate neuroses. New scientific interpreters, marching out behind their quotation marks as if they were shibboleths, aim to acquire an inner freedom to act—any role; this freedom renews the most ancient dexterity, the liveliness with which a human can step aside, as if no particular act represented the responsible I in the middle of his head. Putting all the god-terms and their necessary enemies, the transgressions—'defilement', 'impurity', 'lust', 'untruth', whatever breaks through—between quotation marks, the new interpreters, improving upon both science and democracy, have made ambiguous and entirely problematic all orders in which we might conceivably live. Our feasts of commitment grow more and more swiftly movable; eternally young and unsettled, we teachers ourselves engage in the most acrobatic hopping from one order to another. Yeats was mistaken: all centers hold equally well. Therefore, there is no center. To be radically contemporaneous, to be sprung loose from every particular symbolic, is to achieve a conclusive, unanswerable failure of historical memory. This is the uniquely modern achievement. Barbarians have never before existed. At the end of this tremendous cultural development, we moderns shall arrive at barbarism. Barbarians are people without historical memory. Barbarism is the real meaning of radical contemporaneity. Released from all authoritative pasts, we progress toward barbarism, not away from it.

Barbarism means more than radical contemporaneity; it means playing at being 'Man', or 'Human'; barbarism means the universality of those reeducated or brutalized out of membership in the binding particularities of their culture and, being able to entertain all, inhibited by no new god-terms. One perfectly reasonable reviewer of a recent nonbook of oracles backed me accurately into my historical corner, along with others:

> Philip Rieff . . . comes over with a touching nostalgia for the educated man who once could place himself in a usable tradition. Now, the barbarians are taking over—the barbarians being classically defined as people without a history, and dwelling most naturally in America, a country dominated by "an ingenuous will to transform, without regard to what is being destroyed and what is being constructed." The source of the trouble is the revolutionary activity of the bourgeoisie, for the bourgeoisie is both greedy and rational, reckoning that neither God nor nature nor human nature set any limits to what it might do with the world. Against this Gadarene Rush, intellectuals are powerless; Rieff mentions in an aside that history is only stopped by "prophecy," but that dark saying is left unilluminated.
>
> Indeed, even under some pressure from their interviewers, the contributors who are asked for prophecy invariably back away. Werner Heisenberg talks some calm good sense about the silliness of the demand for "new values" and about the idea that science can or ought to provide them. He is plainly right.[1]

* *

It is out of a highly differentiated society, spheres of action separate, none subject to the same interdicts, and all to fewer, that

---

1. See review by Alan Ryan, "Conference Smog," of G. R. Urban ed., *Can We Survive Our Future?* (1972), in *New Statesman*, February 11, 1972, p. 182. Note, however, that I am not quite so ardent a bourgeois-basher as the reviewer makes me out. Bashing the bourgeois is the Marxist version of baiting the Jews. Do not blame the bourgeoisie. They are talented expressionists of the law that to those who have, more will be given; the law is applied, at times with a vengeance, by have-nots. To be realistic about the propertied is not to grow sentimental about the less propertied. There is no special virtue in either of these conditions.

The Bourgeois-Jewish Question will not wash out of the Marxist symbolic. If you do not believe that bourgeois-bashing is the Marxist link, backwards and forwards, to Jew-baiting, then read Marx on goods. There are other equally infamous passages in the Marxist synthesis of bourgeois-bashing and Jew-hating. Bourgeois-bashing and Jew-hatred aside, the distribution and redistribution

the therapeutic has been born. This ideal-type is free, in the first place, because he can live his life among authorities so long divided that none can assert themselves strongly even in their own sphere—quite the contrary of Durkheim's quasi-syndicalist hope. There is, however, something new about the therapeutic: a conclusive freedom, all interdicts evaginated, so highly surfaced that none can survive. Why should the therapeutic feel anything deeply when he can exhibit his sensibilities? The contemporary man of feeling is equipped with a hidden weapon, his pseudo-sensibility; he demands, he appeals, he does whatever needs to be done, under whatever slogan, to assert himself. A slogan is an unrooted saying. Slogans are the language of a radically contemporary people. The American language has become a grab bag of slogans. This massive abnormality has become the norm.

Living on his surfaces, as he does, the therapeutic is an acutely sensitive man; it is only deep down that he has learned to be less vulnerable. I was struggling toward this point in a passage from *The Triumph of the Therapeutic* of which you reminded me in your interpretative paraphrase of it during our exchange:

> With Freud, the individual took a great and final step toward that mature and calm feeling which comes from having nothing to hide. To live on the surface prevents deep hurts.

It takes a certain genius to survive the deepest hurts. Freud favored asking less of people, most of whom are not moral geniuses or any other kind. Most of us cannot transform our hurts into anything that does not hurt (ourselves or others) more. A true culture imposes certain limits on itself; it does not ask ordinary men to make extraordinary renunciations. But in a true culture, a genius is not considered a criminal, nor is criminality honored as genius.

---

of wealth remains the stuff of the struggle for power. But wealth, as the Jews should know best, is not identical with power or even its predicate. It is as ridiculous to imagine a ruling class that is merely wealthy as it is to imagine a ruling class that remains poor. Property is an infinitely extendable entity. Stalin made the greatest of political fortunes; no one had more servants. It is not clear that Stalin enjoyed owning Russia. Alas, the rich are not happy; they have such responsibilities and they must live in fear of having less.

Life is not confused with Art. Terribilità should remain an aesthetic, not a political, capacity; it rightly belonged to Beethoven and Michelangelo, in their work, not to the condottieri, or Hitler, in theirs. An extraordinarily rare talent does not emerge in transgressions; rather, in works of art, or science, that control their own spheres with full interdictory force, called 'form'. Within its culture, every artwork constitutes a system of discrete limits, each a paradigm of how a culture works; none are sovereign beyond themselves. A universal culture is a contradiction in terms. We Jews of culture are obliged to resist the very idea.

Confusing spheres, modern aspirants to freedom from all authority have produced a parody terribilità in all spheres. Our reeducated classes, rich consumers of everything available, are scarcely competent to perform the most elementary decencies—yet they are urged to fulfill themselves, as if each were a Beethoven, perhaps a little deaf to his own music and in need of some third-ear hygiene. Freud called psychoanalysis a "reeducation." In our own time, post-Freudian, everything new is a reeducation; mind fawns over mindlessness and tries to find fancy names for it. So the therapeutic teaching of transgressive behavior confuses art and life, rare genius and common faith, public life and private. Encounter-group teachings, for example, mainly by therapists of the revolutionary rich, follow the precedent set by the technological radicalism of those same rich in their earlier scramble: for more.

That the opposing sides of the American scene, deviants and straights, are both suspicious of authority is mainly the fault of what passes for authority in our nation; the officers themselves are so often inferior persons that their offices cannot conceal the absence of any reference beyond themselves to a presiding presence. Modern revolt has no authority and is all the more dangerous because there is no authority against which to revolt; we are stripping politics to its barest form, struggle for power after power, violence. What Mill called "savagery" and "barbarism" scarcely applies so well to his notion of static societies as it does to our own dynamic one. We and our students shall have to be reminded that "discipline, that is, perfect co-operation, is an attribute of civilization," not of mass rationalization. Mill tells us that to be capable of discipline in great things, "a people must be gradually trained to it in small."[2] Such training cannot be politicized without inverting the meaning of discipline, from civilization to barbarism—from a not-doing of what is not to be done to a routine doing of precisely that.

Presences have never been encouraged to preside—now less than ever before. The therapeutic has no presence. It is impossible to revolt against him. All revolution worthy of the name has been against authority, giving rise to a new presiding presence, without which authority cannot exist; for example, Jews cannot exist without the Mosaic presence (as Freud understood, in making his attempt at a resolutive interpretation of the Jewish historical character). Suppose, however, there is no authority—only power and its theatrical affects? How can there be a crisis of authority? Among our reflexive sorts, there is much fashionable talk of crisis, of our times of trouble. I doubt the gravity of the crisis, not least for all the crisis talk; the time seems to me less gravely troubled than some others. What can 'trouble' mean if our society is growing cultureless, without presiding presences and a public order of meaning? Guilt is much overestimated as a working force in the new society, usable mainly as a tactic toward its continuing dissolution. During a year in Germany, I met precious few guilty people. My German friends were having an authentically good time. My American friends seem equally guiltless, although they throw up their hands regularly as if aghast at their sense of guilt. I think they are playing games. To feel guilt takes a certain submission to authority. There can be no transgressive sense without someone (and his theory) to transgress.

No guilt is true except as it subserves the interdicts. Guilt is false, 'neurotic', as Freud taught us to call it, when it subverts the interdicts. Far from separating crime and morals, the radical psychologizers treat certain kinds of crime as (politically) virtuous; in the name of 'humanization', false guilt subverts the interdicts

2. John Stuart Mill, "Civilization," *Westminster Review*, nos. 5 and 48 (April 1836): 3.

by proclaiming that everything human is permitted. The radical psychologizers have greatly increased the incidence of false guilt because culture cannot tolerate such direct openings of possibility. Our politicized therapists are the sickest people among us— and our most liberated. Their quest for health has generated an acute dis-ease, 'Liberation', the latest mockery of all god-terms, including the pagan.

We professors of the present have in stock a large supply of god-terms and can conjure orders galore, from the grab bag of things past, passing, and to come. Precisely in the age of the therapeutic, the dead gods cannot rise from their graves. None are alive; any may be talked up, for an occasion, if the talkers like to drop those kinds of names. Our god-terms mock their ancestors, the gods, in one special respect: no god-term worth using can be merely heuristic, a device for extending intellectual reach. God-terms must have binding authority, compelling not merely intellectual interest but also suspicion of that interest. Our God can only reveal as he conceals himself; ask that, concealment with every revelation, and you have understood why the major questions must always continue as if unanswered.

Without concealments, revelations yield none of those compromises which make life tolerable. Imagine the length of the casualty list when a universal publicity reveals everything to all, at once, when nothing is handed down slowly, in generational dances of time. Sociology awaits its theorists in the classic style. Since the positivist takeover, in the first third of the nineteenth century, my discipline has tried too hard to remain permanently advanced, young enough to produce an endless barrage of orginalities. Such youthfulness and originality—trendiness, some call it— are fatal to the life of the mind. Violent excursions toward death and perverse behavior are occupations most fit for the young, when they will not think through what their predecessors have thought. To leave the great past unremembered is to be lost in the howling present; then the best an intellectual can do is shoot off his mouth.

When the god-terms lose their inhibiting dynamic, then they become protean. ('Protean man' does not descend from the god

Proteus. He has no descent, and therefore no existence.) The barbarian who is emerging, stuffed with tactical advice culled from
the ages, can hop from order to order, committing himself, as in
modern marriage, to a serial monogamy that is massively polyga-
mous. ('But I'm always true to you, darlin', in my fashion'—what
is the name of that old hymn? I will not remember. Was it: "A
Mighty Fortress," as Erikson believes?) To say this barbarian is
universally faithless is only to say that no character becomes authoritative in him. Only cultureless societies can exist without
presiding presences. No presence can preside when all are subject
to abandonments quick as their adoptions. Our passionate truths
are so provisional, they move so quickly with the electrified times,
that none can prepare us to receive them deeply into ourselves,
as character; they do not become compelling in their interdicts
but endlessly attractive in their remissions. Where creeds were,
there therapies will be. Our new way, reeducation, is an unlearn-
ing. What, then, have we to teach?

It is as the typical creature of a cultureless society that I have
imagined the therapeutic. I do not imagine him as a serious man.
Seriousness is a state of possession by god-terms, even to the negation of justified violence in their defense. Serious attacks on authority must breed new authority. In the therapeutic, I imagined
someone who takes nothing seriously. Of course, a therapeutic
can resonate empty militancies that signal an acceptance of their
emptiness. Opposing this experimental life, in which all god-
terms can be taken lightly, rather as heuristic devices, there can
be only a culture of militant, opposing truths—god-terms that
are interdictory before they are remissive and thus to be taken
seriously because humans will oppose the interdicts with all their
wits. (To take a god-term seriously, however, is not to be without humor; on the contrary, as I have said, no justification worth
calling to mind ever sets it at rest. What may be taken lightly
is not the god-term, but oneself. Luther called this the joy of
the faithful.) A culture of truth opposing self—what culture is,
understood sociologically—abides experimental lives only in
its own service; thus, for example, monasticism, which opposed

the corporate self-glorification of the church, served culture. Except through institutional services, before they harden into further glorifications and false guilt, experiment belongs in the laboratory and to art, most rarely to publicized individuality. Our continuous publicity for experimental living predicates that totalitarian disorder of which fascist movements gave one premonitory flash. I shall return, below, to the important point that, as Mussolini grasped, fascism is not a creed but an opportunity.

Now I am in position to answer the question for which you prepared me before our interview (perhaps the result of our happy misunderstanding): whether the coming of the therapeutic is to be welcomed insofar as he is free from any need of a common faith. With this emergent type, you ask, will we be delivered from the nightmare history of the last half century, and spared its mass brutalities? No; I suspect we will not be spared. Violence is the therapy of therapies, as Dr. Fanon, the political psychiatrist, suggests. There is less and less to inhibit this final therapy, least where the most progressively reeducated classes seem ready to go beyond their old hope of deliverance, from violence as the last desperate disciplinary means built into the interdicts, as punishment, to violence as a means toward a saving indiscipline, as self-expression. Geniuses of this saving indiscipline roam the college circuit, selling their guidance toward a cultureless society, without interdicts deeply installed.

Which cadre of putative guides to the new freedom will you follow: our rationalizing functionaries[3] or our functional irrationalizers?[4] Never mind: they will meet at the end of their roads. The functional irrationalizers are well on their way to becoming our next rationalizing functionaries. Both cadres will produce endless therapies. With the end of authority, no violence will be illegitimate. Rather, as they destroy the civilities basic to cultured society, the brutalities of direct action will be differently understood. Victims are being taught their complicity, their role, in brutal acts. Let every actor play his variable part, without indignation—except when indignation promotes the part. The new society al-

3. E.g., engineers, social and material, of control.
4. E.g., therapists of release.

ready has the look, both in America and in the Soviet Union, of a hospital-theater—in contrast to the old society, which had the look of a church. The successor to our failed credal organizations will not be another credal one, not even Marxist, which names the last major credal effort to reorganize Western society; we shall be dominated by anti-creeds and think ourselves free.

Our own culture has taken form in credal organizations. Priesthoods and intelligentsias are but two of the forms credal organization, ancient and modern, may take. However, the defense of it, implicit in my theory of culture, does not make me an advocate of some earlier credal organization. In particular, I have not the slightest affection for the dead church civilization of the West. I am a Jew. No Jew in his right mind can long for some variant (including the Party)[5] of that civilization. Its one enduring quality is its transgressive energy against the Jew of culture; those transgressions have been built so deeply into the church-organized interdicts that they survive even now, after the main interdictory motifs of Christendom are dead. Christian transgressions are still so vital that the recent well-publicized statements of Christian remorse are likely to be a condition of further transgression, as the Jews continue to resist their assigned roles and, worse gall, refuse to disappear into the universalist future 'Man'. The gospels were not good news; the ungospeled present has its supremely pleasant feature, the death of the church—or, less pleasant, its conversion into naïvely therapeutic institutions, hawking a few antique graces to ornament our triumphant gracelessness. A contentless faith in 'faith' is but one of the rather noisy rhetorics of commitment to movement—any movement—that characterize the superego turned against itself, against inhibition and for action. As in space

5. But see, on the concept 'political religions', my remarks on functionalism below. I doubt that the Party, which Gramsci saw as the Prince of this world, can be understood as a 'secular' (i.e., successor and functional) equivalent of the church. Indeed, I doubt that penetrative thrust inheres in the concept 'secularization'. We can do better without 'secularization'. The concept obscures interdictory-remissive shifts of indirective content. Secularization especially encourages false homotonalities, an ease of transitions that may falsify true oppositions: as between pastors and professors, for example—as if becoming a professor really does express in another form (perhaps updated, superior because updated) earlier religious aspirations.

science, so in the new reforming amorality, to be distinguished from the old Reformation morality, the countdown slogan is "All systems go."

I, for one, am not keen on being where the direct action is; there brutality and the horror of total politics, uninhibited by any presiding presence, will be. One necessary thing that we inactivists, we academic men, suspicious of all politics, have to teach our students is how not to invest in the nostrums of direct action now being hawked. It is our duty to protect and nurture, in our academies, a few enclaves within which to practice an inhibiting subtlety, to think in something like late Jamesian sentences.[6] If we are not allowed indirections, slowly ordered, if we must serve some program, one side or another, then the academy has no unique service; it is least fit of all institutions to take stands or rationalize them. The more directly political it becomes, the more certainly the university must commit itself to shifting positions, in the endless war for advantage, and so destroy its intellectual integrity. To resist endless politicizing is made more difficult when politics and therapy merge in fancies of a student culture opposed to study. Yet, despite the erotic incitements on campus, some of our students remain ardent to be students.

The threat to study is double: not only from masses of students who do not study but from faculty who will not teach. By their

6. Then, after James, we may graduate to Proust, who grasped Chardin, master of the ordinary and of still life. Prepared by Chardin, Proust could grasp Vermeer, master of that little patch of yellow wall and, more profoundly, of the ordinary moment, quietly revealed. To receive Vermeer's revelation is to become quiet oneself. Looking at a Vermeer, Proust saw how inhibiting are the supreme subtleties and how hierarchical, orderly, beautifully precise, and commanding those subtleties are. This praise is not for old Art. Modern art can be equally inhibiting. It is mere ignorance, parading as traditionalism, to praise the formalities of a Raphael, or the eighteenth-century painters, while dispraising the formalities of modern painting, which begin with Cézanne (to whom Roger Fry makes the best introduction, still, I think) and continue, through Braque, to our best contemporaries in painting. But exclude—from my canon, at least—those talented impresarios (e.g., Duchamp) of a constantly innovative art who, as innovators, lead what is tantamount to a campaign for the abolition of art. Duchamp's *ready-mades* intend that (1) everything is pleasurable; (2) because the pursuit of pleasure can be totally democratic, everything is art. This is cultural egalitarianism with a vengeance, first against art itself.

gurus and Research paymasters, the collegiate young are being reeducated before they have been educated. From our collegiate ranks, the therapeutic will appear a reeducated man, one who can conquer even his subtler inhibitions; his final know-how will be to irrationalize his rationality and play games, however intellectualized, with all god-terms in order to be ruled by none. In their moral modesty, therapeutics will be capable of anything; they will know that everything is possible because they will not be inhibited by any truth. Far more destructively than earlier interdict-burdened character types, the therapeutic will be the warring state writ small; he may be even cannier, less sentimental, stronger in ego, shifting about his principles and his impulses like so many stage props.

Of one condition that could make him less capable of brutality, the therapeutic, conqueror of his feeling intellect, is likely to be incapable: *inwardness*, the quality of self-concealment. That has become, as Kierkegaard predicted, an aberrancy. The growth of this aberrancy is linked to the mistaken idea, held by both rationalists and sentimentalists, of an autonomous inner man. What is referred to as 'inner' and 'autonomous' expresses responses of obedience to interdictory-remissive predicates that are as complex before as after they are taken in as character.[7] Cultures are constituted by interdictory contents, and their remissions, in multiform cults. Few of those cults are recognized in their multiformity, now that all have been overwhelmed by the cult of personality. Within

7. E.g., Jewish moral demands have a complex *We-They* order that, when taken into character, are not entirely defensive, according to my judgment. *I-Thou* is too pure a symbol to cope with the interdictory-remissive dynamic of *We-They*, in the ordinary life of Jews. The *and* between Buber's primary word, *I-Thou*, signifies, for him, an "act of pure relation" which, in its 'purity', comes too near that emptying-out of revelation and its credal order characteristic of nineteenth-century idealism before it led toward its counter, the anticredal order of our time. I suspect a language in which "Man receives, and he receives not a specific 'content' but a Presence, a Presence as power." That sounds to me like the late Protestant emptying out of the interdicts, by a too general affirmation. Historically and sociologically, in this way, 'Meaning' is anything but assured. Quite the contrary of Buber's vision, mine is that nothing can any longer be meaningful when 'Man' receives a 'Presence' without "specific 'content.'" See, Buber, *I and Thou*, trans. Ronald Gregor Smith (Edinburgh: T. and T. Clark, 1937), 109–10 et passim.

those cults we are free to choose among authority relations; authority generates, as culture, its indispensable interior flexibility.

* *

Perhaps our radical student movement should have a memorial essay written to honor its deadliness; call that essay "The New Joodey-ism." What Self-serving hutzpah to speak of 'Judaism' as if the faith of Israel were disembodied by its progress into the Christian era, when, after millennial resistances, synagogue began to imitate church. What Christians still sometimes grasp as faith cannot survive the end of Israel; Israel cannot survive the end of faith. The fate of our high culture is inseparable from the relation between the past of faith and the future of Israel. 'Judaism' represents contemporary Jews to themselves as they are, still in their massive fugue, fleeing that interdictory genius for which the gentile world, like the Jews themselves, cannot be expected to show gratitude. One major form of ingratitude is the act of forgetting. A disproportionate number of young Jews are members of various angry brigades, a just reward to their doting parents for having forgotten the God of their Fathers; this forgetfulness is so acute that it does not include a language of denial.

* *

The American social order is neither ancient nor stable; Americans have experienced no specially crowded rush hour of the gods; the revivalist period ended long ago. Such spiritual traffic jams, as Japan knew for a generation after my war, were expertly dispersed, in our own culture, by the late Protestant faith in criticism. Nietzsche was traffic manager, raised to the intensity of genius. But he declined to be an apostle of understanding. Here was a critic who warned away all followers. Our apostles of their own criticism behave differently. Going about their lucrative business of saying everything, stars in their new very heaven, they can recommend themselves to the new earthlings. Their recommendations are followed. Thousands among our young have taken the paratherapists seriously and, moreover, take their courses in order to relieve—in school, of all places, and in courses, of all things—frustrations. Under this tutelage in soullessness, of use and movement identical with faith and apathy, the therapeutic, as a characterless type, appears loyal solely to the promise of the next possibility. So far have we been taken down the road by the cultists of experiences.

What is Jake?* Neither Jew nor Greek, Left nor Right, and certainly not Christian or rationalist progressive. He is nothing in particular. The Morgans wonder whether Jake exists. Because Jake is a special kind of virtual reality, Barth can begin his novel with the classical intellectualizing cop-out of the therapeutic interpreter, who, while he can be emancipated by any interpretation, can be bound by none. Barth's opening sentence is a master stroke: "In a sense, I am Jacob Horner."[8] Whenever it was that Jacob broke through to Jake, he had to concern himself chiefly with whether he was still all right; the problem of his name becomes a clinical apprehension about his state of mind, which is identical with the insoluble problem of his identity. A sociological definition of a Jew: he who resists—that is, resists the very problem of his identity.

What unsociological nonsense it was for Marx to write, trespassing (unwitting) on the problem of identity, with special re-

8. 'Jacob Horner': how sociologically precise. Jake is probably an ex-Jew, but well beyond the earlier conditions of being an ex-Jew—e.g., a Party member, a rootless cosmopolitan, anything you please. An ex-Jew is someone who, having stopped going to synagogue, declines to go to church. The therapeutic has advanced beyond such negations. Why not synagogue *and* church? Party *and* commune? Jackboots *and* long hair? Masculine *and* feminine? Why not Walt Whitman as Lincoln's assassin?

---

*Jacob Horner is the protagonist of John Barth's second novel, *The End of the Road* (1958). Rieff takes Horner to be a literary exemplar of the burgeoning therapeutic character. *The End of the Road*, Rieff writes by way of introduction to his interpretation of the novel, "is the story of a naked man, entirely exposed—and yet, not quite so. Something remains concealed, even from himself: a still unyielding truth of resistance. . . . Jake is no judge; equally important, there is no god-term by which he need be judged. Unjudging and unjudged, a therapeutic can achieve his perfection." Rieff explains that Horner is not quite a full therapeutic, however: "Barth's Jake does not yet exist in this new state, without reverence and justice. He exists between orders, where death is casual and not a judgment. Some residual reverence in Jake, unacknowledged, makes death an inexplicable foolishness and not a sentence" (*Fellow Teachers*, 55–56).—*Eds.*

spect to money, that the "name of a thing is something distinct from the qualities of that thing. I know nothing of a man, by knowing that his name is Jacob." I say we know that that man, Jacob, to whom Marx referred is, most probably, an ex-Jew. But the sociological pressure remains, its residuum enough to cause *Jacob/Jake* his historical identity crisis. The trace of historical memory has not yet been wiped off proper names; some scent of the past still goes with the name.

In Marxist theory, memory traces mean 'value relation', which Marx associated, particularly in its terminal stage, with the making and having of money. How ardently Marx desired the destruction of historical memory, and its metamorphoses, which he termed "ideal existence." The name 'Jacob' occurs, to this day, under the authority of its ideal existence, although, in this day more acutely than ever, only 'in a sense'.

Marx's ardor for the destruction of ideal existences, which do more than survive in the cycle of primal history because they can only survive as presiding presences, is hidden in his denial of reality to the 'sabbath Jew'.[9] For Marx, the real Jew is an en-

---

9. See Karl Marx, "On the Jewish Question," in *Early Writings*, trans. and ed. T. B. Bottomore, foreword by Erich Fromm (New York: McGraw-Hill, 1964; Marx's italics):

> Let us consider the real Jew: not the *sabbath Jew* . . . but the *everyday Jew*.
> Let us not seek the secret of the Jew in his religion, but let us seek the secret of the religion in the real Jew.
> What is the profane basis of Judaism? *Practical* need, *self-interest*. What is the worldly cult of the Jew? *Huckstering*. What is his worldly god? *Money*.
> Very well: then in emancipating itself from *huckstering* and *money*, and thus from real and practical Judaism, our age would emancipate itself.
> An organization of society which would abolish the preconditions and thus the very possibility of huckstering, would make the Jew impossible. His religious consciousness would evaporate like some insipid vapour in the real, life-giving air of society. On the other hand, when the Jew recognizes his *practical* nature as invalid and endeavours to abolish it, he begins to deviate from his former path of development, works for general *human emancipation* and turns against the *supreme practical* expression of human self-estrangement.
> We discern in Judaism, therefore, a universal *anti-social* element of the *present time*, whose historical development, zealously aided in its harmful

tirely contemporary man and, therefore, entirely sabbathless. The metamorphosis *Jew/bourgeois* of Marxist theory, assessed in my sociology, is, in reality, a symptom of the contemporary identity crisis through which, Marx thought, classed men would evolve

---

aspects by the Jews, has now attained its culminating point, a point at which it must necessarily begin to disintegrate.

In the final analysis, the *emancipation of* the Jews is the emancipation of mankind from *Judaism*. . . . [P. 34]

It is because the essence of the Jew was universally realized and secularized in civil society, that civil society could not convince the Jew of the *unreality* of his *religious* essence, which is precisely the ideal representation of practical need. It is not only, therefore, in the Pentateuch and the Talmud, but also in contemporary society, that we find the essence of the present-day Jew; not as an abstract essence, but as one which is supremely empirical, not only as a limitation of the Jew, but as the Jewish narrowness of society.

As soon as society succeeds in abolishing the *empirical* essence of Judaism—huckstering and its conditions—the Jew becomes *impossible*, because his consciousness no longer has an object. The subjective basis of Judaism—practical need—assumes a human form, and the conflict between the individual, sensuous existence of man and his species-existence, is abolished.

The *social* emancipation of the Jew is the *emancipation of society from Judaism*. [P. 40]

What radically contemporary Jew can fail to deconvert himself into a Marxist and, for the sake of society succeeding, at last, commit what may be called (politely) 'identity suicide'? Marx's denial of reality to the sabbath Jew is widely shared among Jews; it is the open secret of their 'faith'. It is this denial of reality to the sabbath in them, by contemporary Jews, that makes them sick with hatred of the terrible historical fact of their birth, against which all their reeducated self-interpretations—Marxist, Freudian, whatever bizarre suicides their integrity can be made to suffer—struggle. The struggle—call it, in many cases, 'Judaism'—makes these radically contemporary Jews the least educable Jew-haters, in the classroom or outside. Of course, there are many brilliantly radical contemporaries who are not Jews and still manage to be Jew-haters, in their very defense of the Jews. See, e.g., J.-P. Sartre, *Anti-Semite and Jew*, trans. George J. Becker (New York: Schocken Books, 1948). Fromm's foreword to the Bottomore edition is beneath comment (see iv–v). Against all these disgusting untruths stands the great question of old Gedali, "the little proprietor in smoked glasses": "The Revolution—we will say 'yes' to it, but are we to say 'no' to the Sabbath?" Read on:

"Yes, I cry to the Revolution. Yes, I cry to it, but it hides its face from Gedali and sends out on front nought but shooting . . . "

"The sunlight doesn't enter eyes that are closed," I answered the old man. "But we will cut open those closed eyes . . . "

"A Pole closed my eyes," whispered the old man, in a voice that was

into Man, without class. In Nietzsche, the metamorphosis *Judeo/ Christian* becomes yet another grandly articulated gesture by the reeducated classes to erase their historical memories.

Among our famous artists and social designers of contemporary 'values' schlock, metamorphoses of therapy grow less and less grandly articulated, downright crude. In the temporal open space between Jew and some hated after-Jew, there preach impresarios of unconscious Jew-bashing, innocent purveyors of a tradition they would excoriate if they knew about it.[10] One of the latest bashers uses the metamorphosis *Judeo-Christian/Mother Nature– destroyer.* Another uses the metamorphosis *Jew/Science.* If one or the other of you is, as I suspect, a Jew, however unwilling, then be glad you are still held by your name, responsible for practically everything, under the metamorphosis *good/evil,* by a lot of pip-

---

barely audible. "The Poles are bad-tempered dogs. They take the Jew and pluck out his beard, the curs! And now they are being beaten, the bad-tempered dogs. That is splendid, that is the Revolution. And then those who have beaten the Poles say to me: 'Hand your phonograph over to the State, Gedali . . . ' 'I am fond of music, Pani,' I say to the Revolution. 'You don't know what you are fond of, Gedali. I'll shoot you and then you'll know. I cannot do without shooting, because I am the Revolution.'"

"She cannot do without shooting, Gedali," I told the old man, "because she is the Revolution."

"But the Poles, kind sir, shot because they were the Counter-Revolution. You shoot because you are the Revolution. But surely the Revolution means joy. And joy does not like orphans in the house. Good men do good deeds. The Revolution is the good deed of good men. But good men do not kill. So it is bad people that are making the Revolution. But the Poles are bad people too. Then how is Gedali to tell which is Revolution and which is Counter-Revolution? I used to study the Talmud, I love Rashi's Commentaries and the books of Maimonides. And there are yet other understanding folk in Zhitomir. And here we are, all of us learned people, falling on our faces and crying out in a loud voice: 'Woe unto us, where is the joy-giving Revolution?'" [Isaac Babel, "Gedali," in *The Collected Stories*, trans. and ed. Walter Morison, introduction by Lionel Trilling (New York: The World Publishing Co., 1960), 70–71.]

Later in this book, I ask you the essential question about proprietorship: what is it you keep and do not keep?

10. I know for a fact, being one to all of them, that some of their best friends are Jews. Of course, it goes without saying that among the bashers are a large proportion of ex-Jews, reeducated, fairly rich wretches.

squeak successors of poor, unsteady-in-his-faithlessness Nietzsche. A sabbath Jew knows enough never to look so far forward
that he loses the sight of the past.

* *

By his very effort to end the Mosaic revolution, the formative
event, as he knew, in his primal history, Freud could not conclude
that Jewish morals were self-evident still. Other therapists are
not bound by the primal history in which Freud still belonged,
withal his struggle against it. I shall return shortly to what is at
stake for us, as theorists, in Freud's attempted break through his
primal history, an attempt about which he made a rather strangled
announcement in a preface, dated Rome, September 1913. In
his book version of the four essays composing *Totem and Taboo*,
what Freud announced as an "assured and exhaustive attempt" at
the solution of the "problem of taboo" was neither assured nor
exhaustive. Freud admitted that "social and technical advances
in human history have affected taboos far less than the totem."[11]
Finally, it was the social and psychological imperatives of the Mosaic revelation, continuing to operate as it did among Jews in a
compulsive fashion and rejecting certain unconscious motives,
that Freud blamed for his attempt to break with his primal history. Yet he himself asserted that his break left him still, psychologically, a Jew in the "very essence"[12] of that ancient condition,
which has resisted all deep-down change, until practically the end
of Freud's own era—and ours. For Freud shares with us the wish
to have our past and eat it too: the wish to break through and
remain the same in "very essence." Here is the chief among neurotic facts of the immediate past.

Fellow teachers of resistance: do not wait in suspense for the neurotic facts to reverse themselves. I do not doubt that they can be
reversed—and I would prefer them so, because I prefer a more
humane, less dynamic world, deeply graven interdicts etched in
superior and trustworthy characters. Do not count on me; I am

11. Freud, *Totem and Taboo*, SE, 13:xiv.
12. Ibid., xv.

not one of those characters; moreover, I do not know who they are and prefer not to know those who would tell me, straight out, they are the ones whom I, too, merely seek—never to find. I am at one with all you heterodoxologists. For me, too, orthodoxies of all sorts smell of the narrowness that they permit in their characters. Beyond all orthodoxies, rejected, the therapeutic is already widely accepted, beyond my power to stop. I am not an apostle and so cannot redirect the modern wish to obey some leader in a cult of disobedience toward a new learning of old obediences. My ideal-type consumes my meanings, which can have no authority on their own; the therapeutic can treat all meanings as equally authoritative. He is even capable of spraying himself with the smelliest little orthodoxies, ancient and modern, one treating with another in general assemblies of views.

* *

Applauded by academic and media enactors of preposterous entertainments, the dancers to any beat, each alone, compete against all, and all against self-denial, under various new, impersonal names; 'instinct' is only one new name for the original therapeutic dissolution of law and order. That dissolution had an institutional name: orgy.

Our orgies are highly intellectualized, like our mass-spectator sports. We are self-conscious orgiasts. Sex manuals sell profitably, even to the sophisticated. Conflicts among the 'risen gods' are our universal popular entertainment, the football of the reeducated classes. I prefer to watch football. What old cultic exercise is not now being practiced, under some newfangled name? Every cult, and cult object, has its rotating membership. But it is the rare old god who gives away shiny new interdicts; these are old coins, and not Rockefeller dimes distributed to cover some younger stinginess. We have long been told what is not to be done. Meaningful interdicts survive only as they are taught. To be constantly learned, by many, never once for all, they must be retaught by relatively few guiding cadres that practice what they teach and are willing to suffer, demonstrably, the consequences of their own inevitable malpractice.

Freud has given us a superb hint of a nonresponsible cadre, the therapists. In his theory of the inward historical genesis of morality, Freud mimed his own ancient, dying, interdictory father-god carried like law inside the psyche of the guiding cadre, the followers of Moses. His story of culture, in its origins, both reveals and conceals the end of a moral order first settled upon us, as our inheritance, by the history of Israel. Freud raised his ambivalence to bequeathed authority into an act of analytic genius: no one has concealed that act more artfully. It is in Freud's last testament to his own prototypal history, *Moses and Monotheism*, that we discover the ultimate murderer of Moses: Freud himself. His reluctance to publicize his hidden will is understandable; he almost succeeded in denying himself this model resolution, which might also have served the purpose of reviving the authority of his own past. In his way, ambivalently, Freud's own creative sense of guilt, his deepest reaction to the achievement of an imaginative repetition of the crime specific to his primal history, the 'crime' against the authority of Moses, survived in him to the absolute end of his life.[13] In the brilliance of his imaginative repetition of the primal crime, followed, inevitably in his case, by an immensely creative sense of guilt, Freud knew he was performing *like* but not *as* a criminal of the worst, most original kind.

* *

I have said that *there are no aggressions except as transgressions*; that is Rieff's first sociological law,[14] applicable to all public life. Against that first law, of public life, the most cultivated classes—our most progressive intellectual, scientific, and aesthetic cadres—have

13. See *Totem and Taboo*, 159, for Freud's speculation on the origins of the concept of 'crime'; the quotation marks around crime are Freud's, of course.

14. Rieff's first law of private life reads: *You only live once, if then*. Further exploring Rieff's first sociological law, of public life, the tragic fact seems to be that militant faiths (to be distinguished from therapies of militancy) have built in their transgressive operations as elaborately justified defenses of their own interdictory institutions; but, here, the militancy of the Communist state-party apparatus ought not to be confused with any church militancy. The two types of militancy are quite different, yet there is always a potential of connection between the militant and his opposite number, the military man. Trotsky's

been schooled to trust the interdicts only as dead god-terms: their death is the price of our trust. Here lies the Enlightenment. For the sake of law and order, justice and reverence inseparable from their god-terms, we mere teachers, Jews of culture, influential and eternally powerless, have no choice except to think defensively: how to keep ourselves from being overwhelmed by that unique complex of orgy and routine which constitutes modernization and

---

mythic image was so compelling because he combined, in his swift dramatic career, the apparently clashing roles of emancipative militant and disciplined military man. It is the fate of the successful militant to put on a uniform, and to exchange his credal discipline for an organizational one. The pathos of the Trotskyist movement was that it was truly a credal discipline, and therefore at war with its own organizational discipline. What the Trotskyist despised most in the Stalinist was his complete sellout of credal discipline for organizational; yet the confusion of inner and outer, creed and institution, is devastating in Trotskyist theory, deriving as it does from the Marxist optimism that there is no inherent tension between inner meaning and outer expression.

Trotsky remains the legendary non-Jewish Jew, like Marx, essentially interested in what there is to defeat, not in what there is to win. I fully expect our home-bred revolutionary gurus to rehabilitate one of the big winners in the world-historical *Masses/One* elimination tournament, Stalin, as a great chief who did his thing in order to get The People together. The white militants have taken up their positions outside, and against, what they mean to denounce as well as describe under the title "White Civilization"; in particular those denunciations are against ideals in all their disguises—and, in the self-hatred of the white militants, against all white chiefs. At last, in the third (i.e., 'colored') world, the revolutionary gurus have found a place that is beyond good and evil. It is 'whiteness', the abstraction of Life color, that is to blame for everything that is not beyond good and evil. The struggle for power within the third world is acclaimed as the healthy expression of repressed instinct, while in our world that struggle is denounced as the unhealthy repression of instinct. Revolutionary rhetoric changes into therapeutic: proletarian, black, and id become a triune deity of vengeance against white, repressive ideals. It is this triune deity that dominates pop culture. For a number of years, thanks to a French movie, Algiers became the New Jerusalem, even for those who had never had word from the old. You see how, in *Algiers*, as the churches were once the Bible of pious illiterates, so now the mass media, staffed largely by paratherapists, self-selected for their mission, express the instinctual and organize the higher pathology. Everyone knows there is a link between publicity and pathology. Temporarily, I trust, the publicists of principled transgressive behavior have won their long struggle against capital punishment. The logic of their struggle, and their victory, has depended upon a widespread acceptance of the criminal ritually burdened with his role as a Cain figure. In his role, the criminal becomes the *victim/hero* of The System, driven to a propaganda of the deed against it for the sake of The System itself. What reactionary idiot does not know, after

its totalitarian character type, using the language of trust against authority—without which trust cannot exist.

* *

To move backward, along the old road, is not possible. We know that old ideals do not simply repeat themselves; they are reborn. Should they be reborn? Have we departed from positions so far better than those toward which we are moving? Beyond saying 'Inquire', who dares say 'Return'?* Prophetic orders and their

---

introductory sociology, (a) that The System makes us all criminals; (b) that the criminal is he who is caught, for the sake of our continued success in remaining uncaught. Thus the late twentieth-century metamorphosis, liberal and pre-therapeutic, *hidden (or abstract) criminality/normality*. What is then confessed, normally, is *false guilt*, the form of testimony against The System.

---

*This is a reference to the closing paragraphs of Max Weber's 1918 essay "Science as a Vocation":

> To the person who cannot bear the fate of the times like a man, one must say: may he rather return silently, without the usual publicity build-up of renegades, but simply and plainly. The arms of the old churches are opened widely and compassionately for him. After all, they do not make it hard for him. One way or another he has to bring his "intellectual sacrifice"—that is inevitable. If he can really do it, we shall not rebuke him. For such an intellectual sacrifice in favor of an unconditional religious devotion is ethically quite a different matter than the evasion of the plain duty of intellectual integrity, which sets in if one lacks the courage to clarify one's own ultimate standpoint and rather facilitates this duty by feeble relative judgments. In my eyes, such religious return stands higher than the academic prophecy, which does not clearly realize that in the lecture-rooms of the university no other virtue holds but plain intellectual integrity. Integrity, however, compels us to state that for the many who today tarry for new prophets and saviors, the situation is the same as resounds in the beautiful Edomite watchman's song of the period of exile that has been included among Isaiah's oracles:
> He calleth to me out of Seir, Watchman, what of the night? The watchman said, The morning cometh, and also the night: if ye will enquire, enquire ye: return, come.
> The people to whom this was said [i.e., the Jews] has enquired and tarried for more than two millennia, and we are shaken when we realize its fate. From this we want to draw the lesson that nothing is gained by yearning and tarrying alone, and we shall act differently. We shall set to work and meet the "demands of the day," in human relations as well as in our vocation. This, however, is plain and simple, if each finds and obeys the demon who holds the fibers of his very life.

(For full citation, see introduction, n. 12.)—*Eds.*

compelling god-terms have ceased to recall us; therefore, it may be said that they have ceased to exist. We exist only inside orders from which we can depart; that is the sociological sense in which all 'gods' may be said to exist. Our contemporaries discovered long ago that the prophets were really our forerunners, quite progressive chaps, perhaps revolutionary, as Jesus was. Thus Marx is in 'the prophetic tradition'. Again: what rubbish! Critical praxis has no descent from prophetic recalling. In a contrast every talmudist will recognize, the Talmud is an infinitely rich document, the assenting continuation of infinitely rich documents; the Talmud is not critical commentary. True criticism is constituted, first, by repeating what is already authoritatively known. The great teacher is he who, because he carries in himself what is already known, can transfer it to his student; that inwardness is his absolute and irreducible authority. If a student fails to re-cognize that authority, then he is not a student. A teacher is not a teacher in the degree that privileged knowledge is not in himself. 'Charisma', that which cannot be criticized, always gathers around the rich. What money means in the world outside, privileged knowledge should mean in the academy. In a true academy, the teacher is not to be criticized, except as he has not become authoritative enough, in himself, repeating to his successors of what was repeated to him, the knowledge that is in repetition.[15]

* *

In our time, theater, too, may become a social science. Such an advance, beyond the unseriousness of art to a superior make-believe, the sociodrama of everyday life, would be yet another

---

15. "When R. Meir died there were no more makers of parables. When Ben Azzai died there were no more diligent students. When Ben Zoma died there were no more expounders. When R. Joshua died goodness departed from the world. When Rabban Simeon b. Gamaliel died the locust came and troubles grew many. When R. Eleazar b. Azariah died wealth departed from the Sages. When R. Akiba died the glory of the Law ceased. When R. Hanina b. Dosa died the men of good deeds ceased. When R. Jose Katnutha died there were no more saintly ones. When Rabban Johanan b. Zakkai died the splendour of wisdom ceased. When Rabban Gamaliel the Elder died, the glory of the Law ceased

final solution to a problem left to us solution-spotters by our pre-decessors, the Christian cultists, remissive spiritualizers of Jewish law and order, for the sake of deeper interdictory thrusts by Jesus: what constitutes greatness? A therapist would be just 'great' in a sense special and functional: for the relief of his client from the prototypal series of relations to figures of authority.

Older and obsolete versions of the problem of what constitutes greatness are hidden in such innocent remarks as Buber's: "To claim to be the Messiah is fundamentally incompatible with Messiahship." We longtime students of grace know how truly Buber once spoke—if he meant by messiah a transgressive behaviorist. But Jesus was a tremendous re-cognizer of the interdicts. He tells us that he came explicitly to deepen law, which he thought had grown too external, not to abolish it. Our modern claimants are mere products of messiahship situations, of the distress caused by failing interdicts. How health-giving it is to have so many messiahs, proclaiming unambiguously, as Jesus never did, their fundamental compatibility with messiahship—totally reversing the meaning of messiahship, which is inseparable from interdic-tory re-cognition. We ordinary, everyday transgressors—we can all be messiahs now. Nothing is easier; we need only publicize our transgressions with our distress. If we can add stress to distress (things must get worse before they can get better), then the most transgressive may even become professional counselors to others on how to get beyond the old messiah role. Barth's black doctor is a messiah transmogrified into a therapist. Why not Caliban as Prospero? It cannot matter, no more to Barth as novelist than to Weber as sociologist, whether the black doctor is a hoaxer or not. In these proclamations, both artistic and scientific, we can read the historical transition from nineteenth-century religions of criticism to late twentieth-century therapies.

* *

---

and purity and abstinence died. When R. Ishmael b. Piabi died the splendour of the priesthood ceased. When Rabbi died, humility and the shunning of sin ceased." [Text from the Mishnah.—*Eds.*]

A radical aestheticizing of life, the established culture of the rich, Gala indeed,* is very near the anti-creed of therapeutic action that I have tried to imagine here, as I did first in the final chapter of *The Mind of the Moralist*, then further in the two main theoretical chapters of *The Triumph of the Therapeutic*, and yet further in my essay "The Impossible Culture."[16] Compare this man, new in his willed pursuit of whatever presents itself to pursue, to Babel's naïve old Jew Gedali, so obstinate that, though almost blind, he refuses the saving new vision that is The Revolution brought to him by a sophisticated young Jew, equipped with spectacles. Old Gedali knows, as you recollect, that The Revolution respects no sabbaths; and, though weary of his resistance to the relentless move of History, Gedali remains a sabbatarian.

How are you on the trivial old question of sabbath keeping? Is any order worthy of the name without its strict sabbaths? *No* is the first word of resistance; it remains the word that needs deepest, freshest, most constant relearning—and those learned in its ways—to articulate any culture. *No* has to be studied and interpreted almost without break, although it too must exist in a sense heavily qualified, under the sabbath rule of remissions. The Galas and Jakes of our virtual reality have gone a long way toward

16. See my introductory essay to Oscar Wilde, *The Soul of Man under Socialism and Other Essays* [reprinted below, pp. 142–65]. See, further, everything I have written, and may write, of course. I cannot discuss here the meaning of speed in the culture of the rich, except to point out that everything speedy contradicts the pace of life in the academy.

---

*Gala refers to Leone Gala, of Luigi Pirandello's 1916 play *The Rules of the Game*. For Rieff, Gala and Jake Horner both represent "premonitory expressions of infinite plasticity." "Considered typologically," Rieff has explained above (*Fellow Teachers*, 127–28), "the earlier construct, Leone Gala, is an advance over the later Jacob Horner. . . . Pirandello is the greater theorist because Gala is already his own therapist. The doctor, in *The Rules of the Game*, is reduced to the familiar type of naïve old positivist sawbones, with his bag of shiny surgical instruments and no more idea than Watson of what is going on in his friend's mind. Gala has long solved the mystery of his life. To keep up the pretense that he has something more to learn, Gala engages in a parody of an aristocratic agon with his invincibly ignorant, scarcely literate chef; that agon runs parallel to the play, showing the audience how anyone has an equal and instantaneous right to any part, or role, however unprepared they are to act it, so long as there are others to interpret it according to need."—*Eds.*

inverting the authority of the sabbath into the danger of immobility. The answering *No* of our credal culture has become—in its uniquely profane, anti-credal context—a questioning neurotic inhibition. Viewed from a position inside Gedali's old credal culture, Jake and his sort are the most malignant strain of all, young men who, having accepted the disenchantment of the world, would act out the functional equivalents of all enchantments: preposterous sexpressional parodies of infinite 'values'. We are on the verge of solving the ancient problem of what is a good society. When orders of authority, uniquely unchangeable, are resolved into therapies, entirely changeable, then the 'good' will no longer be a problem—the good is resolved into the metamorphosis *input/output*. A good man is one who knows how to keep changing inclusively, which is to say—thrusting toward everything.

You may wish to call this vitalist tactic after one of its more portentous names: *existential freedom*. Such freedom involves the embrace of meaninglessness, entirely unauthorized decisions to do that which has not been recalled. Jake's decision to try to prevent Rennie's suicide, after she has conceived by his most casual act, appears entirely unauthorized. His decision for Rennie's life resembles one of Forster's casually announced deaths: what-is-not suddenly appears and takes over the action. Free as we are, why not suicide? What—more precisely, *who*—is to prevent us? Where there has been no personal justification, uniquely unchangeable and only elaborately interpretable, there is no authority.

* *

By this time, there are no messages to receive from our arts, not even indecipherable ones; instead, there are scenarios. Who among us older folks can forget the scenarios acted out by the Nazis? That was art transferred to life, marvelous scenarios. More scenarios will be acted out, I think. The genius of mass political dramaturgy passed to the New Right in the 1930s; in the 1970s, theatrical genius is entirely the prop of the New Left. Extremes meet in the age of the therapeutic, doctrinal rigor displaced by its functional equivalent—a psychotechnics of acting out. Angela Davis is billed as the lovely leading lady of the progressive American and world-historical stage. To act professionally in the real world is to protest, something or other. Even verdicts in favor of one's own side must be protested; this is what it means to be a political kunstler. The emergent role-player will be capable of stepping beside himself or herself and, at the same time, roar indignantly against anything. Hitler put this acting ability in all its power to work wonders when he answered an early, earnest follower's inquiry about what to tell uptight bourgeois[17] when they asked what the Nazi movement stood for. "Tell them," roared Hitler, "that we are against them!" There spoke the uniquely modern revolutionary. Anything transgressive is creative. As a slogan, 'Make Love' is as transgressive as 'Make War'. It is aimed *against* an interdict and proclaims none; 'Not War' patently excludes guerrilla war and terrorist activity. Moreover, 'Make Love' is the original slogan of universal private war, each against each. These private warriors, my young radical acquaintance who would 'Make Love Not War', are ardent public supporters of Fatah and the PLF. (And most of my young radical acquaintance are 'Jewish'.) At this historical moment, you may choose this transgressive style: *sexual/political.* There are others: *economic/political,* for example. In due course, the various transgressive styles will converge in public actings out, as they did, premonitorily, in the Nazi movement. What splendid erotic manicons those Germans were: upon being selected for the Feldkorps, my aunts committed suicide. Beautiful women they were; the eroticism of the National Socialists was the key to the deadliness of their politics. Unbounded love makes death. Admitted: I may lean a little toward the oversensitive side, on the *love/death* metamorphosis.

After "to act or not to act" the next sociological question not to be begged is: "What humiliations shall humans tolerate?" (Put negatively, this question would read: "How are ordinary men to bear the future, without their stigmata?") That all have to tolerate some goes without saying; none of us shall live entirely self-assured, within stable reciprocities of respect. To be humiliated

---

17. The precedent, confident rather than pejorative, 'value-relational' name for our class was 'proper'.

is to accept the experience of being treated disrespectfully by an other. The question appears in the degree and quality of humiliations we shall tolerate. Some humiliations may serve us well; others make us ill; all therapies include some tactic of humiliation and, therefore, are themselves hazards the ill run in attempting to get well.

Think of what it is to be totally humiliated. It is a positive absence of respect, a lowering, some sixth hour so complete in its inferior treatment of those made superior by it that the one resistance still possible at such a time, the possibility that remains, to defend your self-respect, the utopia of all resistances, is suicide. When life becomes impossible, yet unconstrained by the utopian possibility of death, then the experience of being lowered is best seen through therapies of survival. Here is the alternative utopian possibility, not survival in itself but the guiltlessness that may develop best through therapies of survival. If such therapies succeed, then a survivor would be in the position of knowing perfectly well what he ought not to have done and yet having done it; this transgressiveness would be the one possibility remaining in the field against its utopian contrary.

My aunts died promptly at their own hands; they declined absolutely to tolerate their therapy of survival, which, after all, would not have been so terrible, if you come to think about it. By way of developing a contrasting model of conduct, think for a moment of their father. In Dachau he appeared to tolerate every brand of humiliation lowered upon him without thereby seeming lowered. On his behalf, I can say of my grandfather that he did not think to resist. On the most generous interpretation of it, my grandfather's act of resistance went no further than to pray to his Sovereign for an end to his life, to be spared more. He was not spared.

* *

Who are to be our truth tellers—better say, our guilt provokers? I do not know. I am without authority; moreover, I do not seek what cannot be sought. Authority is given or it is fraudulent; it cannot be taken by force or ambition. That was one of Weber's main errors in his theory of charisma.[18] In the absence of truth tellers, however, waiting their reappearance, we teachers can give some preparatory thought to how we may defend ourselves against a culture destroying itself in the dynamics of contempt, dissociating justice from reverence, associating charisma with publicity and power. We must begin to know again that lawful authority is being progressively destroyed by criminal power, which is no monopoly of the 'Right' but equally of the 'Left'.

In the absence of a supreme interdictory figure, another Moses, with his disciples, a defense by Jews of culture against our democratic orgiasts[19] may be reordered, their preposterous position-taking constrained, from the outside in—by a revival of severe codes of law. It is barely possible that interdictory forms, without which relations between reverence and justice, culture and social system, cannot be maintained, may be prepared from the outside in, as if by the Stanislavsky method. Imagine reinstalled, as among true primitives, a severe code of role limit that would carry with it severe penalties for deviation. Such a code would have to be strictly retributive. To prepare for this return, and renewal, of

18. That theory is best interpreted under the book-laden metamorphosis *Protestant sentimentalism/modern sociology.* I have tried to make this interpretation in a cluttered eruditional warehouse of a book, complete with a passionate chapter on Lutheran jurisprudence, titled *Charisma,* not to be published until it is as tight as a drum and yet without sounding in the slightest 'charismatic'; I shall probably fail to make it so—but one thing the academy is for, precisely, are such failures. [Eventually published as *Charisma: The Gift of Grace, and How It Has Been Taken from Us* (New York: Pantheon Books, 2007).—*Eds.*] I might learn something in the attempt, over the years. Ours is a fast pace in a slow business. But this is only to say how we enchant ourselves with our breakthroughs; privately, I make about one a day. Is writing a fertility ritual? Then file away your children, where they are safe from harming. Why publish? That is a real question for all scholars of meanings; for all intellectuals, as well. The world is broken-through enough. With so many authors, who remains behind to read? Every man his own original: that is democracy sold out, and an impossible culture. Where do I return my vote? The more original the book, the less justified we are in publishing it. Do not blame the publishers for your thrustings; justifications are not their business.

19. That orgy is the one, only and original, totally democratic institution—the common utopia of all our gurus, 'fascist' and 'liberationalist'—is the key to a revival of interdictive knowledge.

the interdicts, we scholars in the humane studies might begin by examining the culturally subversive idea of rehabilitation. The result might be to replace rehabilitation by repayment in kind for transgressions committed; there is an original idea.

* *

What happened was bad enough. The Christian mystery cult evolved into the most terrible rationalizing of transgressiveness ever to curse our culture. Nietzsche knew that Christendom's love was a covert form of making war on culture in any form, an expression of the most terrible hatred, envy, revenge. How sad that Nietzsche remained Christian enough to blame the proud, elitist culture of Israel for this curse, derived, not from Hellenism, but from ex-Jewry. Jew-hatred remains the deepest transgressive motif of Christian Love—and, in succession, of Western organizations of Humanity, including the Marxist. This terrible hatred was directed at the highest, the noblest aspects of human achievement: it challenged the order of reverence and justice. Nothings would be instant everythings by imposing a love that was entirely mendacious.

Nietzsche might have learned more than he did from the case of *Saul/Paul*, that ultimately concerned, universalizing democrat of spirituality, genius taking its supreme form as an apostle, credal organizer, founding church father and still enemy-in-chief of the Jews. Nietzsche missed the point that Jew-hatred rests its case on non-Jewish Jews; they were non-Jewish Jews who first confirmed to the world at large a fundamental change in the classical pattern of hatred, Rome against Jerusalem. It was in rejecting their very own messiah that Israel became proud, stiff-necked, a distancing people.

For persisting in their interdictory-remissive way—despite political defeat and amid the inducements of a more entertaining culture—the Jews were despised by the ancient Romans, who were the most political of people and knew, therefore, how to use culture as well as religion politically. There was something different, however, about the early Christian animus against the Jews. The subject of the Christian cultus was himself a non-Jewish Jew, a victory in particular over every particularity, beginning (and ending) with the particularity of the Jews. In his victory, Jesus represented the defeat of the Jews in their particularity, as Jews; this is very different from representing the defeated Jews. (Cf. the Nietzschean symbolic.) On the contrary, all that a Jew now needed to do in order to escape his defeat was to join in the victory cult of the non-Jewish Jew. What a tempting model, both of humiliation and of deceitful escapes from humiliation. Equally deceitful: assertions of Jewish 'faith' as a matter of pride in a resistance at least as necessary to the cultus as to the Jews themselves. The humiliation of Jesus went no further, according to the Christian cultus, than the irony of his sovereignty over the Jews, who had rejected Him. 'King of the Jews' intended to deprive the Jews of their spiritual kingdom. In his millennial resistance to that deprivation, the Jew became a negative and implicit performer of the positive and explicit cult. By whatever they appeared to do, the humiliation of the Jews was deepened. According to the Christian symbolic, which Romans learned to understand well enough, the Jews had not only lost; more important, as Jews, they could never win. Who can bear to be on the side of a loser as perpetual as history itself? All the world hates a loser or, at best, condescends to him. To be a loser does not imply defeat in the simple sense, during every round of history; rather, it implies having to walk through history as if on eggs. The early Christian Jew-hatred, integral to *Saul/Paul*'s victory over the 'Judaizers', expresses a fundamental egalitarian Christian rancor against the internal distancing symbolic of the chosen people and, at its full transgressive implication, against the Christ of the ex-Jews and their democratically accepted cult followers. It is in this sense that faith in Christ—and the organization of that faith—is ineluctably anti-Jewish.

* *

Conrad's personifications, in *Heart of Darkness*, mind us to the emptiness of the man of power. In the vacant immediacy of Kurtz, Marlow witnesses for us a mystifier of flesh, consuming flesh. Kurtz dies erotically, of power exhaustion. Desire has fed fully on itself. Kurtz's case was moral cancer, the total consumer consumed. European man achieved the 'natural' by carrying 'civilization' to unprogressive cultures; those cultures sometimes even appeared to welcome the 'natural man' (who, often between the sixteenth and twentieth centuries, could achieve nothing back home in Europe), perhaps even allowing him a self-deification, as in the case of Kurtz. Compare this perfection of the transgressive with the mysterious restraint Marlow believes must be at work inside his black (sometime cannibal) boatmen.

The Africans who sacrificed themselves, perhaps fascinated, to Kurtz had not that resistance which is the object of Marlow's journey toward Kurtz—precisely to test himself, his resistance, against the announced fascination of Kurtz's transgressiveness. Although their defenses are entirely incomprehensible to him, Marlow sees how his boatmen endure the ultimate temptation: of survival. They will neither kill nor eat him in order to survive. The reasons for his safety with them, however precarious, remain concealed—concealed even from Conrad, godlike as he is in his authorship. Marlow is privileged to know a moment in which the interdicts stripped bare, to their form, hold—without the passage of a word, in silence. (My paternal grandfather, the aforementioned old grad of Dachau, a presence among his junior colleagues, told me of moments in that institution when the interdicts, stripped bare, held. Tell me: did you imagine I pick my theories out of a bag of books? Books are, at best, mere life analogues; do not trust to books. But how privileged we are to enjoy the concealments of the book.)

* *

As if to specify the target of this course, the student acolytes of these holy men have concentrated upon the destruction of our temple of feeling intellect. Make no mistake: the figure under siege in our culture is not Johnny Carson but Lionel Trilling, superior teacher and leading American Jew of culture. For us pedagogically inclined Jews of culture, England was Zion, the fantasy fatherland; perhaps it was only the Pax Britannica, seen from the top of the Hawksmoor towers.

Authority attracts; authority long established, woven into manners that cultivate men, has the virtue of attracting those who need a shelter from the crudities of power not yet refined. High culture must stand a political test: what brakes, not counterpower, there are in it against both anarchy and the warring state. A warring culture is bent on its own resolution, in politics. A culture can be 'strong' only in a sense related, but not reducible, to politics. I have opened the question of this relation early in this text, specially in reference to academic side taking. I do not doubt that English high culture has declined with the decline of empire. With the dissolution of the Pax Britannica, the manners of young Oxonians grow visibly more American, specially among those who, suffering identity shrinkage under the retreat of English authority, talk themselves into easy hostilities against its callow successor, American power; those Young England hostilities are easy and, at the same time, imitate the worst in American society because American authority does not yet exist, while its parent, English, has failed. Our power is resented not least because it does not present to the less powerful anything in it superior to its mere existence. On the other hand, American culture is more therapeutically advanced, without authority, and precisely for this reason it is not resisted in other cultures less advanced in our way. While the others hate us politically, they imitate us culturally.

I sit, some part of each year, looking out on my defaulted second Zion from its Masada, All Souls. My participant observations have taught me something about the arbitrariness and pathos of old authority when it will not stay far enough in arrears; it is there, at the old top, where revolutions, cultural and political, begin, visible everywhere except in the blind eye of the defaulter. Marx knew this; his revolutionary theory, in the name of the proletariat, was addressed to the young intellectuals at the old top, or near enough to that top for the management of inverting movements. With what art Marx wrote and schemed. He is an original. For his revolutionary purposes, the first explicit task of Marx, as theorist, was to make the bourgeoisie ridiculous in its own mind's eye. His form of argument makes massive mockeries, which have become a staple of the bourgeois style. You see that there is *fame/money* now in the Revolution move. Poor Marx; he was born too soon.

So far as the privileged youth of England, as in America, continue to be taught to feel relieved by their disinheritance, authority in default raises itself to a pedagogic principle. Under the pedagogy of defaulting authority, a suicide in principle, the young can assume, without trial, the experience of being a self-deceitful Jacob: these Jacobs celebrate their fatherlessness even as they adopt new fantasy father figures and lands. The most aggressive and least psychologically stable[20] among the reeducated young have adopted that most ambiguous fantasy father figure of revolutionaries: History itself. Our Jacobs aspire still, as the Marxists did, to become the favorite children of History, the father enacting his own defeat in order to prepare the sons for unbroken victories; under this default of authority, victory becomes final. These young, being doctrinally young, cannot think how they can win and yet lose at the same time.

From its beginnings, Marxist theory was toned by this fantastic response to the default of a History it read too easily and with too great an interest in conclusions: however unkindly the father predicate may act, its secret struggle, hidden from itself, as in 'ideology', is to produce the conditions of its own defeat. A defeated parent, training children to reciprocate with victory, is the most helpful kind. The one and only reason that the 'proletariat' will not be defeated is that it constitutes the youngest class; after its victory, primal history will produce no more favored sons. What

---

20. Sociology, my discipline, has a special problem: the disproportionate number of disturbed young people who seek to study (i.e., change the world) under this rubric. Much of modern sociology is part of the symptoms to which its concepts are addressed. Sociology, if it succeeds, demands situations, roles, and the like. By the very spread of its own namings, modern sociology treats the world as if it exists between quotation marks. 'Value' is the main term in that treatment, money its scarcely concealed reality. Abusing the science of sociology, you may become famous in one of two ways: by investigating 'values' or by being investigated. Better be the investigator; the investment is high, but the returns greater. Investigators, like chaplains in the army, are not the sort of people to whom you want to go when you have a problem; but they are likely to seek you out. Who is not now playing an investigator and investigated? This is the sociological meaning of being both master and crippled pet.

romance could be more childish, more self-deceitful, than that of the Jacobs? Yet our Jacobs celebrate their 'honesty' and each is inclined to pronounce himself a more ethical I than Thou. What an orgy of a dream: each kid his own authority. Imagine grandfather Abraham reduced to saying: "Play nice."

Under the most extreme pressure, survival in the world as it is, as in the case of Sodom, grandfather Abraham pleads brilliantly against the strictest and most complete punishment of broken interdicts. Although Israel becomes Jehovah's favorite people through, and only through, the commandments revealed—and in the establishment of a cult proper to those commandments— grandfather Abraham understands that there are saving concealments in that revelation. At least so I understand Abraham's brilliant defense, standing before the Chief Justice, pleading in the case of Sodom. That defense is not of Sodom—that goes without further saying. But Abraham grasps the tragic danger of judgment: "Wilt thou sweep away good and bad together?" There follows the grandest and most concise of all theoretical efforts in defense of culture: Abraham's supposition after supposition, qualitative and quantitative, that for the sake of first fifty and finally ten just men who may be found there, the city is not to be destroyed. This is grander than anything Plato imagines about justice, because it is so indecisive; Abraham's brilliant casuistry will never make political sense.[21]

Abraham assumes that those ten are also hidden from themselves, that they do not know they are God's favorites and are still in the doomed city, their goodness unremarked. Yet a true Jew is he who is such in externals.

This is to point out, as best I can, how complex is Abraham's call. The old rabbinical truth tellers grasped the intricacy of Abraham's call and tried to teach it in their own interpretations of what the original story means. One of these stories has Abraham teaching God that if he wants to maintain the world, then the interdicts cannot be maintained without specific remissions. Supreme authority, according to *Abrahamic/rabbinic* theory, cannot

21. Genesis 18:23–33.

be simple; it must be cultivated in its judgments or the world cannot endure. Fanaticism is not superior to the absence of convictions—as we interpreters of the original Abrahamic case might reconstruct it.[22]

I am merely retelling motifs from Israel's family romance. Under the Freudian conception of family romance, we can grasp in a very different and competing way the psychodynamics of the principle that authority attracts: the romancing child invariably adopts fantasy parents from classes or characters higher than those of his biological sponsors. Who among us has not been switched, however momentarily, in the cradle? My parents were not nearly good enough for me; I was lucky to have grandfathers. Father figures do their difficult job best if sons, with them, are subject to grandfather figures, who, in their own submission to a tradition at once credal and oral, will stand for a strictly limited amount of new nonsense from their successors.

22. In my theoretical work, I have not yet been able to cope with the prototypal Jacob metamorphosis. How to grasp the original Jacob's revolutionary bout of disrespect: imagine wrestling with God—the real and ideal God—as the central act of your 'identity crisis' and demanding to be blessed by name! Abraham knew that even argument (his or any other) has its limits. What follows from the fact that Jacob is the most successful of our founding fathers— and a rather questionable brother? How should I know? I am not learned in the tradition.

The Impossible Culture: Wilde as a Modern Prophet

I shall begin by quoting at length from Edward Carson's[1] cross-examination of Wilde during the first of the three trials when Wilde was still plaintiff in that ruinous case of libel he brought against the Marquess of Queensberry. Then we shall see at once the quality of Wilde's wit, his view on certain aspects of culture, and how far we have come toward Wilde's view in the three-quarters of a century since he became something less than a martyr and more than a victim.

> *Wilde:* "I do not believe that any book or work of art ever had any effect whatever on morality."

1. Edward Henry Carson, Q.C. (1863–1928), later Lord Carson. Carson had been Wilde's contemporary at Trinity College, Dublin, in the seventies and probably shared a general reluctance to take Queensbury's defense. The case taken, he attacked, through Wilde's art, the doctrine of life celebrated in that art.

All three trials of Oscar Wilde were of a man who "stood in symbolic relations to the art and culture of my age." Knowing himself to be a "symbolic figure," always on stage in a life representing the art of brilliant comedy, Wilde rightly took as the vital issue his justification of life as an aesthetic, rather than moral, phenomenon.

Edward Carson, too, was a symbolic figure. The philistine barrister represented life justified as a moral phenomenon. With the instinct of a great advocate, Carson took aim at Wilde's artistic acceptance of all experiences. That acceptance required a tone of subtlety and nuance, a nobility of manner that would limit the danger of moving in strange perspectives. The tone of Wilde's homosexual affairs, not least with Queensberry's son Lord Alfred Douglas, appears ignoble. Lord Alfred was a bad actor and made ugly scenes. In the Bosie affair, Wilde found no brilliant comedy; rather, "a revolting and sinister tragedy . . . stripped of that mask of joy and pleasure" behind which he saw, too late, the horror of that carnality we, with him, have learned to call "hatred."

Through Carson's questions, we may see represented articulate old suspicions of the truth of masks that have all but lost their voice in our culture. Car-

Carson: "Am I right in saying that you do not consider the effect in creating morality or immorality?"

Wilde: "Certainly, I do not."

Carson: "So far as your works are concerned, you pose as not being concerned about morality or immorality?"

Wilde: "I do not know whether you use the word 'pose' in any particular sense."

Carson: "It is a favourite word of your own?"

Wilde: "Is it? I have no pose in this matter. In writing a play or a book, I am concerned entirely with literature—that is, with art. I aim not at doing good or evil, but at trying to make a thing that will have some quality of beauty."

Carson: "Listen, sir. Here is one of the 'Phrases and Philosophies for the Use of the Young' which you contributed: 'Wickedness is a myth invented by good people to account for the curious attractiveness of others.' You think that true?"

Wilde: "I rarely think that anything I write is true."

Carson: "Did you say 'rarely'?"

Wilde: "I said 'rarely,' I might have said 'never'—not true in the actual sense of the word."

Carson: "'Religions die when they are proved to be true.' Is that true?"

Wilde: "Yes; I hold that. It is a suggestion towards a philosophy of the absorption of religions by science, but it is too big a question to go into now."

---

son stood square for those external sanctions and sacred commands that Wilde would not admit: unadmitted even as necessary fictions of limit upon his search for modes of "self-realization" so fresh that they aspired to self-creation. For all his cold questioning, the victorious philistine kept a merciful sense of fair play. "Cannot you let up on the fellow now?" Carson asked Sir Frank Lockwood, the Solicitor-General. "He has suffered a great deal."

So far as he realized himself in the Wilde affair, Lord Alfred Douglas, too, rises to the rank of a symbol. It was from this nemesis that Wilde suffered the hatred of father figures complicit in "the love that dare not speak its name."

Suppose Wilde's love life, with both sexes, exemplified a law in which this self-proclaimed "born antinomian" believed: the enlightened modern law of continuity, rather than opposition, between evil and good. Then might "all men kill the thing they love." It was under this profanation of "thou shalt not kill" that Wilde became the victim of his lover and, in turn, Constance Wilde became his victim.

Carson: "Do you think that was a safe axiom to put forward for the philosophy of the young?"

Wilde: "Most stimulating."

Carson: "If one tells the truth, one is sure, sooner or later, to be found out?"

Wilde: "That is a pleasing paradox, but I do not set very high store on it as an axiom."

Carson: "Is it good for the young?"

Wilde: "Anything is good that stimulates thought in whatever age."

Carson: "Whether moral or immoral?"

Wilde: "There is no such thing as morality or immorality in thought. There is immoral emotion."

Carson: "Pleasure is the only thing one should live for?"

Wilde: "I think that the realization of oneself is the prime aim of life, and to realize oneself through pleasure is finer than to do so through pain. I am, on that point, entirely on the side of the ancients—the Greeks. It is a pagan idea."

Carson: "A truth ceases to be true when more than one person believes in it?"

Wilde: "Perfectly. That would be my metaphysical definition of truth; something so personal that the same truth could never be appreciated by two minds."

Carson: "The condition of perfection is idleness: the aim of perfection is youth?"

Wilde: "Oh, yes; I think so. Half of it is true. The life of contemplation is the highest life, and so recognized by the philosopher."

Carson: "There is something tragic about the enormous number of young men there are in England at the present moment who start life with perfect profiles, and end by adopting some useful profession?"

Wilde: "I should think that the young have enough sense of humour."

Carson: "You think that is humorous?"

Wilde: "I think it is an amusing paradox, an amusing play on words."

Carson: "What would anybody say would be the effect of *Phrases and Philosophies* taken in connexion with such an article as *The Priest and the Acolyte?*"

Wilde: "Undoubtedly it was the idea that might be formed that made me object so strongly to the story. I saw at once that maxims that were perfectly nonsensical, paradoxical, or anything you like, might be read in conjunction with it."

Carson: "After the criticisms that were passed on *Dorian Gray,* was it modified a good deal?"

Wilde: "No. Additions were made. In one case it was pointed out to me—not in a newspaper or anything of that sort, but by the only critic of the century whose opinion I set high, Mr. Walter Pater—that a certain passage was liable to misconstruction, and I made an addition."

Carson: "This is in your introduction to *Dorian Gray:* 'There is no such thing as a moral or an immoral book. Books are well written or badly written.' That expresses your view?"

Wilde: "My view on art, yes."

Carson: "Then, I take it, that no matter how immoral a book may be, if it is well written, it is, in your opinion, a good book?"

Wilde: "Yes, if it were well written so as to produce a sense of beauty, which is the highest sense of which a human being can be capable. If it were badly written, it would produce a sense of disgust."

Carson: "Then a well-written book putting forward perverted moral views may be a good book?"

Wilde: "No work of art ever puts forward views. Views belong to people who are not artists."

Carson: "A perverted novel might be a good book?"

Wilde: "I don't know what you mean by a 'perverted' novel."

Carson: "Then I will suggest *Dorian Gray* as open to the interpretation of being such a novel?"

Wilde: "That could only be to brutes and illiterates. The views of Philistines on art are incalculably stupid."

Carson: "An illiterate person reading *Dorian Gray* might consider it such a novel?"

Wilde: "The views of illiterates on art are unaccountable. I am concerned only with my view of art. I don't care two-pence what other people think of it."

Carson: "The majority of persons would come under your definition of Philistines and illiterates?"

Wilde: "I have found wonderful exceptions."

Carson: "Do you think that the majority of people live up to the position you are giving us?"

Wilde: "I am afraid they are not cultivated enough."

Carson: "Not cultivated enough to draw the distinction between a good book and a bad book?"

Wilde: "Certainly not."

Carson: "The affection and love of the artist of *Dorian Gray* might lead an ordinary individual to believe that it might have a certain tendency?"

Wilde: "I have no knowledge of the views of ordinary individuals."

Carson: "You did not prevent the ordinary individual from buying your book?"

Wilde: "I have never discouraged him."[2]

Wilde correctly said: "A great artist invents a type, and life tries to copy it, to reproduce it in a popular form, like an enterprizing publisher." He also agreed that "literature always anticipates life." Nowadays, the type Wilde created, not least in himself, has been reproduced in very popular form. I like to think that Wilde would have despised all the cheap reproductions of his prophecy, especially among the young. Perhaps Wilde might have agreed that there should be limits, not on a great artist's invention of a type but, rather, on the enterprise of reproducing it in popular form. Certainly, Wilde was suspicious enough of the ways in which new character types are commercially exploited and, in their success, cheapened almost to the point of contradiction.

Can invention and reproduction really be separated? I suppose the imaginative invention of a type, and its reproduction, inseparable from the cultural process of choosing a pastoral guide for the conduct of life. This supposition on the changeable character of human types in any society specifies the power of art, even as Wilde wanted to use it—and even as others, at least since Plato, have wanted to censor precisely that power.

There are no neutral powers in the permanent war of cul-

2. See *The Trials of Oscar Wilde*, ed. H. Montgomery Hyde (London: W. Hodge, 1948), 122–24.

ture. In his own way, representing the ordinary and established hypocrisies, Carson knew he was attacking one of the great commanders of the forces subverting his culture. Now Wilde's subversive spirit has been made obsolete by the cheap and massive reproduction of that spirit throughout the educated and televisioned strata of Western society. It is the Carsons, now, who are on the defensive. But Wilde can never win. For he imagined an impossible culture, one inhabited by consummate individualists, freed from the inherited inhibitions necessary, at least until our own time, to culture itself. As a guide through the future maze of choices, leading nowhere but attractive in his activity of choosing, Wilde named a type he imagined opposing all conformities: the "artist." In certain great artists of the past and present, including himself, Wilde found intimations of a future at once socialist (universally rich) and free (universally expressive). This artistic dream is, perhaps especially in advanced technological societies, more revolutionary than the dream of Marx.

For Wilde, the artist is the true revolutionary figure. Only the artist is fit to play the role of guide in the next culture. He is fit because "he expresses everything." Wilde italicized that sentence. The artist, radically different from any revolutionary figure preceding him, precisely by his special freedom to express everything, plays the prophetic role in Wilde's entertainments. Indeed, in the artist, revolutionary and entertainer merge.

Nothing is more contemporary than Wilde's imagination. Almost a century after his time, young revolutionaries in advanced industrial orders conceive themselves more artists than proletarians: their aim is to express everything.[3] But here the resemblance between Wilde and his epigones begins to fade. These latter-day epigones are, mainly, failed artists, relying on their assertions of freedom to express everything rather than upon the wit, grace, and reticence with which Wilde believed everything should be

3. In America, the allegiance of these young revolutionaries has shifted from proletariat to black *Lumpenproletariat*, because in blacks they believe they see a culture even less inhibited than their own parental one. I consider the Negroes, at least in the young white artist's understanding of them, by far the most powerful influence in contemporary American culture.

expressed. Yet, precisely as failed artists, his successors follow Wilde in asserting the primacy of the artist as a guide to the next culture. What separates them from Wilde may be fatal to their art but vital to their success in a society increasingly uncertain about what it will, and will not, permit. Indeed, some confuse this uncertainty with civilization itself.

In every culture, guides are chosen to help men conduct themselves through those passages from one crisis of choice to another that constitute the experience of living. Once criteria of choice are established, guides are often self-chosen. Shamanry becomes hereditary; priesthood becomes an institution of those who would be ordained. The bandwagon effect operates in every culture. Men enjoy best those roles in which they can exercise an authority which is not their own and yet does not belong to the people they guide. Power may come out of the barrel of a gun; but authority comes out of the projection—and introjection—of ideals.

The rank-and-file members in idealizing institutions of guidance used to be called "laities": laities were those who listened to whatever the mouthpieces of idealizing institutions had to say. A crisis in culture occurred whenever old guides were struck dumb, or whenever laities began listening to new guides—new, because they encouraged their laities to do what theretofore they had not done (and not do what they had done). The crisis of modern culture adds something new to the history of such crises: the defensiveness and guilt of those who now know that they have nothing to say is compounded by the ascendancy of those who say that there should be no guides. Wilde is one of those permanently putative guides, ordained by his art, who have helped our culture advance beyond its unsuccessful Protestant phase in which every man would have been his own priest.

In the next culture, there are to be no priests, not even secular ones; we are not to be guided—rather, entertainment, stimulation, liberation from the constraints drawn around us by narrowing guidelines, become the functional equivalents of guidance. Where creeds once were, there therapies will be. Oscar Wilde was a brilliant herald of therapeutic culture when, near the turn of the century, the promise of it seemed dazzling. Neither the design nor implications of Wilde's heraldry are obvious to the naked eye. Wilde entertains so well that a guest at one of his feasts of words may easily forget these pleasures have a purpose beyond entertainment. The philistines wanted only entertainment, to be reassured by him in an amusing manner. And Wilde used his talent to entertain, precisely in his most popular plays, such as *The Importance of Being Earnest*. It is in his best essays that he tried to achieve the other purpose of art, which is not to entertain but to insinuate alternative prophecies of how men ought—and ought not—to act; and to make these insinuations at a level of character deep enough to help transform a culture. Plato was the first to acknowledge the seriousness and power of art in the transformation of character and society. Wilde denied this penultimate power only when he was in the public dock; there he defended the purity of art in a vain effort to save his life from the vengeance of philistines. But the philistines, who had him cornered, knew almost as well as he the power of art and its differences from entertainment. As entertainer, Wilde threatened nothing; only as an artist was he a threat to established culture. There is pathos in the separation of Wilde's talent as an entertainer from his genius as an artist; that genius appeared more in his life and essays than in his plays. He was a relentless performer, intent mainly upon himself and the impression he made. It was only upon those who knew him that Wilde made his greatest impression. We who come long after his performances are left with his supreme talent as an entertainer. But there is that other side of Wilde: his subversiveness as an artist.

A culture survives the assault of sheer possibility against it only so far as the members of a culture learn, through their membership, how to narrow the range of choices otherwise open. Safely inside their culture—more precisely, the culture safely inside them—members of it are disposed to enact only certain possibilities of behavior while refusing even to dream of others. It is culture, deeply installed as authority, that generates depth of character; indeed, "depth" is an edifying word for the learned capacity of rejection and acceptance. Members of the same culture can expect each other to behave in certain ways and not in others.

As culture sinks into the psyche and becomes character, what Wilde prized above all else is constrained: individuality. A culture in crisis favors the growth of individuality; deep down things no longer weigh so heavily to slow the surface play of experience. Hypothetically, if a culture could grow to full crisis, then everything could be expressed and nothing would be true. To prevent the expression of everything: that is the irreducible function of culture. By the creation of opposing values[4]—of ideals, of militant truths—a seal is fastened upon the terrific capacity of man to express everything.

Priesthoods preside over the origins of a culture and guard its character. If they did not preside, then a culture could be established without the mixed blessing of authority. A priest is whoever guides men by teaching them truths, or ideals. Sociologically, a truth is whatever militates against the human capacity to express everything. Repression is truth. God is not love, except as he is authority. When Wilde declared himself against authority, he did not know how he weakened what he was for: love. Authority will not be separated from love. To be for love and against authority is a paradox upon which no institution, socialist or otherwise, can be built.

Wilde tells a different story. In a culture without authority— Wilde called it "socialist"—the artist would teach each man, even the least talented, how to become more like himself. Freed by technology from labor, and by socialism from bondage to private property, each man would become what he can be: an individual, enjoying his own life, not degraded by poverty, not absorbed by possession. Imagine: not an art that has become popular, but a populace become artistic. We would entertain ourselves; self-entertainment is the final human autonomy.

Is this Utopian? A map of the world that does not include Utopia is not worth even glancing at, for it leaves out the one country at which Humanity is always landing. And when Hu-

4. "Values": whenever I hear the word, I reach for my pillow. It is a poor, misleading word and belongs to a marketing culture. In order not to expand the argument with my search for a better word, I beg leave to use "values" sparingly in this essay.

manity lands there, it looks out, and, seeing a better country, sets sail. Progress is the realisation of Utopias.[5]

We will have to tease out this new kind of prophet, the artist as every man who would inhabit Wilde's Utopia—until he spies a better country. Certainly, the new prophet will be more witty and less serious than any who came before him. This is not a small point toward the understanding of Oscar Wilde. The artist is he who can take all god-terms lightly. Because Wilde's new prophet possesses the comic spirit, he is self-possessed—as no other man has been before him. The alternative to self-possession is to be possessed by some god-term.

By "god-terms" I mean values that forbid certain actions and thereby encourage others. "God-terms" express those significant inhibitions that characterize us all within a culture. They are compelling truths. To take god-terms unseriously, while admitting their existence, seemed to Wilde the main, saving "pagan idea." Wilde put himself entirely on the side of the pagans, against Jerusalem, because he knew that the terms in which our particular God was conceived could exist only so long as they limited the capacity of man to express everything; the "pagan idea" was treated, in the nineteenth century by a small group of supremely talented European minds, as the refusal of this limit.

That Wilde had a most inaccurate notion of any actually pagan idea is beside the point. Like others gifted with revolutionary imaginations, Wilde meant by "pagan" some ideas that he considered would release men from their impoverishing inhibitions. To believe that man is the supreme being for man—supreme even over those primordial powers to which real pagans submitted—this is a subversive idea of modernity without precedent in any "pagan" culture. Like Marx, or Nietzsche, Wilde is a very modern man. What characterizes modernity, I think, is just this idea that men need not submit to any power—higher or lower—other than their own. It is in this sense that modern men really believe

5. Oscar Wilde, *The Soul of Man under Socialism and Other Essays* (New York: Harper Colophon Books, 1970), 246.

they are becoming gods. This belief is the exact reverse of the truth; modern men are becoming antigods. Because, as I have said earlier, the terms in which our God was conceived can exist only so long as they limit the capacity of man to express everything, our old God was never so uninhibited as young man. Our God was bound, after all, by the terms of various covenants.

Thus, we can imagine all too easily Wilde's parody priesthood of de-inhibitors pitted against the repressive elites left over from the god-terms and institutions of the past. In Wilde's time, the struggle was still unequal; and Wilde himself has been considered a martyr in the struggle. That martyrdom, the trials and jail sentence, was due less to the repressive elite of English culture, which was more than willing not to have its hand forced, than to Wilde's own imperfect artistry. He intruded deeply into a struggle of son against father—Bosie Douglas against the Marquess of Queensberry—without realizing what it was about. More important, Wilde may have been led into the fatal step of prosecuting Queensberry for slander (the Marquess was naïve enough at first to accuse Wilde merely of *posing* as a homosexual with his son) by his own sense of guilt. A more perfect artist of life should have been able to shatter the connection between guilt and culture. But the repressive culture was still enough alive inside Wilde, I think, to destroy him when he blundered into a direct confrontation with its official inhibitions. Wilde lost his personal battle, in 1895, the moment he went to court against his own knowledge (not admitted to his lawyers) that he was a practicing homosexual. That battle lost, Wilde's side appears now to be winning the war, even in the courts.

In the history of Western culture, churchmen have played the leading role of pastoral guide. By Wilde's year of success and wreck, 1895, all except the obtuse understood that the clergy had lost whatever sense of direction they once may have had. The office of guide, the most important in any culture, was vacant. Why should not literary men, artists, scientists, try to step in? Wilde commended this seizure of moral power. Such a seizure was in no way bizarre or out of the question; the modern political struggle appears to urban sophisticates an enlargement of their own personal struggles: over distributions of the privileges and deprivations that determine differences of style.

Of course, at the turn of the century, many churchmen were still unaware of their default. Ibsen's Pastor Manders is an immortal characterization of a guide upon whom it never dawns that he has nothing to say. Mrs. Alving twice appealed to him as her figure of authority only because her own conversion to the art of life is bookish, a matter of idle chatter; deep down, she still submits to the old authorities. Oswald is doomed by the fact that he is her son, the child of a destructively fictionalized past. The culture that Ibsen denounces so heavily, and that Wilde dismisses so wittily, must be called neurotic. But Wilde, and his circle, are products of that very culture. They are examples of posh bohemia, deviant entertainers whose subversive attitudes can be at once supported and denounced by the philistines in imperial cities. Posh bohemians become a pseudoelite, easy to sacrifice and replace if they go too far out of line and forget that they are not really heralds of a new culture but entertainers of a society in search of kicks.

What has changed since Wilde's time? First, the artist has become a popular type, reproduced now in massive numbers among the young in Western societies; second, the philistines are less self-confident and more easily persuaded that the bohemian lifestyle is something more than shocking entertainment, exhibitions intended chiefly for their embarrassed pleasure. The philistines can now read *The Soul of Man under Socialism* more sympathetically than in Wilde's time. Even so, he remains the kind of figure who attracts philistine hostility precisely by asserting a near relation between artistic genius and deviancy.

Not only respectable philistines feel hostility to those who challenge their established sense of limit, particularly on the range of allowable deviancy. Prostitutes danced outside the Old Bailey, and lifted their skirts in mock salutes, when Wilde was convicted. Were they mocking Wilde alone? The respectable philistine prosecutors of Wilde might well avert their eyes; they too were being mocked, I think, for reaching up to the talent of their own most celebrated entertainer and destroying him for a deviancy he had kept quite private.[6]

A culture in control needs first of all to preserve that control by not reaching its legal arms too far into the labyrinths of private life. The guardians of any culture must constantly protect the difference between the public and private sectors—and encourage forms of translation between the two sectors; that is the meaning of ritual in all traditional cultures. Wilde never advocated his private deviancy through his public art, as it is done nowadays. On the contrary, stage Bunburying masks and transforms very different home truths. Wilde dealt brilliantly with the relations between art, lying, and truth. (See his duologues on "The Decay of Lying.") It is the stage honesty of his successors that makes them failed artists. Their failure to realize the superiority of stage Bunburying, in all its forms, is a subversion of art itself and inadmissible in any culture. By their failure to respect the rights of privacy and its sovereign deceits, respectable philistines have played into the hands of the new revolutionaries who, unlike Wilde, use honesty to oppose culture itself. For the very life of every culture depends upon its powers to mask and transform private motive into something very different, even opposite, when it appears in public. In this sense, art, including Wilde's art, ought to function as an equivalent in modern culture of our lost opposing values. Art should be expressive and repressive at the same time. This, after all, is what is meant by sublimation.

In Wilde's time, as a side effect of their humorless insistence upon honesty, the philistines (this was what Wilde called the great propertied public) had created a high-mindedness that they mistook for culture. In this kind of culture, with the space between public and private sectors of feeling too narrow, anything of beauty was likely to give its viewer a case of what Wilde once called the

---

6. Wilde was punishable under a bill that almost casually included a section that created as a new offense indecencies between male persons in public *or private*. The clause making deviant behavior in private an offense had become law only in 1886.

"Protestant jumps."[7] Early in his life, Wilde determined to escape high-mindedness. The philistines, even those who called themselves socialists and engaged in good works,[8] were his natural enemies. The one difficulty with this ethic of escape is that it has become so easy; it can be achieved without the slightest talent. To be an escape artist without talent contradicts the meaning of art, installs things that are ugly as equal with anything beautiful, and smashes up those structures of conformity from which alone art can emerge. This helps us understand why all those failed artists among the contemporary culture revolutionaries shout as one of their favorite words, "Smash." On walls everywhere in Western societies, graffiti invite us to smash this and smash that—solemn calls to an iconoclasm undignified by the slightest hint of alternative achievements of public meaning. Our young revolutionaries might learn from Wilde the real worth of wit. His genius lay in doing away with both the solemnity and incipient violence of serious argument. What should a free man, an artist, do when he is arguing against authority as such? Wilde's wit and good humor, his style, are the essence, not the ornament, of his case.

Under the needling of such wit, under those comic revelations of the Tartuffery of ideals that come from the best writers of the nineteenth century—Marx, Freud, Nietzsche, Wilde, among the more strictly literary—we moderns have fled all militant ideal conceptions of our own character; those conceptions once supplied bridges between the private and public sectors of our experience, without abolishing the difference. On the contrary, a bridge of militant ideals functioned to establish and maintain the difference between what is private and what public, although the price was certain necessary tensions, now variously called "guilt," "alienation," and other current curse words. Against those separations of public and private, installed inside ourselves as our good name, we once learned to fear even the faintest dispraise and will-

7. *The Letters of Oscar Wilde*, ed. Rupert Hart-Davis (New York: Harcourt, Brace and World, 1962), 30.
8. The highest-minded socialists have also been philistines; the Webbs, and other fighters for humanity in the abstract, come most easily to mind.

ingly put up with a diet of admonitions as our earliest form of moral nurture. Personality was identified with an idealized image of itself.[9] Wilde was an early modern opponent of militant ideal conceptions of the self, despite the fact that by such conceptions the private and public sectors of experience are kept discrete and in order, the one a transformation of the other. That order cannot be established, as art or society, if no dialectic of translation occurs between private motive and public experience. Without thereby eliminating what is an eternally renewable difference between culture and morality, the point at which they meet and become inseparable is wherever a transformation of private motive occurs. A culture that does not moralize is no culture at all.

Militant ideals are not another name for public poses; if they are that, then they become the outward and visible signs of some private hell. A transformation forbids what would otherwise be allowed. A deceit, so far as the joke is not on the deceiver, allows precisely what it would forbid. Tartuffe was a poseur, immediately comic, at least to maid servants and theater audiences. But not all poses are comic. Kurtz, for example, made "Civilization" to mean "exterminate the brutes." The best way to read every cultural translation is backwards, from public experience to private motive. Thus read—backwards—too many translations evoke laughter, if only in order to avoid tears. Wilde chose laughter. As a guide, his artist is deliberately intended to suspend belief; he must ensure his own harmlessness.

To emphasize the harmlessness of the new man, Wilde shifted from the artist to the more traditional image of the child. In his greatest essay, *The Soul of Man under Socialism*, Wilde offers for our guidance both the artist and the child.

It will be a marvellous thing—the true personality of man— when we see it. It will grow naturally and simply, flower-like, or

9. In contrast, modern children are often educated early in a rejection of authority and hear little about themselves except praise. At the same time, militant ideal conceptions of character are mocked as injurious to the creative potential of the child. This revolution in child-rearing has occurred mainly among the educated classes in Western societies.

as a tree grows. It will not be at discord. It will never argue or dispute. It will not prove things. It will know everything. And yet it will not busy itself about knowledge. It will have wisdom. Its value will not be measured by material things. It will have nothing. And yet it will have everything, and whatever one takes from it, it will still have, so rich will it be. It will not be always meddling with others, or asking them to be like itself. It will love them because they will be different. And yet while it will not meddle with others, it will help all, as a beautiful thing helps us, by being what it is. The personality of man will be very wonderful. It will be as wonderful as the personality of a child.[10]

This is one of Wilde's more sentimental passages. Nothing in it hints how human personality can stabilize its ambivalences except by installing oppositional ideals. Wilde's sentimentality derives from the ancient logic of so-called antinomian thought: if nothing is prohibited, then there will be no transgressions. But in point of psychiatric and historical fact, it is *no*, rather than *yes*, upon which all culture and inner development of character depend. Ambivalence will not, I think, be eliminated; it can only be controlled and exploited. Ideal self-conceptions, militant truths, are modes of control. Character is the restrictive shaping of possibility. What Wilde called "personality" represents a dissolution of restrictive shapings. In such freedom, grown men would act less like cherubic children than like demons, for they would disrupt the restrictive order of character and social life.

Anyone who so disrupts a restrictive order is performing a demonic function. Just such disruptions seemed to Wilde the mission of the artist. The main, sociological question is never whether such disruptions occur but only whether they occur in the public or private sector of behavior. Wilde understood this difference between public and private disruption; we must understand the difference between public and private therapies—and, moreover, understand the dynamics by which every powerful private therapy tends to become public. In public, the art of Bunburying meant

10. Wilde, *The Soul of Man under Socialism*, 237.

one thing: in private, it meant quite another.[11] Like any pastoral guide, the artist is a bridge between the private and public sectors of a culture. Therefore, by Wilde's implicit argument, the artist becomes a dangerous and necessary figure—dangerous because he disrupts the established order by casting doubt upon it, necessary because through such doubt progress occurs toward another mode of expressiveness.

We are now better placed to understand the precision of Wilde's wittiest and most famous interpretation of himself. André Gide had asked him how it happened that Wilde had failed to put the best of himself into his plays. Wilde replied: "Would you like to know the great drama of my life? It is that I have put my genius into my life—I have put only my talent into my works." Wilde understood that in the established society this was an inversion of the energies appropriate to the private and public sectors. In our culture, any man who exercises a genius for intimacy is bound to find it becoming public and therefore scandalous; he may be rewarded by public martyrdom. If some rare individual should be cursed with genius, then the safe course, in any society, is to put that genius into work, while reserving his talent, which can reassure friends and entertain associates, for living. So Kierkegaard arranged his life, after all, in the critical case of his genius versus Regine. In this way are preserved the sacred distances between desires and their objects. Ordinary men will rarely tolerate, except occasionally in politicians or prophets, a steady confusion of the public and private spheres. Yet it is precisely men who aspire to confuse the public and private sectors, putting genius into their lives, that become putative guides toward a different way of life. Following Weber (but with Freud's help) we now title such men "charismatics." This merely argues the uncharitable character of charismatics, for they will not leave people alone in their privacies. Western society is again crawling with would-be charismatics; and they have a ready-made audience. With all their experience of default among candidates for the office, ordinary

11. Just as in public the word "artist" might mean one thing and in certain private circles another. In one of Wilde's circles, the word "artist" also meant homosexual; "renter" was yet another term Wilde used with the same meaning.

men still crave guides for their conduct. And not merely guiding principles. Abstractions will never do. God-terms have to be exemplified in order to be taught; or, at least, vital examples must be pointed to and a sense of indebtedness (which is the same as guilt) encouraged toward the imitation of these examples. Men crave their principles incarnate in enactable characters, actual selective mediators between themselves and the polytheism of experience.

Until recently, it seemed true that without imitations of compelling characters, *character* itself could not develop. Morality abhors impersonality. In this sense, so far as science develops through a transfer of truths impersonally, there can be no such cultural phenomenon as a scientific morality. In science, a truth ceases to be ideal and militant. Wilde had some premonitions of the dissolving effect of science upon culture and, as an artist, declared the amity of art and science—and both with socialism. Only under this triumvirate—art, science, and socialism—could the New Man exist as anything more than an occasional rebel sport of the world as it is. But under the triumvirate of art, science, and socialism, Wilde looked forward, with a messianic smile, to a culture of many truths, none of them set up as ideal and none militant. In this way, authority as such—not merely this or that authority—would be defeated.

There are counterarguments. What Wilde dismissed as mere imitation of authority, as well as authority itself, may turn out to be the one way necessary to decide questions of internal development; culture must always come to each man with certain claims ready-made, to set deep within him answers that can prevent disorganizing questions from arising. To conceive of an individualism that "does not come to a man with any claims upon him at all" destroys the established meaning of culture. Wilde could accept this destruction because he conceived of authority as completely external, like the cross he had heard of being carried through the streets of Jerusalem by some madman imitating Jesus. That madman seemed to Wilde acting out all "lives that are marred by imitation."

Wilde's attack on all authority is too easy. When authority

becomes so external, then it has ceased to be authoritative. The heaviest crosses are internal, and men make them so, that, thus skeletally supported, they can bear the burden of themselves. Under the sign of this inner cross, a certain inner distance is achieved from the infantile desire to be and have everything. Identification is a far more compelling concept of authority and includes imitation. True individuality must involve the capacity to say no, and this capacity is inseparable from the genesis of no in authority. A man can only resist the polytheism of experience if his character is anchored deeply enough by certain god-terms to resist shuttling endlessly among all.

Wilde uses the traditional, god-term-determined rhetoric of the inner life against the inner life itself. The logic of Wilde's opposition to all authority depends upon his prototype of a new prophet, the artist. He imagined himself and others, each with his sovereign calm, self-centered, submitting only to the authority of experience—never predisposed by the experience of authority. By the grace of his opposition to militant truths Wilde helped lead an aesthetic movement away from the dominance of inwardness and toward an externalization that works against all our received conceptions of character. The genius of modernity is in Wilde's cleverness. That genius is only now being caricatured by a culture that produces revolutionaries who are less oppressed proletarians than failed artists.

The history of the struggle to fill the vacant office of guide to what men may not and may do has taken a remarkable turn. There are powerful movements that proclaim some version or other of the doctrine that the new guiding character must make his presence felt only in order to abolish himself. By virtue of his essays, Wilde belongs in the pantheon of this movement.

Of course, there are larger figures in the pantheon. But they are faced in the same direction. Nietzsche's future philosopher, as a humorist, is not far from Wilde's artist. The New Man for whom Marx was so impatient, and without whom the revolutionary process that he found in the hands of the unprincipled bourgeois could not be complete, is another near relation to Wilde's artist. Freud made a different and more cautious case in the character of the therapist, who is inseparable from his theory. I shall review the Freudian case briefly, for the background lighting it casts upon the Wildean case of the artist as our New Man.

For Freud, the power of decision over the internal redevelopment of a crippled, or arrested, individuality could be acquired, or extended, in that last phase of therapeutic suffering which constitutes the psychoanalytic relation. In correct Freudian time, after necessarily protracted resistances against his own opportunities, a patient should become able to seize on the opportunity presented by the fact that the sources of his suffering are evaginated. Those sources are uncovered precisely in the patient's relation to the analyst. In the resolution of the transference, certain internal guides lose their authority and the patient therefore becomes that much freer to be his own guide. The analyst played a virtually silent critic without whom a patient could not re-create his own character, at least to say something on his own behalf. Psychoanalysis may be viewed as much a branch of moral letters made over into a unique process of therapy as it was of medicine.

But, with all his interest in the relation between case and collectivity, Freud never made therapy a model for culture. On the contrary, therapy can be understood as the model for anti-culture. Precisely here is the tension between Freudian therapy and his theory of culture, of which authority, incarnate in character, is a necessary part. Freud never dreamed that his genius would be used to assert a culture in which there would be no figures of authority against whom youth could react and thus achieve their own sense of the limits that define any truly human existence. Such a dream, if he had it, would batter against Freud's own colossal creation of himself as a figure of authority locked in immortal combat against his final rival, Moses.

Wilde shared with the other most sensitive spirits of the late nineteenth century what is now public knowledge: that whatever makes authority incarnate in our culture is no longer available to it. No creed, no ramifying symbolic of militant truths, is installed deeply enough now to help men constrain their capacity for expressing everything. Wilde understood that internalizations from an earlier period in our moral history no longer held good.

Western men were sick precisely of those interior ideals which had shaped their characters. The New Man has no choice except to try to become a free character. Viewed from within any among the precedent cultures of commitment, the character of the New Man must be anticredal. Wilde's artist is another version of the anticredal character around whom other, more notable heralds of the future have announced their designs. No less than Marx's New Man, Wilde's artist is anticredal because he too is conceived to live free from ideals. All the most important revolutionary movements of our culture, including the Marxist, represent various strategies of attack upon the inwardness of the Western character. They are efforts to evaginate those militant truths, functioning mainly as inhibitions, around which men learn to negotiate their elaborate dodges toward pleasure. Freud, Marx, Nietzsche, Wilde: these are some of the chief evangels associated with new ways toward the realization of self.[12]

A new way has to be shown, at least until laities are so practical in it that they can find the way for themselves. But contemporary culture is in such a turmoil of new ways that none of them can show to advantage. The field is too crowded. Even more in the era of anticreeds than of creeds, prophecy and deviant performance have become closely related and lucrative arts. Where individualism is so highly prized, charisma can be reproduced cheaply and becomes a highly profitable product. Wilde reckoned that, until the advent of socialism, full expressive individuality could occur only "on the imaginative plane of art." He reckoned without the cultural effect of the mass media—and without an alliance of art with the most philistine commercialism. Bohemia is more posh than ever, and more inclusive, in a society that will buy everything. The revolutionary arts are now mass entertainments.

By standing the artist "outside his subject," Wilde tried to make the artist revolutionary in a less easily corrupted manner. Such a lack of identification with his subject implies that the artist

---

12. New ways, in order to appeal the more readily, can be supported by intimations from an ambivalently rejected past. Wilde considered Jesus as a forerunner, rather as Marx considered the utopian socialists. This branch of literature once came under the rubric "apologetics."

is a very special kind of personality. In Wilde's conception, the dissent of the artist becomes a kind of deviance. It is because he is detached from his subject that the artist can be trusted to defy authority. Such a mistaken conception of the relation between dissent and deviance permitted Wilde to indulge in some very sentimental writing, about criminals as well as artists. It helped him locate the revolutionary animus in psychological rather than social relations.

This is not to dismiss all thought on the psychological origins of revolution. The animus of all revolution may well be summed up in one passage from Marx, where he invokes that "revolutionary daring which throws at its adversary the defiant phrase: 'I am nothing and I should be everything.'" No phrase could be more defiant, and none could better express the infantile unconscious— if the infantile unconscious could express itself. But animus is not action. The artist who stands outside his subject is himself a subject. He is neither nothing nor everything, but, like all other men, a significant something. Culture is a tremendous articulation of compromise between equally intolerable feelings of nothing and everything.

The claim of the artist to express everything is subversive in one especially acute sense: the claim to express everything can only exacerbate feelings of being nothing. In such a mood, all limits begin to feel like humiliations. Wilde did not know that he was prophesying a hideous new anger in modern men, one that will render unexcited, peaceable existence even more utopian than before.

To criticize Wilde's prophecy of the soul of man under socialism is not to defend a dying culture. Indeed, men who aspire to express everything can exist only in a culture grown so superficial that it can no longer perform its proper preventative functions. A culture that penetrates deeper into the interior, creating its own interior space rather than growing ever more disposable, is not made to order. Professors do not renew a culture. The sources of renewal are no less irrational than the sources of revolutionary death sentences against it. We can only wait and see which character will dominate the future: the credal or anticredal.

Wilde would have had the future liberate itself from the authority of the past. But, in the absence of sustaining opposition from its credal parent, the anticredal character compounds for its own defeat, as Wilde's did; that character, instinct in his and all comic art, proved tragic to the life.

Near the end of his life, Wilde reaffirmed its aesthetic justification: "Whatever is realized is right." His homosexual realizations had a pyrrhic air about them. From the affair with Lord Alfred Douglas rose a miasma of ugliness. Wilde's laudations of the pederastic glory that was Greece, its pedagogic eros, bore little upon his relations to homosexual prostitutes. His feastings with those "panthers," as he called them, appear to have been nothing like Plato's *Symposium*, in which he must have read, expertly in the original: "diseases of all sorts spring from the excesses and disorders of the elements of love."

On his own report, Wilde's homosexual affairs were lowering. Low life mocked high art. Wilde transgressed in life against the one god-term, Beauty, to which he would have remained faithful. We Pharisees of culture know the world is justified neither morally nor aesthetically. Yet we need trouble no more than Wilde about Leviticus 18:22; or any other of those sacred commands to disobedience from which we may acquire our own compassionate understandings of faithlessness. Wilde's homosexuality is condemned by his own aesthetic, which he took too seriously, as if it were his true religion.

In his great confession, *De Profundis*, Wilde almost realized what had "lured" him from the "beautiful unreal world of Art . . . into the imperfect world of coarse uncompleted passions, of appetite without distinction, desire without limit, and formless greed." His aesthetic justifications of life scarcely survive their translations into life.

Asked how he endured prison, Wilde's riposte plunged deeper than any other he ever delivered: "I was buoyed up with a sense of guilt." That sense true, it is more spiritual than legal; it is more trustworthy than ego; it is more profound than reason. If shallowness is the supreme vice, as Wilde believed, then his true guilt began in the clever insolence of his approach to art as if it were

supreme reality. The most insolent and contemporary of cleveri-
ties must follow: an approach to life as it were an endless choice
of styles; modes of fiction contrived by any with wit enough and
will for such contrivances.

Tragedy reminds us that true condemnations of the self cannot be pronounced by the self alone. I shall end by quoting two
sentences that may be taken to constitute Wilde's verdict upon his
life as work of art. Taken one after the other, they show a movement inevitable as that in a tragedy.

> What the paradox was to me in the sphere of thought, perversity
> became to me in the sphere of passion.

> Everything to be true must become a religion.

Is Not the Truth the Truth?

I

1. In its meaning as a defense of Freud as a lifework, the year 1989, that of Yerushalmi's lectures, takes on its own weight. The numbers of our years carry their own specific gravities of memory. Freud published his deathwork in the year of a larger and more material deathwork against the Jews, 1939. In my Jewish memory that year is engraved with the turning of the German version in what had been largely an assault of fighting images and words against the Jews into the firing of their very bodies. That more material deathwork against the Jews began in the symbolic. Always and everywhere the symbolic is a propaedeutic for a more material reality. The symbolic is not less real for being preparatory. Freud's Jewish memory must have carried the image of men with a death's-head insignia on their uniforms invading the sanctuary of his own house in Vienna. These death's-head men were agents, in Freud's own language, of one of two 'Heavenly Powers'—in the power of his primary imagination. Freud always limited that sense of two primordialities of power, the primacy of his imagined duplicity of the primordial, by putting the phrase for death and life, the latter a passing disturbance of the former in

Title is from *Henry IV, Part 1*, 2.4.230. I thank Michael Scott Alexander, at the time of this writing my research assistant at the University of Pennsylvania, for his crucial writing and research through the course of my work for this finger exercise for a trilogy titled *Sacred Order/Social Order.*

[Rieff's original subtitle was "Ten Commentments on the Jewish Question, of True Worlds and Ourselves in Them, Drawn From, among Other Texts, Yosef Hayim Yerushalmi's *Freud's Moses: Judaism Terminable and Interminable.*" Roman numerals reflect Rieff's original section divisions; the editors' selections are indicated with arabic numbers.—*Eds.*]

its eternity, between quotation marks. That sense of their fictive existence qualifies the primordiality of both 'Heavenly Powers'. The year 1939 lives in my memory as a deathwork in its material firing against the Jews, the firing that became a literal war of the worlds at the moment the German armies crossed the Polish border, the German third world* in its chief purpose devoted to conquest and destruction of the Jewish second world in all its variations, sacred as they are secular; and the number of that year, 1939, standing as well for the Jewish world assaulted from within, that assault constituted by the publication of the deathwork that is Freud's *Moses and Monotheism.*

In the Jewishness of my memory, Yerushalmi's *Freud's Moses,* delivered in 1989, carries now a double truth in the echo of that year. Now, its inwardness, 1989 means the year of Yerushalmi's lifework against Freud's deathwork, its tactic of partial incorporation of symptomatic death, representative of what it is not into the truth of life, which is what it represents—namely and in brief, sacred order in its partial incorporations as social order. The second of the two truths in the number of my year 1989 echoes the year in which the third world of deathworks against the Jewish second emerged in its founding political movement, the French Revolution. The year 1789 is bracketed by the year 1989. The closing year marks two centuries of struggle for the world, by more or less dominant politicizings of deathworks in the name of the rights of man as denials of the right of God.

The Declaration of the Rights of Man constitutes a wrong turn in history. *The Rights of Man* developed then and there, in the French Revolution, as it turned against sacred order in the name of human emancipation from that predicative order. That *Declaration* can be read best, in the proto-Marxist manner, as the rage and futility consequent upon the double truth of an earlier call to a turning that would constitute the truth of a humanity freed as the self-constituted agent of He who calls. *Turn Thou us unto thee, O Lord, and we shall be turned* (Lamentations 5:21).

---

*See *My Life among the Deathworks* and pp. 169–75 below on Rieff's technical usage of "third world."—*Eds.*

There are revolutions and there are revolutions. At its cutting edge, the French Revolution, opposite of the American (which led to the greatest of undeclared wars in the eighteenth century, between America and France), constituted a revolution against the Lord, Creator and Commandant of the Jewish world as it was, is, and ever shall be, Israel, in one *historical* truth or another; however those truths claim supersession of their predicative Israels. No movement in world history before the French projected, even festively as well as mortally, a social order without a predicative sacred order. The pamphlet published by the Marquis de Sade, *One More Step*, proclaims the necessity of a sexual and moral revolution if the political revolution he saw coming was to found a new world. De Sade's fictions of profanation take their significance only from their heraldry of fictions that in art are admirable, such as Mozart's *Don Giovanni*, which was first performed in 1787, but are less memorable in life. Those fictions of profanation, in their social and political realities, have been directed specially against the Jews. The eighteenth-century literature that constitutes a heraldry of an entirely profane world has its own components of Jew-hatred. Voltaire's work is only one instance of that heraldry.[1]

That the literature of profanation includes the work of both Marx and Freud suggests the complexity and confusions in the matter that Yerushalmi takes up in these superbly calculated and graceful lectures.[2] But the context in which these lectures were delivered, the foreseeable historical context in which this book will be read, is scarcely more than hinted. That context, with the war against the Jews[3] as an apparently permanent part of the context, is most concisely described as a war for the world. *Kulturkampf* is the compound German word, now used increasingly, to

1. See Arthur Hertzberg, *The French Enlightenment and the Jews: The Origins of Modern Anti-Semitism* (New York: Columbia University Press, 1968).
2. Yosef Hayim Yerushalmi's *Freud's Moses: Judaism Terminable and Interminable* (New Haven: Yale University Press, 1991).
3. Lucy S. Davidowicz, *The War against the Jews, 1933–1945* (New York: Holt, Rinehart and Winston, 1975).

describe the permanent form of our advancing third world's wars against our Jewish second world; as ever on the defensive.

I take 'culture' to be, in its credibilities, the mediating matrix by which sacred orders have been transferred into the substance of social orders. That substance, except in its cultural artifacts otherwise invisible, all cultures, and the social orders of which they are symbolic have had as their predicates sacred orders. For purposes of concision and clarity I must treat these forms of mediation typologically. Typologies carry their own striking implications. As world-creating, culture is the form of fighting before the firing begins. In the historical typology I shall use here, as the context for my comments on Yerushalmi, let there be three types of world creation. After all, as a theorist of culture as world creation, I pun on my third world self as a self-referential god-term. Therefore, let there be what follows.

As a type of world creation, first worlds constitute, in their god-terms, the All, primacies of possibility from which all realities derive. Gods derive from the All no less than the grains of sand in which William Blake saw being in its primordiality. Freudian theory constitutes a vision of the highest as a primordiality in its form delivered by the single word "ambivalence," and in its content delivered by the single word "sexuality," of which all sacred orders are themselves derivative and, as a matter of *historical* truth in its latest eventuality, that are derivative in its disturbances symbolic enough—i.e., representative of what those disturbances are, life as the passing disturbance of death. This All, death as the being given, forms the world elsewhere to which every life, in the individuality of the disturbance, must return. The degree of investment by the primordiality of death in the disturbance that is life reflects a duality in the Freudian sense of being that is not Jewish in any canonical reading of the truth of being in its Jewishness. In the alternative, such a duality reads life as an ephemeral denying of death. By contrast, the creation of life is not derived, in its Jewish truth, from death.

In its typological character as our second world, Israel, the turn to life is the creation of the world itself. In the beginning there is no primordiality, there is only the caller and his call toward which life is the turning. Beginning with *The Declaration of the Rights of Man* and its celebrations integral to the French Revolution, a new turn occurs. In that turn, and in all the others after, the call is itself a deathwork against the life of the second world. The year 1989 represents what may be the synergies of a turn against the death-works of our third world, represented by the longer of the two surviving political expressions of that deathwork in the twentieth century, the communist denial of second world life, by a confused resurgence of those second worlds. The Israel founded in 1948 represents the earliest of those resurgences: a Jewish *Machtstaat* to protect the Jew in his fictive primordialities as well as in his *Kulturstaat*. Here, the *Kulturstaat* within Israel pivots on the un-answered question: who is a Jew? Yerushalmi responds to that question with the case history of Freud and Freud's *Moses*.

Freud's *Moses* belongs, in a way Yerushalmi leaves ambiguous, as the consequence of his softening of the struggle between the Jewish second world and the anti-Jewish third, to the anti-canon of our third worlds. That anti-canon is constituted by its nega-tions of the second world canon, whether Jewish or Christian. Neither first nor second world creations, whether typologically primordial or theonomic, can be read so that they project a world entirely without predicative sacrality. Rather, the profane or secu-lar, the world in its everyday thereness, is there to realize, as of-ficers realize orders, the directive orders that are the substance of sacred orders.

Substantial realizations of sacred order in social are constituted by their first secularizations as being given, directively, in human life. *This word is your life* (Deuteronomy 32:47) is the symbolic of human life in social order; life in its *is-ness*, the representation of what life is in its truth. Second world truths can have other virtu-ally immortal representations. The word takes on this reciprocal life of human repetition, each repetition unprecedented in its au-thenticity or originality. Every word that addresses the Thou of Lamentations or celebrations is uttered for the first time in the truth of its address. A cathedral may be centuries old. In its there-ness it is always at its first instance of being: *ad majorem gloriam*

Dei. The church, both visible and invisible, is what it represents. Reality is no less the secularity of stone than the sacrality of words humans use in the extraordinariness of their everyday lives.

Every human being, secular only because the substance of his being constitutes a sacred self, registers as life history the enactments of his being given. The continuities of that being given are inseparable from the discontinuities of consciousness in the agency of every being given. That agency cannot be conscious, completely aware of that agency and of everything represented in it, at every moment of his life. Continuities are no more completely conscious than discontinuities are completely unconscious. Life registers, like the flights and perchings of consciousness, in the offices and those offices unperformed, in the world of commanding truths known even as they are unknown in the restlessness of human life itself.

As the highest secular office of life in sacred order, human being is given in what is at once the substance and the subtlety of the worded life: conduct.[4] Unworded, the conduct of life in our Jewish second world loses the name of action in the precise sense of an act being both true and good or not worthy of the name. To lose the moralizing names of action is to deny human life at its height and truth in obedience to the word. Where the word is, there is life, in Jewish human being given as the one and only agency of life in the word. No animal, nor any thing or creature else, carries, in its life, the responsibility of agency. The secular world is the world of sacred agencies. Not that such agencies have been shut off historically from other cognate apprehensions of life as the agency of truth.

Certain cultural mediations of primordiality, our first worlds in their metaphysical representations, as they have been incorporated into the world of the living and lawful word, are matters of historical fact. The theonomic, the mythic, and the philosophical have a long history of reciprocal and partial incorporations. *Logos, hidden harmony, Law as the opposite of the word falsified, hu-*

---

4. Matthew Arnold had the foundation of our second world right when he remarked, in *Literature and Dogma,* "The bible is almost all conduct."

man existence as a battle — Israel is the nation that gives battle against untrue worlds — nevertheless, in later intellectualizing Israels, by way of examples the worlds of Philo and Maimonides, represent first world theories assimilated into the theonomic second world of the Jews.

In this historical sense, there are no secular Jews until both worlds of sacred order begin to be treated as mystifications of the real and only and profane world. That last world *is* the world of Yerushalmi's Freud, who is both *godless* and a *Jew*. What accounts for this late historical paradox of the Jewish world in its embattled existence? I suggest, in these comments on Yerushalmi's *Freud's Moses*, that the historical period denominated by the words "Freudian" and "post-Freudian" may be understood as periods of cultural history characterized by the repression of revelation.

2. The shifting sense of distance in both the Jewish and Christian sense of a distancer reports a reality that can never be rendered static. The dynamic of truths that are sacred implies the fear, at once sacred and profane, of the distancer. Distancings of truth can never be abolished. They may be argued endlessly. But the argument is always about *Something*, not nothing.

> Not, I'll not carrion comfort, Despair, not feast on thee;
> Not untwist—slack they may be—these last strands of man
> In me or, most weary, cry *I can no more*. I can;
> Can something, hope, wish day come, not choose not to be.[5]

That "last strand of man" is the sacred self in my meaning. It cannot be undone except by choosing not to be. There, in Hopkins's phrase "not chose not to be" is the second world affirmation of truth in its lifework. The Christian doctrine of the Christ, in his resurrection, represents a syncretic version of the Jewish world-word "lifework." That the Christian and the Jewish represent unfusable second worlds rests entirely on the doctrine of the *god/man*. Whether such a fusion can be considered a historical truth or not is the line drawn, never to be withdrawn, between the founda-

5. Gerard Manley Hopkins, "Carrion Comfort" (1918), in *Poems and Prose* (1953; New York: Penguin, 1985), 60.

tional Jewish second world and the more expansive Christian; expansive because it included the first world of heroic apotheosis, a double truth that the Jews rejected and the gentile nations accepted. Freud's primal father has its own incarnational character, entirely different from the Christian. The lifework of the resurrection is a return, in mythic memory, of the primal crime and its after-affects in a group sensitive to those after-affects in a way that includes languages of constraint dependent upon an unstable culture of repression and the repressions admitted.

No complete fusion is possible between first world *logos* and second world creation in either its Jewish or incarnational meanings. The reason of that incompleteness in the Jewish second world is the Jewish rejection of all doctrines of primordiality as untrue. The Jews have seen the deadly risk of truth assimilated into some primordial of the natural or historic rules that then become truth incarnate and primordial. But the Jewish truth remains, in its doctrine of man as an *imago dei*, very near and yet irreducibly far from a fusion of man and truth. The human remains an image of God, merely. An image represents what it is not, commanding truth itself. The sacred self must remain modest in its imagery and never represent itself, even in imagination, as a god-term. The god-relation is not representative of more than obedience to the truths conveyed in that relation. Once those truths are reduced to a secondary object of a historic event, the primal crime, the way to a third world as other than a variation of seconds or firsts becomes open.

The greatest theorist of that way made possible, the way to third worlds, is Freud in a way that represents both the strength and weakness of Yerushalmi's lectures on Freud, his defense of the true Israel, embattled as ever within its own world, registers an attack on Freud and yet does not register the contextual crescendo of the noise of war except as an echo of the year 1939 as the beginning of the most powerful deathwork yet to be inflicted upon the Jews and their lifework.

3. All is not one in the second world of sacred order, being given to the Jews in their irreducible culture of commanding truths. In that culture of commanding truths, the oppositional

sense will not abide in the doctrine that life and death, good and bad, upward in the vertical of authority and downward, are one and the same.[6] In its office as the agency of sacred order, executing those orders in the everyday life, human being cannot assert the oneness of opposites. In their meaning as the founding nation of mediators between sacred order and social, the survival of the Jews depends upon their maintenance of the *either/or* of reasonably distinct conditions, from the *both/and* of first worlds recycled into the ambiguous egalitarianism of thirds.

In the directive character of its truths, second world being, self in its unique time of life in sacred order and social, is given through offices that are themselves concealing as they reveal the truths they conceal. Those truths are not there in the clouds, pillars of fire, darknesses, burning bushes, that constitute the offices of delivery. Directive offices are not themselves what is delivered through those offices. Freud had the genius to take up a German word for the indirective character of offices well known, in the character of the deliverances, to his biblical predecessors: offices are indirections through which direction is delivered unawares in its third world meaning and aware in its second. The German word is *Verdrängung*. The English translation of that word has become infamously diffuse in its application: *repression*.

Third world repression is to revelation as third world movements of denial are to second world institutions of truth received. The family is the primary institution of revelation received. Freud's image of the world as suffering, the Oedipus complex, is of the family divided within itself against itself. Whether the family is the primary organization within which human suffering takes place can now be seen, not as the question of parents Freud made it, but rather as the parent question of humanity. The second world creator asks, through the fifth commandment, at the very center of the shortest codex of second cultures: *Am I thy Master, or thou Mine?*

As near as the teaching authority of fathers and mothers, but

6. See Deuteronomy 30:15, 19.

of fathers in particular—teaching authority belonging to the father as nurture more naturally belongs to the mother—ultimate authority is no more distant than the natural officers of direction: parents. By his doctrine of transference neurosis, authority concealed behind a primordiality of sexual competition for the mother, Freud created the very distancings and distortions that characterize the repression of revelation. In the family institution of command, in which parents lay down the law, from generational time to time, the offices of direction, action taking its name from the fathers and mothers, crossing the distancings and distortions there are in the distinction between the giver, who is wholly other, and the receiver, who is gifted with the receiving instrument, the sacred self. That sacred self emerges in its secondary characteristics as a 'superego'. On the contrary, the sacred self is the true self. It is the feeling intellect given in human being, and in this being given entirely unlike animal being.

Third world visionaries of the highest, theorists of the transition from the late second to our early third, Freud the greatest of those theorists, de-create the second world in its commanding clarities of direction, however unclear the circumstance of execution may be, by reducing those clarities to a primordiality of conflict between fathers and sons. In the necessary sexuality of its continuity, the family becomes, in the Freudian reading, the unit of primal suffering. In its agency, as the mediating institution of commanding truth, the family, in Freud's reading of that institution, suffers the gravest of reductions: the truth it mediates becomes the interest payment of guilt in sacred order by sons who can only imitate their fathers by repressing the primordial will to imitation into the constraint of that will by commanding fictions they may call fate or, in the supersessive history of true fiction, the Word. In either history, of our first worlds or seconds, suffering acquires a primordiality that remains the reality principle, in Freud's reading, against the resolution of that reality in any sovereign good.

4. Even so, the credal truths that mark the Jewish authority of the past, in its "enormous weight [and] gravitational pull . . .

whether it be felt as an anchor or a burden"[7] are represented symptomatically by Yerushalmi in an All-inclusive sponge word, a sovereign symptom, representing what it is not: *Jewishness.* That word represents a sea of pseudosacralities and amputated secularities on the surface of which Yerushalmi rides at anchor too easily. Yerushalmi carries his burden so gracefully that this reader would swear that the Jewish past is brought into the post-Freudian present without more than occasional noises, offstage, of the war within the Jewish camp Yerushalmi conducts. The war for the Jewish world, conducted here within the Jewish camp, is almost noiseless. Yet, hovering as the hidden reality, just off Yerushalmi's stage, is the world in all its bloody mess and gore, ourselves ever on the move in that mess.

Yerushalmi's *Freud's Moses* intends an irenic lifework against a brilliantly concealed deathwork. This deathwork exercises, in its particularity, a resolution of the Jewish culture of commanding truths into the therapy represented exactly in Yerushalmi's subtitle: *Judaism Terminable.* With *Moses and Monotheism,* Freud became the ultimate murderer of Moses. That this murder is symbolic, the supersession of a primordial event repeated, the murder of the father as the *donnée* of all culture in its moralities, does not lessen the deadliness of this deathwork. Symbols are what they represent.

The *is-ness* of a symbol is not less real than the material death of bodies. *Judaism Interminable* represents what it is, the lifework of Yerushalmi's faithful intellect. It is a symbol of Jewish life in its particularity of resistance to the gentilism represented by Freudian theory in the irenics of psychoanalysis as a 'godless Judaism'. *Freud's Moses,* on the other hand, is a vast symptom. It represents what it is not, the Judaism in its ineliminable god-relation. That God will not be turned, except in an antic version of which Joyce is the better artist than Freud. Comedy can conceal the tragedy of every deathwork. There is nothing funny about Freud's *Moses.*

5. The fratricidal animus of Christian culture in its Jew-hatred

---

7. Yerushalmi, *Freud's Moses,* 31; further citations are in parentheses in the text.

carries the weight and gravity of *historical* truth. But that truth is far from eternal. Confronted by the deathwork proposed by third world movements against both Christian and Jewish eternities of truth, the prudence of alliance is far more reasonable than the imprudence of the misalliance repeated in either convention: patricidal or fratricidal. There is no hint of this proleptic theme of truth as it is called for in the material and spiritual condition of the deadly movements both Christians and Jews cannot but confront. Both face a tale of two truths in their negational enactment: the repression of revelation as the diagnosable command of all deathwork movements in our advancing third world. To truth, duplicitous in Shakespeare's art as it is repressive in Freud's, I turn in my second commentment.

II

6. Auschwitz may be read as an instrument of darkness that told the Jews an eternal *truth:* no one who belongs to the Jewish *Kulturstaat*, however secular in his Jewishness, and however remote the territory may be to which he has fled from that historic truth of his particularity, can be safe without a protective *Machtstaat.* The lesson is delivered artistically in Macbeth, who becomes the king of a killer state. All struggles for the world are historical. The truths of that struggle argue blood. That truth was told at Sinai and incorporated into the canon in Exodus 32:27. In defense of the arguments of truth, against first worlds as they were danced out even as he brought them those truths in their briefest codification, Moses must resort, in the reality of the condition there and then, to the argument of blood.

The difference between the Mosaic resort and the German is that blood was not Moses's argument. Blood is not only life, its shedding can be an instrument of darkness. War is not a godterm, as it was made in both the German doctrine of racial war and the communist doctrine of class war; that latter derived from the primordiality of class war, no less than German racial war. Holy war is something else again; as is just war.

Macbeth is sacred drama. Macbeth has transformed the Scottish social order into an instrument of darkness. The struggle for the true world in the Scotland of Shakespeare's imagination includes the reality of blood. Particular distances between social order and its predicative commanding truths may require something bloodier than *kulturkampf.* I have remarked that culture is the form of fighting before the firing begins. A true culture will not be so much the liar to itself that it permits the fighting to become a firing without resort to its own arms. The doctrine of *historical* truths that require the abolition of eternal *truths* is a form of disarmament. No *Kulturstaat* in our second world can afford to disarm itself.

7. The two truths, repressive and revelational, of the war against the culture of commanding truths, constitutes the war against the Jews only in its hidden predicate: the war against the King that was and is the question of these wars. The question of the death of God is inseparable from the question of the after-affect produced by Freud's *Moses.* Graceful as he is in his treatment of the question, Yerushalmi becomes an accomplice in the third world deathwork of all seconds by the sheer concision of his noble aphorism: "Freud *was* godless and he *was* a Jew" (8). That aphorism may conceal a deadliness in the after-affect of such a *historical* truth turned into the predominant form of modern Jewishness. After all, it represents the fusion of godlessness and 'Jewishness'.

The fight for our second world, in the variety of its stands against thirds, turns on the parent question of commanding truth as it has been given, in its historic particularity, as Israel. Put in that particularity, the paradox of godlessness and Jewishness fused is more than absurd. The paradox risks an entirely new Jewry: 'Jewishness' and expression of some more or less ephemeral tradition of taste. Bagels-and-lox Jews may be less ephemeral than nationalist Jews, but cut off from the godly Jew, Jewishness becomes a stopping place on the way out. The history of Jewishness may have ended in Auschwitz. Unspecific as Yerushalmi is in drawing this implication in more than such dark ends as his reference to the dark end of the Jewish romance with German culture, he risks a certain subtlety of participation in the various cults of Jewishness that such delicacy allows the reader. Taste, whether political or gustatory, supplies no foundation for Jewish life in any of its canonical stipulations.

In its generational warfare, Freudian doctrine empties all canons of commanding truths, primary in its Jewishness and tertiary in all its other canons. That the struggle is at times made oversubtle is equally apparent. *Freud's Moses* is wonderfully subtle, but the subtlety weakens its otherwise firm opposition to the Freudian deathwork popularly titled *Moses and Monotheism.* An oppositional lifework, of the kind toward which *Freud's Moses* strains, needs some more direct and directive address to the post-Freudian consequences of Freud's deathwork *Moses.*

8. Both Freud's primordial world and Kafka's strange world of a Gregor Samsa who wakes up one day to find himself a monstrous insect, is the world of the indifferent All, moral only in its consequent remorse. The world as it is, for both Kafka and Freud, is not differentiated in its deepest is-ness into either good or evil. Nor is it both good and evil. The primordial world is not paradisiacal. Far from it. Freud recorded his sense of smell, his nose for the primordial world even as it is now, in a letter to his then confidant and fellow doctor, specialist in diseases of the nose, Wilhelm Fliess. The letter is dated December 22, 1897. The English translation of Freud's sense of the primordial world smell, even now, reads as follows: "I can hardly tell you how many things I (a new Midas) turn into—filth."[8] Freud wrote: *Was sich mir . . . in Dreck auflöst.* A more candid translation may be: *How many things turn to shit before my eyes.* To put the primordial of our third world in a four-letter world that may be familiar even to the most un-American reader: *shit.*

There should be no deodorizing *Dreck.* Freud does not know what he knows: how profoundly he himself has contributed to the turning of our second world into our third, the world as shit. This is the world of the Jews as the Nazis would un-create them. *Lump*

8. Sigmund Freud, *The Origins of Psycho-Analysis: Letters to Wilhelm Fliess: Drafts and Notes: 1887–1902,* ed. M. Bonaparte et al., trans. E. Mosbacher and J. Strachey (New York: Basic Books, 1954), 240.

was a word for the corpse of a Jew after the first death had been consummated in its chamber. *Lumpen* had to be dragged out for burning by what might now be called *neo-Lumps.*

9. However execrable the politics of the *Haredim*, as agents of sacred truth, the truth remains: Israel is inseparable from the traditions of commanding truths, if not in the life of the *Haredim* then certainly in the classical Jewish texts that secular Jews have abandoned. Those classical Jewish texts have not been abandoned in the secular school curriculum of Israel. As I understand the Israeli school curriculum, sacred history, in those classical texts, is taught as the history of Israel. If not, then the *Machtstaat* of Israel will have no foundation in a *Kulturstaat.* Without question, the predicate of the here and now is, in space-time, the there and then.

Given the radical psychologizing of diaspora Jewry in America, the future of the Jews depends upon the maintenance of its holy nationality. That the maintenance is frozen in the amber of ultra-Orthodox lifestyle, its black caftan and *peyot* betrayed by patently third culture body language unconscious as it is vulgar, suggests one answer to the question of *kulturkampf* in contemporary Israel: the ultra-Orthodox do not represent tradition. They represent one tradition that, in its political desperation, parallels the last hurrah of Islamic ultras. The difference is encapsulated in the Freudian phrase "a narcissism of small differences." Ultra-Orthodoxy is the facade of deadly earnest political gamesters. Seen in its political context, ultra-Orthodoxy, on its own terms, is less than earnest. There is no more relation between the two kinds of earnestness than there is between Freudian doctrine and commanding truth. We can read that absence of relation in a passage so significantly shallow that I remain shocked when I am forced to recognize that it is by Freud. The man was not shallow. Yet the emptiness of his sense of Israel as a "tragically mad land"[9] parallels the shallow conviction of Gertrude that her son was mad.

9. Freud, in a 1932 letter to Arnold Zweig, in *The Letters of Sigmund Freud and Arnold Zweig*, ed. Ernst L. Freud, trans. Elaine and William Robson-Scott (New York: Harcourt, Brace & World, 1970), 40.

III

The oppressive feeling of the longevity and irremediability of being Jewish. (32)

10. The burden of being Jewish is irrecoverable except in the negation of third world "Jewishness." Whether that burden has the "same psychological structure" (12) in the repressive mode of guilt substantiated in the Jewish culture of our second worlds is a question of recoverability implicit in both Yerushalmi's book and the book it addresses. Whether psychological structure can replace objective correlative is implicit in Yerushalmi's ambiguous assertion that "in some profound sense [Freud] remains a Jew" (14). There is a legitimate and tragic sense of that godlessness I read as entirely different from Freud's. That sense of difference is in the oppressive feeling inseparable from the Jewish identity of a great poem of that condition alive in the deathworkworld. "God of Mercy" expresses the condition of Jewish lifework I read as well in the poetry of Paul Celan. But first, in respect of the despair, a godlessness incomparably truer to that being than Freud's, I shall quote entire the poem by Kadya Molodovsky, "God of Mercy."

God of Mercy

O God of Mercy
Choose—
another people.
We are tired of death, tired of corpses
We have no more prayers.
Choose—
another people.
We have run out of blood
For victims,
Our houses have been turned into desert,
The earth lacks space for tombstones,
There are no more lamentations
Nor songs of woe
In the ancient texts

God of Mercy
Sanctify another land,

Another Sinai.
We have covered every field and stone
With ashes and holiness.
With our crones
With our young
With our infants
We have paid for each letter in your Commandments.

God of Mercy
Lift up your fiery brow,
Look on the peoples of the world,
Let them have the prophecies and Holy Days
Who mumble your words in every tongue.
Teach them the Deeds
And the ways of temptation.

God of Mercy
To us give rough clothing
Of shepherds who tend sheep
Of blacksmiths at the hammer
Of washerwomen, cattle slaughterers
And lower still.
And O God of Mercy
Grant us one more blessing—
Take back the divine glory of our genius.

—Kadya Molodovsky, 1945[10]

Tenebrae

We are near, Lord,
near at hand.

Handled already, Lord,
Clawed and clawing as though
the body of each of us were
your body, Lord.

---

10. Kadya Molodovsky, "God of Mercy" (1945), trans. Irving Howe, in *Penguin Book of Modern Yiddish Verse*, ed. Irving Howe, Ruth R. Wisse, and Khone Schmeruk (New York: Viking, 1987), 330–33.

Pray, Lord,
pray to us,
we are near.

Wind-awry we went there,
went there to bend
over hollow and ditch.

To be watered we went there, Lord.

It was blood, it was
what you shed, Lord.

It gleamed.

It cast your image into our eyes, Lord.
Our eyes and our mouths are so open and empty, Lord.
We have drunk, Lord.
The blood and the image that was in the blood, Lord.

Pray, Lord.
We are near.

—Paul Celan[11]

Taken together, these poems answer Adorno's famous declaration that after Auschwitz there could be no serious art. Both
poems take the god-term of the Jews most seriously. Neither are
deathworks. Molodovsky's plea for the mercy of being unchosen
depends upon the truth of being chosen. Celan's inversion of the
Christian archetype, the Jews as the crucified rather than cruci-
fiers, without implication of incarnation, does reincorporate in an
effectual partiality the Christian tradition into the Jewish.

If I were on the liturgical committee of the American Reform
rabbinate, I would incorporate both Molodovsky's and Celan's
poems into the Reform liturgy. But that would risk, again, taking
the presiding presence seriously in the forgiveness such a presi-
dency is invited to ask of the crucified. There is always a risk in
adding to a second world canon. But survival, indeed prosperity, in
modernity suggests the nature of the modern economy at its most

11. Paul Celan, "Tenebrae," in *Poems of Paul Celan*, ed. and trans. Michael
Hamburger (New York: Persea Books, 1988), 113.

courageous spirituality. I like to think that the title of my old economics teacher Frank Knight is entirely applicable in *kulturkampf.*
The title of his essays, eminently readable still and widely applicable beyond economics, is *Risk, Uncertainty and Profit.*

11. Ever at the center of the war for the world, Jews can become deaf to its noise only by the canonical hearing of truth. Radical contemporaneity can develop a category response of avoid-
ance to the credal phrase *Hear O Israel.*[12] As a category phrase, the
Shema can fall on deaf ears. That deafness describes the nature
of Freud's modernist humiliation of the Jewish culture of commanding truths. Form remains intact: Moses and Monotheism, as
it were, emptied of their directive particularities. Here and now,
Joyce's inversion becomes an ally of returning the phrase to its
substantive and directive meaning. Joyce's "hear, O Ismael"[13] is a
kind of oppositional hearing, a parody emptying out of substance
that respects what it parodies.

Third world parody has become more than art. In its own
after-affects, parody becomes a lifestyle internal to the self of a
profane order that carries an enormous weight of complexity. The
world is transformed, as Stevens says, "from substance to subtlety."
The search for subtlety anchors the transgressive lifestyle.

12. In the sense Yerushalmi gives Freud's identity as both godless and Jewish, the fight inseparable from both *historical* truth and
eternal *truth* suffers a self-negation. That negation is repeated
in Freud's further identifications, as "with Yochanan ben Zakkai." The second historical stipulation of Freud's Jewish identity
compounds the mistake made in the first. That Freud "identified repeatedly with Rabbi Yochanan ben Zakkai, the architect of
Judaism after the destruction of the Second Temple" (6) does not
distinguish between the authority of Yavneh and the power of
Vienna. Vienna is to the post-Jewish world of the therapeutic in
transition to anti-Jewish third worlds as Yavneh is to the Jewish
Kulturstaat without the primordiality of a *Machtstaat.* Truth needs
power, not in order to survive, but in order to live well. It is the

---

12. Deuteronomy 6:4: "Hear O Israel the Lord Our God, the Lord Is One."
13. James Joyce, *Finnegans Wake* (New York: Faber and Faber, 1975), 258.

protection of truth empowered that alone can produce ease in Zion if the *Machtstaat* is reduced, yet again, to a *Kulturstaat*. Then the sacred self loses its surround. It is without the completion of that self in the social self that needs its political expression in order to achieve the primordiality that cannot be there except as a conservative and yet variable consequence of sacrality. Eternal *truth* does not derive from *historical*. On the contrary, *historical* truth derives from eternal. Sacred order is far more stable than social order. In fact, all social orders derive such stabilities as they may be given from their predicative sacred orders.

Yavneh and the Vienna of psychoanalysis cannot be conflated. However appealing the rhetoric of Anna Freud's conflation of those two places in her address at the Hebrew University in Jerusalem in 1977, psychoanalysis cannot rightly be described as "a direct product of the Jewish mind" (100). The Jewish rebellion against the eternal *truth* of identity in its personality and incommunicability neither begins nor ends with the de-creation called 'psychoanalysis'. The therapeutic is not a variation of the rabbinic, let alone the prophetic type in the history of the Jews. The primordial self of sexual drives is not the self of Genesis or of Yavneh. In the American experience, therapeutic and rabbinic can be merged only at the risk of a deathwork upon one or another side in that mergence.

We see the fate of such mergences in the experience of the American Reform rabbinate in its suicide recorded in June 1990, in Seattle.[14] No canonical element of the culture of commanding truths can be abolished without the abolition of the Jew in his identity. The abolition of Leviticus 18:22 constitutes a deathwork of the Reform rabbinate upon itself. The constituency of the Reform rabbinate is bound to that deathwork in ways that will drive it out of the temple. Without rabbinical resistance to the major offensive launched by the movement of gay liberation against Jewish identity in its sexual relations, Jews of the Reform persuasion will have little reason to remain members of that con-

14. See "The Kedusha of Homosexual Relationships," in *Yearbook of the Central Conference of American Rabbis*, 1990.

stituency. That the suicide I describe is symbolic does not render it less real than more material suicides. A symbol is what it represents. The decision of the Reform rabbinate to abolish Leviticus 18:22 is a symptom rather than a symbol. The suicide of the Reform rabbinate represents what it is not, the Jews recognizing commanding truths self-evidently not their own. The movement of gay liberation cannot be assimilated to the tolerance special revelation in second world traditions is commanded to offer general revelation. There is nothing in the traditions of natural law that can contradict the traditions of Torah, special as they are to the holy nation.

IV

Both read the same Bible, and pray to the same God; and each invokes His aid against the other.

Lincoln's Second Inaugural Address

13. The Bible is to our second world as the fifth commandment is to the founding nation of that world. Lincoln understood and asserted the canonical foundation common to both armies in that civil war within the American nation. To honor that canon is to engage in a competition of readings. There are times when that competition will break beyond the words of the permanent war, the *psychomachia* and *kulturkampf* endemic in the world, never to be resolved before the *meshiakh*. Those times are tragic. Those breaks are bloody. The tragedy of the American break was deeply engraved on Lincoln's face.[15] The pivotal character of the fifth commandment is clear. The parent question of humanity is mediated by every parent. I have treated the parallel of that pivotal commandment as the canonical one, now largely ignored by all except the unregarded 'fundamentalists' of the American nation. That canonical and functional equivalent of the parents to be honored at the very pivot of the Mosaic code is that very Bible to which Lincoln referred in his pivotal paradox of the Civil War in its absurd truth.

15. See Garry Wills, *Lincoln at Gettysburg: The Words That Remade America* (New York: Simon & Schuster, 1992).

A holy nation must live somewhere. Lincoln thought America a sacred space not to be divided within itself. Thus Lincoln put the American *Machtstaat* in the service of the *Kulturstaat* which mediated the true sense of an American nation. In the Palestinian case, the leaders of the putative Palestinian *Machtstaat* are trying to reinvent themselves as a *Volkstum*. Whether they can do so or not, without recourse to Islam, is highly dubious. Nor do I think that they will long accept whatever boundary may be drawn between their space and Israel. That Arab *Volkstum* is too deeply penetrated by the Islamic sense of sacrality.

Analogously, in Lincoln's Second Inaugural, the space in which the same Bible was read and the same God received petitions was at war within itself. The oneness of the nation was inseparable from the oneness of that God, however the truths of that Creator were being misread. As it represented what it was, the last best hope of mankind, that nation could not be divided.

Upon the firing at Fort Sumter, the defense of the national self seemed to Lincoln indivisible as it was measurable. Defensive purpose, national as it was personal, seemed to Lincoln indivisible as it was measurable by the distance between defense and offense in the complex world binding *historical* truth to eternal *truth*, mixed as they were inextricably together; indeed, in the here and now, mixed as they are still.

Freud essayed a supersession of that inextricable mixture, *historical* truth in its national character, one and the same as eternal *truth* in its national character. Second worlds are divided into nations. The ancients of Israel referred to the larger world as "the nations." Freudian analysis offers a *therapeutic truth* that resolves the connection between nation and truth by examining the Jewish case. In *therapeutic truth* all worlds, as creations of culture, receive their energies from transgression and its repetition. The world is founded on a primal crime and the denial of that crime in its repetitions. But *therapeutic truth* is negational, merely. Moreover, negational truth is itself resolved by the very process of arriving at it. The war of truth against truth is fought out in the transference neurosis. The therapist becomes, at once, the father of resolutive truth and of its antics—i.e., its lies. Lying, in the undeliberated sense, takes the name of repression. The consummate liar knows and yet does not know the truth. But the entire world of truths that are held sacred stipulates knowledge of those truths and the necessary burden of judgment and action consequent upon holding truths in their sacrality.

14. Freud's *Moses* is established as a book of the counter-canon: a brilliantly internal intellectualization of the third world aesthetic of forgetfulness as if forgetfulness were a reminder. Else, surely, Yosef Hayim Yerushalmi, author of *Zakhor* and thereby commissioned in the highest rank of our second world's elite troops, would not have bothered to address Freud's book as the great and idiosyncratic symptom it is: of the *"gottloser Jude"* at the end of his sacred tether. This specially acute psychopathology of everyday Jewish life can be read even by those untrained in the hermeneutic of suspicion. We are all psychoanalysts now.[16]

At the moment of the door I have tried to open, by quoting it, as Freud himself stands before the Law, Freud's repression of revelation failed him. In his sacred fear, his mind's eye saw what he did not see, his feeling intellect knew what he did not know: the ultimate object of his denial, sacred order. *We must admit.*[17] Those three words carry an extraordinary weight, the gravity of which carries Freud nearest to the objective correlative, hidden behind his singular postulating of a third unconscious and yet not seeing what is there so plainly before his eyes. Sacred fear[18] has intervened to protect him from the truth of his own vision of the highest.

Because that sacred fear is frozen by Freud in its crucial yet preliminary phase of repression, fear does not lead Freud to an act of obedience. 'Third unconscious' can be read to represent

---

16. Who will survive longer as a figure in directive authority, a veritable god-term in third world movements, Marx or Freud? Lord Harcourt once said: "We are all socialists now." That may be true no longer. However, it can be said, as the Lord knows, to his sadness no doubt: "We are all psychologists now."

17. See "One Step Further," the new epilogue to the 3rd ed. of my *Freud: The Mind of the Moralist* (Chicago: University of Chicago Press, 1979).

18. See Plato, *Laws*, 671d. Since all social theory is a footnote to Plato, I consider it important to say that Plato is the first great writer, outside Israel, on the *kulturkampf.*

what it is not: 'supernatural reality' transformed into a symptom that Freud successfully ignores. It is from that symptom, from which Freud himself suffers at that moment, readable in our own here and now if not in his there and then, that the Freudian counter-canon draws its militant character; it is as if the Freudian art, and its prudent lowerings of second world moralities into third world therapies of those moralities, were a "scientific *psychology of the unconscious*" (20). Here I quote Yerushalmi quoting Freud. Any supersessive psychopathology of everyday life in the post-Freudian era would have to see how the Freudian mind's eye turned from the truth of supernatural reality in order to protect the counter-canon in its ultimately militant post-Freudian character. In this post-Freudian present, Yerushalmi has let Freud off lightly enough.

Freud has remarked that it is the fate of revelation, in the permanent war against it, that it will be "changed back once more by science" (21) as either philosophy (*metaphysics*) or Freudian historical psychiatry (*metapsychology*). Implicit in Freud's great assault against sacred order, published in 1901,[19] is the entire doctrine of the repression of revelation rendered, in Freud's last work, his *Moses* of 1939, as the "repression of the memory of the deed" (21).

What is the deed? The author of *Zakhor* might have been explicit. The deed is Oedipal murder, as Yerushalmi says explicitly. The murdered one is the "primeval father," which Yerushalmi says explicitly. The murderers are the "horde" of his sexual rivals, his "sons." Guilt is the "veiled recollection of the murder itself through its periodic reenactment" (21). The last periodic reenactment of the murder to which Freud refers was committed by Freud himself. Yerushalmi conceals in the velvet of his style the knife of his criticism. The grace of that style is wounded by his own version of the velvet revolution. He does not thrust home the truth of his critical exposition. Freud's *metapsychology* constitutes his veiled recollection of revelation. Each of Yerushalmi's criticisms is too heavily veiled. The reader is left to follow a logic too heavily concealed. It is Freud himself who is the ultimate

19. Freud's *The Psychopathology of Everyday Life*.

murderer of Moses. This book represents a literary climax in the history of "Jewishness" as a form of defeat; millennial exile turned into the intellectual exercise of the Jewish war against Israel.

It is the secret of Freud's genius that the strength of his negational intellect scarcely weakened throughout the course of his life. The repression of revelation remained intact not only in his own deathworks, which constitute the *Tendenz* of the canon entire. That strength, hidden as it is from his doctrinal descendants, has now become, in cruder registrations, the force of the therapeutic in all the movements, however otherwise contentious against Freud, that have as their purpose the abolition of our second worlds out of Israel. Even in these sentences, his fear is mediated by his admitted ignorance of what he is saying. In his bafflement, we can see, as well as a second world reader of Yerushalmi's virtuosity, that Freud's repression of revelation has remained intact.

There are repressions and there are repressions. It is an integral part of the biblical canon that repressions, in their subservient mode, the interdicts delivered through some indirection, are themselves threatening. Threat is a protective device. Safety is plucked from the nettle danger. In the service of revelation, images of repression threaten and yet cover the threat implicit in their negational character. Cloud, darkness, a burning bush, a mountain high beyond the reach of other than appointed sacred messengers, the secret or mystery of prophesy—in these instances, as in others I need not cite by way of illustration, offices of indirection serve the purposes of the directives they deliver. The protocols of psychoanalysis probe the secrets behind symptomologies. However kinder and gentler, for reasons of his true and justified respect for Freud, the movement of theory and practice of which Freud has become, in the here and now, a canon rather than a person, much like Shakespeare, is irremissively of our third world. There is the hidden reason for Yerushalmi's book.

In the irrationalizations of its critical reasonings, third worlds must be incorporated at their deepest salients of attack into the countercritical rationalities of a second world in which truth may be affirmed first and yet again by the critical and rational power of those counterattacks. Withal his metatheories in their pure sub-jectivities, Freudian doctrine, the conquistador of the there and then of commanding truths, may be conquered in the here and now. Second world intellect must extend the Freudian canon, like the Marxist, in the manner of partial incorporations that use the energies of enemy truths to revivify their own. To that use, Ye-rushalmi's book represents a useful preliminary form or reconcili-ation between the ambiguities of Jewishness and the precisions of commanding truths.

In his person, Freud remains forever and honorably one of the high officers in our third world armies. The various few who are in Freud's world class can also serve our second world class. That strategy of partial incorporation, at once through the most highly critical and assimilative readings, has always been the object of the humanist tradition inseparable from the traditions of schol-arship. It takes no clown, even one created out of Shakespeare's genius, to say that Freud's concealment of that which his work reveals negationally is the commonplace of modern art. Third world deathworks are the cowl that does not make the mark. "*Cu-cullus non facit monachum*."[20] The cowl does not make the monk. All masters of third world disorder should receive the respect of their genius for "misprision in highest degree."[21] Freud's *via negationis* is the way of all modern art, if not Science. It is the way of modern Science in its positivist cultural history. That way is the way of a defiance not to be mollified by the mere negative attribute, godlessness.

In the tradition of commanding truth out of Israel, as we can see the trajectory of those traditions, godlessness is more than foolery. It is no fool, merely, who says now there is no God (Psalm 14:1). Of course, there is a certain foolery in all godlessness. But the logic of foolery is the drive toward deathworks. Charlie Chap-lin's effort, in *The Great Dictator*, to turn Hitler into a clown, paralleled by Jack Oakey as that clown Mussolini, was Chaplin's greatest mistake as director-actor. Sacred history never repeats

20. *Twelfth Night or What You Will*, 1.5.60–61.
21. Ibid., 1.5.61–62.

itself. It is linear rather than cyclical. In the late twentieth century, we know that the foolery of godlessness has become fatality in all its forms. Those who dine at the banquet table of Fate suffer and produce almost untellable suffering. *Kulturkampf* has shifted from the war of first worlds, sacred orders in all their pluralities against second, to a war of our advancing third worlds against our retreating seconds. The rate of fatality has become astronomical. The fool has become a figure of such intellectual and political power that its misprisions need to be incorporated into our commanding truths. Then and only then is the counterattack of our second world armies against thirds' a lifework worthy of life.

Sacred history tells us, if nothing else, that God does not suffer fools or figures of fate gladly. Revelation is more truthful and commanding than the tolerances implicit in the history of deathworks turned into material reality. The alienation of so many from life itself can be seen in the false righteousness characteristic of third world movements: abortionist, racialist, homosexualist. Revelation promises punishments certain as death itself. Exodus 3:14 is more than self-revelation. That self-revelation is the premise of all the promises and punishments that follow. In their objectivity, commanding truths have their consequences. Else, human knowledge becomes too modest and knows less than it knows in reality. The knowledge of God's attributes is entirely a matter of judging the purposes of God we ourselves enact.

Lincoln knew that much and tried to teach what he knew, in his Second Inaugural, as a teaching to the nation no less publicly than the lessons recorded in Nehemiah 8.* Without that sense of the Almighty in the *historical* truth of his purposes, human knowledge is driven to the *via negationis* in which it now moves downward in the vertical of authority. There is modern reality, scientific as it is aesthetic, in its negational nutshell.

15. The conflation of 'Jewish' and 'Jewishness' with 'Jewish identity', typical in our early third world, is what it represents: the symbolic character of this discipline of truth relaxed characterizes

---

*This chapter reports on Ezra's reading of the Torah to the people gathered in Jerusalem.—*Eds.*

an Israel in exile, stripped of its self-protection by the absence of a *Machtstaat* in service to its *Kulturstaat*. The diaspora is a necessary form of reconciliation with *schlecht Realität*. That this latter phrase is Hegelian German may make the double meaning of 'Jewish' stand away from its apparent, merely phenomenal, reference; as in, by analogy, 'Irish', or even 'British'. The comparison can be driven one clarifying step more. What is 'Irish' without Roman Catholicism in its Jansenist character? The implicit answer is given magisterially by both James Joyce and William Butler Yeats. 'Irish' is either the pre-Catholic and Celtic twilight of paganism, so to release a land and its people trapped in a culture of commanding truths, or 'Irish' becomes another kind of fantasy fatherland.

16. No one, not Freud himself, can know whether Freud thought, even for the most fleeting of moments, that in his *Moses* he lied in every word. Yet the idea of the thinker and artist as virtuoso lawyer is there as early as Plato and late in its greatness in Nietzsche. As if he were his own severest critic, Browning gives his first thought on his own kind of virtuosity in the opening lines of "Childe Roland":

> My first thought was, he lied in every word,
> That hoary cripple, with malicious eye
> Askance to watch the working of his lie
> On mine[22]

17. Israel has had to bear any number of resolutions of the transference neurosis. Readers need only recall Edmund Wilson's *To the Finland Station* and many other books in which Marx becomes one among the Jewish prophets. As the mediating nation between the sacred order of commanding truths and their institutionalizations in social order, the Jews must be a nation of conservatives. The quintessential character of Jews as conservatives may be read in the stability of their transference, from one generation to the next, of an abiding sense that the particularity

---

22. Robert Browning, "Childe Roland to the Dark Tower Came," in *Penguin Book of Victorian Verse*, ed. Daniel Karlin (London: Penguin, 1998), 234.

of commanding truths cannot be distanced from their universality. Given the conservative character of Israel, the dichotomy between particularity and universality reconciled by the commanding truths themselves, Yerushalmi rightly remarks on the expressed morality of candor in the Jewish canon.

18. Third world messengers and their messages admit neither special nor general revelation. Either or both: the message is unreadable, as in Kafka's "In the Penal Colony," or it is undeliverable, as in his "An Imperial Message."

Wallace Stevens gave Kafka's emperor, the writer of the undeliverable message, a marvelously comic term. He is no longer Kafka's dead Commandant, no more than he is Freud's primal father. Rather, the emperor of emperors may be characterized as "the roller of big cigars," the cook of "concupiscent curds." The emperor has become a supremely harmless figure of fun. What more American delectability of an anti-creed can there be than the creed, once milestones on the road to truth, become ice cream. True as Stevens's lament, in his "Notes toward a Supreme Fiction" that "the death of one god is the death of all," there is a death sentence of celebration in the last sentence of "The Emperor of Ice Cream": "The only emperor is the emperor of ice cream." The seriousness of the imperial theme has gone out of thinking about it. The poet of "The Emperor of Ice Cream" is as amused and sane as Nietzsche's madman is grim and insane. There is nothing amusing in Nietzsche's image of the institutions in second world order as sepulchres. I think there is something in the death sentence, the key line of "The Emperor of Ice Cream," Stevens pronounces upon our second world. It is as if the Commandant had become a theatrical director. The world scene calls for this final commanding truth, reality a derivative of fiction: "let be be finale of seem."

What a long way this third world creation, as a stage direction, is from Genesis. Seeming is no longer an accusation of deception. Imagine an Isabella, once she grasps the intent of Angelo's proposition, delivering her two words of judgment as an admiration: "seeming, seeming."[23] In second worlds this directive toward

23. *Measure for Measure*, 2.4.150.

a supreme fiction could only be uttered in the accusative. In a world in which ice cream is the emperor, this stage direction is uttered as a final celebration. Long live ice cream. The king and his imperial themes are dead. Seeming, as it has turned out, was the truth of socialist realism.

A Jewish joke will deliver, I reckon, the price Jews pay when they play that joke upon themselves: *The Trotskys make the revolution and the Bronsteins pay for it.* There is a systemic mendacity, an especially Jewish disingenuousness, that parallels the canonical candor of the Jews. Jewish candor turned disingenuous constitutes the energy of what I have called the Psychological Jew. That type attaches itself to whatever rebellion is being mounted against whatever particularity of the Jewish culture of commanding truths appears to threaten the disingenuous character of Jewishness as it lives without abidance in the tradition represented by one or another enacted version of Jewish world creation.[24] The disingenuous is to the repressive character of the Jews as the commandments are to revelation. Commanding truths can never be more certain than their enactments. Reality is the proof text of truth texts. Proof texts have their readers.

Every reading occurs in the vertical in authority. Jewish truths live in the sacrality of their vertical relations even as they live in the horizontality of primordial relations such as those between the sexes and between the generations. In every horizontal there is, penetrative in its meaning, the vertical in authority. Movement within that vertical includes a shuffling, or sidling, that is there because truths are ascertained only in their human enactments. The canon of sacred history is closed only in its historicity. Isaiah is canonical. Shakespeare represents a parallel canon. The question of canonicity has been incorporated into our third world *kulturkampf* against second.

Defenders of the historical canon are mistaken to reject such a parallel canon that the proper noun "Shakespeare" represents. It is no parody of the immortal "You don't have to be Jewish to

---

24. On the varieties of disingenuousness among the Jews, see Sander L. Gilman, *Jewish Self-Hatred: Anti-Semitism and the Hidden Language of the Jews* (Baltimore: Johns Hopkins University Press, 1986).

eat Levy's Rye" to say you don't have to be British to be read by Shakespeare. Shakespeare belongs to me, as a Jew, if he reads me. Reading me as he does, when I read him, Shakespeare is part of a parallel canon without which my 'Jewishness' is impoverished.

Being read by Shakespeare opens the Jewish canon to modern reality not less than the Jewish canon itself. The canon is closed but questions occur beyond the reach of that canon. No Jew can live in an entirely Jewish reality. However tightly the wagons of Orthodoxy are circled, the larger reality remains un-Jewish. The Orthodox ignore the larger world at their peril. In my observation of them and it, the larger world, the *it* of modernity, penetrates the very bodies of the Orthodox. That penetration of third world body language into the body of the Orthodox second world Jews became clear to me during a recent visit to Israel. Then and there the third world body language of the ultra-Orthodox, however anachronistically devout their dress, could be clearly read. How deeply third world gracelessness in the body has entered the second world body of the Orthodox. They shamble, in their pieties, very like the shamble of the most vulgar secular Jew. Sacred selves cannot withdraw so far from the profane self that grace achieves autonomy in the body from the gracelessness of the profane.

19. Third world cultures are unprecedented in their absent functions, namely, the functions of mediation between sacred order and social.

What then to make of a liturgical book of repentance issued to the largest Jewish religious constituency in America, the Reformed? There is an unmistakable tension between the partial incorporation of Lear's most despairing reference to a world without an objective correlative of morality, and Psalms 32 and 34 of the Jewish canon, into which the Reform rabbinate has incorporated Lear's remark of despair.

Shall we now consider
The suspicious postures of our virtue,
The deformed consequences of our love,
The painful issues of our mildest acts?
Shall we ask,

Where is there one
Mad, poor and betrayed enough to find
Forgiveness for us, saying,
"None does offend,
None, I say,
None"?
Listen, listen,
But the voices are blown away,
    And yet, this light,
    The work of thy fingers, . . .[25]

The partial incorporation of *Lear* into a contemporary edition, based on Psalms and other canonical passages, of the Jewish canon for the day of repentance makes perfect sense. The two canons are parallel. There are many passages in the Jewish canon of which there are echoes in *Lear*, not least on the repressive mode as it occurs in everyday life. Eyes that do not see and ears that do not hear—which is to say, eyes and ears that see and hear in some way so distorted and distanced from the commanding truths as to be false—occur as well in *Lear*. On the other hand, the positive references to seeing truths otherwise invisible with the mind's eye are also commonplaces in *Lear*. *A man may see how this world goes with no eyes*[26] is entirely incorporable into our second world canons. The untruth in the partial incorporation made by the committee of Reform rabbinate for the liturgical volume of Yom Kippur refers to *kulturkampf* as the battle has been confused in the incorporation made by that rabbinate. World, world, O rabbinical third world: that rabbis should not quite know what they know about *Lear*. It is patent knowledge that Lear's remark represents, not his tolerance of offense and the offenders, but his despair at the world turned into their triumph. The heath is their punishment colony. Lear's world has become a permanent storm of disorder. That disorder applies as well to the bodies, as he sees them in their spiritual truth, of the two eldest daughters as they

25. *Gates of Repentance: The New Union Prayerbook for the Days of Awe* (New York: Central Conference of American Rabbis, 1978).
26. *King Lear*, 4.6.153.

have become themselves world women. *Down from the waist they are Centaurs, / Though women all above.*[27]

20. Such are the vicissitudes before the Gates of Repression. The rabbinical committee recycling Lear's cry of despair into their liturgy has transformed the cry itself. That cry is not for tolerance or for general forgiveness. On the contrary, the despair is passionate and bitter that the vertical in authority should be so leveled that the world itself contains none that do offend. Lear has been humiliated further. His cry has been turned into precisely what it does not represent. This rabbinical misprision mistakes entirely the nature of tolerance in *Lear.* Tolerance and forgiveness are here associated with weakness, with defeat. The dynamics of defeat in which the rabbinate was founded, at Yavneh, proposed no such forgiveness and dealt in no such tolerance as indicated in the Reform partial incorporation of *Lear.* For in second world truth, forgiveness must be earned by repentances of return to the true way. There is nothing mad, poor, or betrayed necessary to the character of the forgiver. Humiliation is not the predicate of charity without resurrection and the life. Else forgiveness becomes romantic, a sentiment rather than an obedience in truth.

Romantic suffering has nothing to do with Jewish or Christian rectitude. Martyrdom is not its own justification. The rectitude of martyrdom calls forth its own reasons of the heart. Those reasons are two. Martyrdom testifies to the truth that obedience in life as in death to the commanding truths is superior to suffering. Suffering is justified in the immediacy of its testimony to truth. Truth does not yield to suffering. Thus, after the Crucifixion is the Resurrection. In His eternal life as living truth, Jesus can say after his first death in his second life, *I am the Resurrection and Life.* It is that eternal life to which suffering, in its rectitude, testifies. The second reason of martyrdom is in its true sense of history. Later if not sooner, the truth to which martyrdom testifies will triumph.

21. This is the first organized action of the *Machtstaat* implicit in the defense of every *Kulturstaat.* Those tribal people knew and

27. Ibid., 4.6.126–27.

yet did not know that the primordialities of power and fertility were made: the making of the artifactual calf representing primordiality in all first worlds, out of one of which they had come, both physically and spiritually as from Egypt and its bondages in the first world as well as physical sense, remains as true now as it was then. The order of the people to Aaron, brother of Moses, at least in Aaron's report—*Make us a God*—suggests the complicity of truth and fiction that has emerged millennia after the fact of that making as the fictive truth of third worlds. Yet that fictive truth is there, complete as given, in the canonical text, Exodus 32:23. The break between the Mosaists, the sons of Levi, and the leaders of a likely return to first world modes suggests that the entire character of the world struggle, in both its modes, seconds against firsts and thirds against seconds, is already there in the eternal truth of the text in its traditions; even as those traditions are forwarded consciously in the intention of my own present sentence. As a function of the *Machtstaat*, nascent in the sons of Levi, as defenders of the *Kulturstaat*, in its commanding truth, power, on both sides whether Baalist or Mosaist, remains the most sensuous and most deadly of human aspirations in their ultimate mode of execution: death. It is not for nothing that sociology, as a discipline in the historical study of culture, understands the state as the agency monopolizing violence, death its ultimate weapon. Third world *Party/states*, in the essential of their *partinost*, constitute the physical application of that ultimate primacy of possibility: deathworks.

22. The Jewish canon makes the baser matter of life clear. There are no idealities. Supreme fictions are treated as working lies, as Abraham's lie that Sarah is his sister is a working lie, a way of muddling through. The living live in the remissive middle, the world mess and each self in its sacrality itself a bit of a mess. To cope with that mess, intellect and passion must grasp the endlessness of that mess. Sacred order is the known world, but that knowledge of the world is of our imperfections in it. God himself is said to suffer moments of regret. God himself is almost of a mind that Moses or Abraham changes. The commandments cannot be lived as if life can be lived academically or notionally.

For this reason, the dead cannot be celebrated for having escaped the mess that is, understood canonically but never hopelessly, life as it is lived in the reality of this known world. I remember my shock, as a young man attending funerals of family and friends, at recognizing that the Psalms being chanted at the graveside were thanks to God by the living for their life. There was no celebration of the dead.

V

For my thoughts are not your thoughts, neither are your ways my ways, saith the Lord. (Isaiah 55:8)

23. The canonicity of the text reaches into the contemporaneity to its applications in the present. The "my" of the sentence in Isaiah refers to a person. The substance reported by that person, thoughts and ways, said rather than unsaid, are not those of any man, nevertheless. The Lord is a person, but neither man nor woman in his personality. There is the tension of reconcilability and irreconcilability between Israel and the church. The truth of the church is the *god/man*. The truth of that selfsame personality, of Israel and the world, is of a God who is not a man. The mediating nation of that truth can never claim any divinity in its institutional life. But that nation must claim the divinity—that is, both the commanding character and eternal *truth*—of truth. Canonicity, as in the passage from Isaiah, cannot be a remembrance of form emptied of its content. In his earlier work *Zakhor*, Yerushalmi defended the particularity of *historical* truth in its universality. By contrast, the universality of *therapeutic truth* opposes the particularity of sacred truth in historic Israel.

Index